GOING UP

Proven Strategies for Reaching Higher Levels in Business

Contributing Authors

Nido Abdo – Shannon Allen – Archer Atlas

Nick Cooper – Aaron Davis - Scott Dudley

Russ Holder – Matthew Lee - Alex Navas

Sam Page - Niki Papazoglakis - LaShonda Steele Allen

Julie Trotter Clark - Jennifer Villarreal - Steve Werner

BEP Business Excellence Press

Going Up: Proven Strategies for Reaching Higher Levels in Business

ISBN: 978-1-939315-14-4

ASIN: B00JU79F3M

Contents

Read This First

Thank you for purchasing our book, *Going Up: Proven Strategies for Reaching Higher Levels in Business.* We hope you find it a valuable resource for building your business.

Register to Win the Following Prizes!

- A $250 Amazon Gift Card

- The fifteen authors of Going Up are each donating an hour of telephone coaching / consulting time in their area of expertise (a $125 - $600 value).

How to Register:

Visit   www.BusinessExcellencePress.com/GoingUp or www.GoingUpBook.com and take the Going Up survey. It takes less than 3 minutes, and you could win one of 16 prizes ranging in value between $125 - $600.

Winners will be announced on May 28, 2014, so don't hesitate and take the survey today at www.GoingUpBook.com.

Chapter 1

7 Simple Strategies for Success in Business & Life

Steve Werner

Strategy 1: Never Quit

How many times have you been involved in a situation where pain or frustration has led you to the verge of quitting? I learned while attending a seminar by famed Peak Performance Coach Anthony Robbins that you never lose at anything until you QUIT.

Quitting is not in my nature or my vocabulary. If it were, I would have quit writing this e-book long ago. I've had the thought to write a book for quite some time now. I procrastinated and found every excuse to not sit down at my keyboard and let my thoughts flow freely.

My guess is that it was probably due to fear. What will I write about? Will I have enough to write about to fill up enough pages? I finally figured out the best method for moving forward to complete this task: I won't quit.

When I originally sat down to write, I thought it would be easy. But, as I sat at my keyboard with all of these thoughts, nothing happened. I realized that, much like living one day at a time, I had to attack this book one step at a time. That way I would never quit.

First, I thought about the best tips I could give someone. I woke up every morning at 5 a.m. to jot down the best tips I could think of. When I reached my goal of 50 tips, I began to narrow it down to 7 that made the biggest impact on my life.

I made a verbal commitment to my coach that I would e-mail her each morning with a new tip on how to Live To Win each day.

I learned that breaking things down and continuing to knock down one barrier at a time would give me the greatest chance for success. It also prevented me from wanting to quit.

Each time I would try to write a chapter I would get so frustrated that I would shut down my computer. But I determined that I was going to make this work - no matter what.

Then, I decided to write one paragraph. Again I came to a standstill; I wasn't sure I'd have enough to write about. When I finally decided to start with one word, I allowed my mind to work freely and conquer the mission. Over the course of my life I have been on the brink of quitting, whether it was school, work, or athletics. Now my spirit won't allow it! I've come to realize that you never know when you are at that critical point - the point where the things are in your favor and all of the hard work and sacrifice pays off.

I always remember hearing the phrase: "If you are not failing, you are not trying hard enough." What I learned is, failing isn't quitting, it just means you need to change your plan of attack.

When you give up or quit, you lose.

Strategy 2: Surround Yourself with Successful People

Success breeds success. That's why I encourage you to surround yourself with people who have been successful -- successful in business, successful in relationships, successful in family, etc. You can learn a lot from successful people.

World renowned Peak Performance coach Anthony Robbins heavily stresses modeling yourself after people who have been successful. He often uses Michael Jordan as an example. Robbins contends that you don't need to reinvent the wheel when it comes to being successful. Following or emulating the methods by which Michael Jordan practices on a daily basis can give a basketball player the greatest chance for being successful.

I spend the great majority of my time in business networking with successful people. Being in a room filled with overachievers gives me the opportunity to pick their brain and see what route they have taken to get them to where they are.

In my opinion, successful folks are more pleasant to be around than people who are not successful. They tend to view the world in a positive way. Successful people look at situations as opportunities, while unsuccessful people look at the same situation as a problem. Successful people create positive energy which inspires me to keep my eye on the prize.

I try to stay away from people who are not interested in success. These types of people tend to be victims and are typically negative, pessimistic, passionless and often very scared. I have many friends who fall into this category. They see successful people as "lucky" instead of understanding what peaks and valleys they might have gone through to get where they are today.

As I get older and wiser it has become easier for me to identify with people who will help me to keep growing as I pursue my goal of success. When I wake up each morning at 5 a.m., I read numerous blogs about success. The stories are amazing. They illustrate what people have accomplished and what they had to endure to get to where they are today.

Remember, migrate to those who you can learn from and distance yourself from those who will bring you down.

Strategy 3: Let Fear Be Your Friend

Why is it that everyone has fear in their life at some point? And why is it that people who learn to deal with fear seem to excel in life, while those who let fear paralyze them seem stuck and unable to move forward?

It wasn't until I realized how fear paralyzed me and my ability to grow and succeed that I decided I was going to take a radical approach in how I dealt with my own fears. I decided to let fear be my friend. How crazy does that sound? After all, fear is supposed to be one of the most restricting factors in our lives. How was I going to embrace this obstacle and actually use it to my advantage?

I have to admit that this did not happen overnight. I needed to understand fear itself, identify the real ramifications of what I was fearful of, and how that would impact my life.

My dear friend and mentor Fr. Frank Cimmarusti used to ask me the same question when I would speak with him on the subject of fear: "And what is that going to do for you?" In other words, now that you have identified your fear you have two choices:

- Curl up in a ball and continue to be fearful.
- Embrace the fear and understand its ramifications.

Being the type of person that I am, I chose the latter. When you decide to make fear your friend, you literally take the situation and use it to your advantage. This, according to my friends and colleagues, was much easier said than done. Since my choices were limited I decided to prove them wrong. The following are the steps I use to make fear a positive tool in my life:

1. Get a total understanding of what I am fearful of. I call this the "deep breath phase."
2. Understand what impact this fear has on me on a short and long term basis. Is the fear limiting me in my success because I am so consumed by it?
3. Destroy the fear by taking massive actions in my life and check off eliminating that fear as another accomplishment.

Many of my clients or prospective clients suffer from the same fear that I did years ago while reinventing myself in my career; the fear of being able to provide for their families while making a transition in the work place.

I discovered that fear seems to hold you hostage in this particular circumstance, but once you have identified your fear you have those two choices I mentioned. You either continue to live in fear or you decide to embrace the situation, attack the fear and overcome your barriers.

The next time fear enters your life, think to yourself "what is being fearful going to do for me?" Get an understanding of what it is you fear and how it will impact your life. Then envision your life once you move past the fear. This will give you a good reason to make fear your friend and your mastery of it a worthy accomplishment.

Strategy 4: Never Allow Yourself to Be Satisfied

The reason for never quitting is simple. You never know when the tide might change and things start to go your way. All it takes is a slight shift, a little luck or the right timing and your world can change forever.

In 1982 I graduated from Arizona State University with a degree in Political Science. My career options were limited at that time. I contemplated going to law school but my desire was to get involved in my father's construction business.

About two weeks after graduation my roommate and closest friend asked me if I wanted to visit a place called the Chicago Board of Trade. There, commodities were traded. An acquaintance who had become very successful as a trader was recruiting young guys out of college to learn his system. To be honest, I had never heard of the Board of Trade, but my father encouraged me to go take a look just for the fun of it.

As luck would have it, 90 days later I was a trader in the largest trading environment in the world, The 30 Treasury bond Pit at the Chicago Board of Trade. With virtually no experience except for a few weeks of simulated trading sessions, I was now thrown into the pit with the best in the business.

Over the course of the next six months I would leave my house in the middle of the night and drive 25 miles to work to lose money on a daily basis. Yes, lose money. That was part of paying your dues in order to learn how the business worked.

Some new guys picked up the art of trading rather quickly and began making back the small amounts of money they initially lost. Not me!

Nothing came easy. Day after day I would lose money and often go home very depressed. Four months into my career I remember thinking "am I cut out for this"?

One morning as I was walking out the door my father got up early to wish me good luck. With tears pouring down my face, I turned around and said "I don't think I'm going to make it." My father asked me what I was going to do. I stated that I would make a decision that next week.

Then something amazing happened. That same day a gentleman named Norm Singer called me into his office. He told me that he had been monitoring my progress and that it was time for me to start making money. Start making money? I was a week away from quitting!

He told me he could see the volume of my daily trades increasing and the ratio of losses diminishing. He told me he was proud of me. He said that I followed his rules, rules that were designed to create discipline and that would keep a trader coming back every day. He also pointed out that 90% of new traders failed. Why? Because they lacked discipline.

When Norm told me I was going to make $10,000 in the next eight weeks I thought he was crazy. But, he was right. I did make $10,000 over the next few months and spent over 18 years in the greatest industry I ever could have imagined.

Strategy 5: Have Your "Go-To" Person

Having a "go-to" person is imperative in any aspect of your life. We often make decisions without thinking through what our potential or desired outcome might be. This happens because we don't have enough expertise on the particular subject we are dealing with.

This can also occur when we don't have that mentor or go-to person who has more experience and can help us make an educated decision. For example, you probably wouldn't make a decision in your life concerning your health without contacting your doctor or a decision that has some legal ramifications without first consulting an attorney.

In essence, these are "go-to" people.

A success or business coach is a great addition to your overall business or life strategy. Not only will coaches help you set up plans for action and accountability, but the right coach will probably have real life experiences to help you think through and solve issues or dilemmas in your life.

I personally am a big believer of having a "go-to" person and coach. A story that I enjoy telling my clients is how once a year I take a friend's father to lunch to review what has gone on in my business life and how my businesses are performing.

A few years ago, while sitting at our annual lunch my friend's father was scanning through my financial statements. Then he looked up and stared me right in the face. He thought for a second and then said "You're a really smart young man." I thanked him, and then asked him why he had that thought.

He said that I was smart because I would seek him out each year, knowing that he had many more years in business than I had and he made many more mistakes. By talking with him I was able to get years of knowledge and wisdom without having to go through some of the same experiences myself. He wished he had a go-to person earlier in his life. If he had, maybe he would have made some wiser or better calculated decisions.

I look forward to our lunches every year, and I am wise enough to come to the table filled with questions or concerns that he might help me think through. I am also wise enough to pick up the tab.

So, who is your "go-to" person?

Strategy 6: Know Your Story

I cannot stress how important it is to know your story. Knowing your story means understanding who you are and where you came from. Knowing your story allows you to look back at your life and gives you the ability to focus on what has helped make you successful or, perhaps, what has led to failure.

Do you know your story? Have you been able to dig deep to understand what has worked for you in life and why? Can you review of some of the biggest mistakes you have made in the past and what you have done to make sure that you will not make them again?

If you know your story you can begin to identify patterns in your life that have accounted for success or failure.

If you are a networking or sales person like myself, you may recall the first sale you ever made. If you are an accomplished manager or leader your story may lead all the way back to your childhood, for example, when you were the captain of a team or leader of a club in school.

We all have our stories but most of us never look back to see what it was that molded us into who and what we are today.

Going forward, do you want your story to play out the way it has up until this point of your life, or do you want to write your story and live it by a plan?

Wouldn't it be interesting to look forward and design your own story? Of course there will be twists and turns, but you've already learned so much. By knowing your story you will be able to deal with life's obstacles and stay on your own designed course.

I always preach to my children to know their story and to design a plan at a young age to live by. My youngest son has a dream to be a college basketball coach someday. Currently he is a high school basketball player. Some days when he may be slacking off or not working to his full potential, I ask him, "do you know your story?"

The first few times he gave me a puzzled look but now he understands. He explained to me that 30 years from now, when he is a high level division 1 basketball coach, he is going to be able to tell his players what he did to get in the best shape of his life. He is creating his story as a fifteen year-old.

Do you know your story? Think hard about all of the points in life/business that got you where you are today. Jot down all of the major hurdles you have overcome and the failures that you have learned from. Then, start writing the script for the rest of the journey.

Be as imaginative as you can. Reach for the stars and create the life that you want in front of you. Once you can visualize your future and begin to write down your goals and dreams you will know your story and start living it.

Strategy 7: Live Your Life in Balance

Several years ago I began to take notice that my life had become part of my business instead of my business being a part of my life.

While attending my child's little league games, I would often find myself on my cell phone, attempting to solve a business issue or close a deal. I committed my time to coaching baseball but there I was diverting my attention to my business.

While watching my daughter perform in a play or dance recital, my phone would vibrate in my pocket. I would get up and leave the room to deal with the business issue instead of enjoying precious moments of my life.

While having dinner with my wife, I would literally be thinking about business while she was carrying on a conversation with me. Half of the time I couldn't even focus on what she was talking about.

Then it hit me -- I was living out of balance. I was devoting so much of my time and energy to my business, that I was jeopardizing all of the other aspects of my life. It was at that point that I began researching life and business coaching.

After hours of research and interviews I hired someone who had a perfect understanding of what my dilemma was and how to attack it. The first thing I needed to do was understand what "balance" meant and what the benefits of being in balance would be. Life is like a finely tuned machine, and it does not run efficiently unless all components are in balance.

In order to live a balanced life you need to identify the most critical components of your life and work on them on a daily basis. My business, marriage, relationship with my children, family, friends, mental and physical health, religion, and spirituality were key components that I needed to have all in balance. I believed that if I sat down and rated all of those components that comprised my life on a scale of 1-10, I was better off being a 6 in all aspects than a 9 in one and a 4 in another.

It takes a lot of soul-searching and self-truth to come clean with yourself on what your balance really looks like. Once you are able to be honest with yourself and identify where you are out of balance you can begin to set action plans and goals to move forward on a daily basis.

In the Free Resources section of my website, locate the Leadership Balance Wheel and find out where you are and decide what you need to do to move forward.

●●●

Congratulations for taking the first step on "The Road to Success." This road is always under construction but does come with many twists, turns and roadblocks. I know, I've experienced many of them.

If you are looking to continue your journey, let me help you find the right path to take.

Visit www.LiveToWinCoaching.com and stay on the right road today.

About the Author

Steve Werner is a Success and Business Coach who engages is clients through years of entrepreneurial experience. As President of Live To Win Coaching, Steve's motto is, "I'm never too busy to become more successful in life and in business."

Over the years, Steve has learned many times to adapt and reinvent himself to keep up with an ever-changing marketplace. With over thirty years' experience in a wide array of businesses, Steve gained the knowledge and expertise to help individuals and business owners develop leadership skills necessary for success.

Steve has found his greatest professional satisfaction as a Success and Business Coach (www.LiveToWinCoaching.com). With Rolodex in hand, Steve leveraged the ups and the downs of his own experiences to evolve into a mentoring coach. It is this role that combines his hard-earned business savvy with his dedication to developing strong leaders and helping rebuild those who have experienced a loss of confidence or who might be in a transitional state. Steve's clients learn to identify their purpose, recognize and eliminate barriers to success, develop the leadership skills and strategies necessary to succeed, and focus on what matters so that they can lead a more satisfying life.

Steve believes his job is not to give answers clients might be looking for, but rather to enable them to think through tough and sometimes paralyzing dilemmas in order to make the best choices when dealing with immediate issues and preparing for future success. As Steve puts it, "My passion is helping people uncover and bring to the surface their ability to fight through issues and solve problems."

Contact Steve at: Steve@LiveToWinCoaching.com

Chapter 2

Stop Making Excuses and Get Real Results Now!

HOW ANY BUSINESS CAN TRIPLE THEIR PROFITS IN AS LITTLE AS 90 DAYS!

Matthew Lee

One Sunday the owner of a small software consulting business received a call. No, this wasn't a call from a customer with a big order. This was the kind of call every business owner hates... this was a call from a creditor. The creditor called to remind him that he was late in paying a rather large bill. On this day, he got a little angry and frustrated, not only because he couldn't pay the bill, but because it was Sunday, the only day he gave himself to relax and spend time with his family. He thought to himself "How dare this snake call me up on Sunday of all days. Why don't they have any decency?" He snapped back at the creditor and hung up the phone. As he slammed down his cell phone he looked over to see his 8 year old son standing near him which only made matters worse. Having his son see him lose his cool was the last thing he wanted. He looked at his son and said, "I'm sorry, son. Sorry you had to see me lose my temper."

In a moment like that it breaks your heart as a business owner and parent to feel as if you may be causing your family stress because of the work you are doing to build a successful business. His son looked up at his father, trying to comfort him and said, "Dad, didn't you tell them that you just hadn't made enough sales?"

We've all had a day when we question if all the sacrifices will pay off and someday we'll hit the goals we set for ourselves in becoming a business owner. And there are even days where we question whether just "grinding it out" another month is the answer to saving a business that is holding on by a thread. Yet it's even harder to find a shoulder to lean on because in most cases our families don't fully understand what it takes to start and run a successful business. It almost feels like you are speaking a different language to them. You tell them how passionate you are about your business and all they can think about is, "What if your idea doesn't work?"

In a business you write your own paycheck. To you it means your income potential is unlimited, but to them it may mean you don't get a regular paycheck, or there are no guarantees you'll have a paycheck at all. You think to yourself, "as if having a job is a guarantee to have a paycheck." In the end there is support as long as you are doing well financially. At the sight of any challenging market conditions or challenges in your business everyone else thinks it's time to walk away and go back to a real job. With all this chatter being put into your head by loved ones no wonder it's so difficult to run a successful business and raise a family.

I wish I could tell you that with a little extra hard work and some focus everything will be fine. Unfortunately that stuff only works for motivational speakers. Motivational speaker I am not. I'm a real "in the trenches" business owner that knows what it feels like to struggle, fail, struggle some more, and still keep on grinding in the trenches. I wish I could tell you that there is a light at the end of the tunnel, and you'll eventually get there, and to just keep your head up. I'm sorry but that kind of advice will only help mask the real pain, and it will eventually get you killed in the real world of business.

So what is the real answer - what does it really take to succeed? I am going to spend the rest of this chapter giving you the framework of The Real Results Now Method™. The Real Results Now Method™ helps business owners unlock the potential lying dormant in their business to be able to live a more fulfilled life. But before I dive into the framework of The Real Results Now Method™, I have a short quiz for you.

Business Quiz

1. True or False: Only 1 out of 5 businesses survives past the 5th year.
2. True or False: Only 1 out of 25 businesses survives past the 10th year.
3. True or False: Only 5% of companies will ever reach $1 million in revenue.
4. True or False: Only .08% of companies will ever reach $5 million in revenue.

All these answers are true- and that is why I have the deepest amount of compassion for you when I tell you I don't think anyone goes into business to face such high odds of failure. In fact it takes someone that is exceptional, who has amazing courage, and is willing to overcome extreme odds to have success. If we know business ownership is not for the faint of heart, then why do so many people naively stumble into business with no plans at all? Even if you had some plan in the beginning why haven't things gone exactly as planned? Are you really living up to your business potential? Are you confident that you know exactly what to do to have the business success needed in order to hit your business, income, and lifestyle goals? Or does it sometimes feel like you're flying by the seat of your pants?

If you're unsure of some of the answers to the proceeding questions then you're in the right place. By the end of this chapter I will lay the framework for a business model that you can use to build a successful business and get the money, time, and freedom you've always dreamed of. Is it going to be easy? No. Will you walk away with more clarity than you've ever had on how exactly you can triple your profits? Yes!

Finding Your Unique Advantage

What is at the foundation of this new business model? Well, it's not about reinventing the wheel. It's not about having a better website or having better closing script, although both of those will help you in the end. It's about taking your greatest skills, talent, and abilities and building your whole business around them. We all have unique skills that can give us a competitive advantage in the marketplace. However, in many cases we take them for granted. We all have experiences – good and bad – that when combined with our skills make us who we are. This combination is what I call your "Unique Advantage."

Now, imagine something with me. Close your eyes and picture that from the time you opened your business you had clarity about what your Unique Advantage was in the marketplace. All your marketing and business activities revolved around this Unique Advantage. Because of how you marketed your Unique Advantage you only attracted your perfect client. These perfect clients go through a pre-qualification process to qualify themselves to work with you. Imagine hand selecting the clients you want to work with, and as a result you only work with clients that will get 500-3,000% returns on their investment with you. Now your business is at capacity and you cannot take anymore clients.

At this point you have a waiting list of perfect clients that want to work with you. With every perfect client you work with you continue to develop your Unique Advantage. As your Unique Advantage grows, so does you confidence about your position in the marketplace. Instead of trying to market to all potential clients you have identified the perfect client profile, and your marketing is so compelling to them they wait in line to work with you. Your Unique Advantage differentiates you so much from your competitor that you are easily able to charge 2-3 times what your closest competitors charge. As a result of this increased income you can afford to hire people that do all the things in your business that you don't really like to do.

Let's be honest, you didn't start a business to do the things that drain your energy. You got into business to do the things that you love to do that give you more energy the more you do them. As a result of the success your clients have in the marketplace you gain increased recognition in your field. This increased recognition inspires and motivates you to develop your Unique Advantage even more so that you can create even greater contributions to the clients you serve.

As a result of your business success you have more fun in life, you have more time with your family, and you're able to go on more vacations. And now, because your business has created this kind of lifestyle, your life is great!

What Happens When Most People Open Their Business

You open up your business with the best intentions. You work hard. You have grand visions of business success. Everything runs smoothly and as a result you knock the ball out of the park. Does that dream seem familiar?

This dream of a successful business running smoothly bringing you your perfect clients is great, but that is not always your reality nor is it most businesses. For a lot of business owners this is not how their life is. I believe that to get rid of an issue you must get rid of the root problem, not cover it up with Band-Aids.

Why You Don't Have Your Dream Business

There are a number of reasons you don't have this dream business and you don't have perfect clients lining up to work with you. One reason is you're not exactly sure who your perfect clients are. You don't know who you should be targeting. Because of this your marketing message is not clear. In fact, a lot of businesses are niching too wide. Instead of having a laser beam focus with your marketing, you market like most businesses and as a result you feel like you must market to everyone.

Next, the perfect prospects don't currently see you as the solution to their problem. You're not standing out enough in the marketplace. You're just like everyone else. You're just like all of your competitors. To triple your profits you must absolutely stand out in the marketplace. Because you're not standing out in the marketplace, you're not comfortable charging what you're worth.

Not only have you not been charging what you're worth, when clients do come to you, they stay a little while and then they leave, like a thief in the night. They got what they think they needed, and then they go. However, they don't stay long enough to get to the results that they really need. You have basically done your clients a disservice because you haven't created a proprietary process that helps them get the best results possible. Because people are not getting the best results possible, you start questioning your ability to deliver on your promise to new clients. And since they're not getting those great results you're probably not generating enough referrals.

Your testimonials, well those are most likely non-existent. If you do have them, they are not pulling in clients for you. They might say something like "He's really nice. He's a great guy. Yeah, I got good results."

The Biggest Problem In Your Business

The biggest problem by far is you aren't closing enough new clients. Think about it the number one activity that is linked to your business's success. It's having enough sales conversations with prospects that are qualified and can write a big check for your products and services. If you're being really honest with yourself you know that this is one area that frustrates you the most. You know if you had a marketing system to line up qualified prospects who could write a big check, you would close the sale 30-50% of the time. The problem is you have no system or consistent process for creating enough sales conversations with qualified prospects. And if you've read any books on sales, you've probably been taught old school methods of closing the sale that make you feel like a used car salesman. Essentially when it comes to having that money conversation, the part when you ask for the check, it's like you become a different person. It's like you avoid that money conversation because you feel icky. Yes?

You're also talking to too many unqualified prospects. You know those tire kickers that come for your free advice, but they never have any intention of buying? Talking to too many of these unqualified prospects affects your confidence. You now hesitate to meet with new prospects because they are likely to be more tire kickers just wasting your time. Worse than that, they drain your conviction in your Unique Advantage and your edge over your competition goes down.

So now your confidence has declined because you haven't been closing many sales. When you show up for your next sales conversation you lack the conviction you need to inspire confidence and generate excitement from your prospect. The result: you don't close the sale. It's a dangerous and self-perpetuating cycle that must be stopped.

Let's Get Honest About Your Marketing Plan

And if we're being really honest you probably don't have a real marketing plan. You have a piecemeal marketing plan. But that's not a real marketing plan.

Your marketing isn't systematic. What I mean by that is you have no automation in place to communicate with your prospects and clients. Instead, you are creating messages from scratch for every communication instead of using automation to do the heavy lifting. You're reinventing the wheel each time you do something.

In addition, sometimes you're inconsistent with your marketing efforts. In fact, you're consistently inconsistent. When you begin to automate more of your marketing messages, you get more time and you do more marketing. What happens when you do more marketing? You attract more perfect clients. You can't generate more marketing if you're constantly on the phone with unqualified prospects or checking social media. You need automated marketing systems. You need proven marketing that is done on a consistent basis.

The Silent Business Killer Nobody Likes To Talk About

I almost forgot – Have you ever gotten carried away with any bright and shiny objects? Come on, admit it. They distract you. When you get distracted, you don't finish what you've started. You begin to feel guilty and overwhelmed. And you feel like that because you know better. You know you are cheating yourself, your family and clients out of the experience they could be having if your business was successful. And what else does it do? It creates inaction. When you have inaction you feel guilty and your level of ability goes down.

It's Not Your Fault

Now that was the bad part. Are you ready for the good part? It's not your fault. And I think it's important to say that because there are a lot of people who beat themselves up for not having figured this out. Here's why you can't beat yourself up and why I won't allow you to: it's easy to be overwhelmed and confused because you were never taught how to build a business around your Unique Advantage. In fact nobody ever taught you how to differentiate between a regular client and a perfect client. Nor have you figured out how to create an offer that your perfect clients would comfortably pay 2-3 times more than what your competitors charge. You've never been taught how to develop a marketing strategy that compels your perfect client to pick up the phone and call you or go to your website and request more information. Last but not least, you've never been taught how to develop a sales conversation that is authentic and flows naturally, so the ideal prospect doesn't even feel like they're being sold. Instead, they can't wait to buy.

The Real Results Now Method™ - Your Blueprint For Success

How many years have you been running your business, trying to figure it out, and simply flying by the seat of your pants? What would you give to go back and start your business over, having been properly trained on how to use your Unique Advantage to attract your perfect clients and develop the income that would have given you the time, money, and freedom to have the lifestyle you've always dreamed of? Only you know the answer to this question, but the truth is that you can't go back, you can only look forward. Take the time to study the framework laid out in the rest of this chapter as it may be the closest you'll get to go back and starting your business over from scratch.

The ugly truth of the matter is The Real Results Now Method™ is NOT for everyone. So before I share with you the framework, let me tell you who it is for and who it is NOT for.

Who is The Real Results Now Method™ NOT for:

- Business owners with no real skills or expertise.

- Business owners who expect to sit on social media all day and earn income with no real work.

- Business owners who are not willing to spend money to market and advertise.

- Business owners who lack a very strong work ethic.

- Business owners lacking drive and determination for success.

- Business owners that have a "get rich quick" mentality.

- Business owners looking for a fast and easy method building a successful business.

The Real Results Now Method™ is only for:

- Business owners who have real skills and expertise.
- Business owners who are willing to spend money to market and advertise.
- Business owners who have a very strong work ethic.
- Business owners that have a high drive and determination.
- Business owners that are willing to experience some failure during the testing phase.
- Business owners looking to build a real business and realizes that takes time and effort.

Before We Get To the Best Part

What is the most important step before you can dramatically change anything in your life? It's being willing to tell yourself the truth. If I entered a room filled with business owners and asked every single one what income they wanted to earn over the past 30 days, and then asked what they actually earned over that period, there would be a dramatic difference. If I had put their business under a microscope for the past 30 days, their actions would tell the story behind why they didn't hit their income goal.

I Have a Confession To Make

Since we're being honest, I should tell you that before I developed The Real Results Now Method™, I too struggled for years in my business. I had some success, if you consider success working 60 hour weeks to be successful. I had no leverage in my business and absolutely no marketing systems. Was I making good money? Yup, I was very much the beneficiary of a great real estate market and a lot of hard work. But when the real estate market collapsed so did my business. At that point I believed the story that it was the real estate market that caused my business to collapse. A few years later I was finally able to see the truth. I realized I never owned a dream business, I owned a job… and a nightmare job at that.

While I earned a great income during the real estate boom, I couldn't develop my Unique Advantage because I didn't realize I had one. I never developed a system for creating consistent results because I had never been taught how to do it. As a consequence, I never had any real freedom. Not exactly the dream business I thought I was creating.

Does this sound familiar? If you're anything like me you may have been in denial about the business you have been building, but today can be your turning point. You can go from the nightmare of feeling like you own a job to owning a dream business with a few simple steps.

My Business Turnaround Story

Prior to my business collapsing I was a 1-on-1 coaching client with several top marketing & business growth coaches. I had read over 500 business books, studied over 3 dozen home study courses, and I had been a member of several high-level paid mastermind groups on marketing & sales. I learned a lot of business stuff that worked, and a lot of stuff that really didn't work as well as advertised. Over 8 years I had spent close to $200,000 and over 10,000 hours learning this stuff first hand. And since we're being honest, I was kind of mad that I invested so much money in programs that never worked when implemented. Also there was no one program that taught all the best marketing and business growth strategies. Instead I had to sit through multiple programs that didn't work to find the strategies that did. That frustration alone was enough to make me give up.

Luckily I didn't, and I continued to focus on putting the puzzle pieces together. I reexamined all of the things that I had learned about marketing and growing my business that actually worked. Then I took out a sheet of paper and asked myself this question: "If I were going to start my business over knowing what I know now, what would I do differently?" I probably spent several hundred hours really thinking over my business and all of the successful businesses I had been fortunate enough to see operate first hand through networking with fellow mastermind members. I compiled a long list of things that worked and things that didn't work. My biggest realization is that there were too many things to implement at once, and to be successful coming out of the gates, I would need to get focused and keep things simple. Then I made my final list of what I'd do to start my business over again.

That process, which I used to rebuild my business is the initial framework for what I now call The Real Results Now Method™. The Real Results Now Method™ has dramatically changed the way my real estate business is run. No longer do I wonder where my next client is going to come from, I have push button marketing systems in place to bring new clients in like clockwork. Before the real estate downturn my clients got free advice and I worked for free until we sold them a home. Now my clients pay my company as much as $5,000 up-front to begin working with us. Before the downturn we worked like every other real estate agent and investment company in the market: focused on chasing down the next prospect to sell them a property. As a result, we focused much more on simply making the sale before the buyer got cold feet. We never sat down and spent time to think about how we could differentiate our business from everyone else. After the downturn we decided to sit down and take the time to determine our Unique Advantage. We then created our own proprietary process, The Path To Home Ownership Blueprint™ for empowering renters who have credit and down payment challenges. Instead of looking like all of our competitors who were always the hunter looking for their next sale, we became the hunted, and our satisfied clients sent their friends and family to us because of our commitment to educate and empower them. We even we sought out by our local media outlets and were featured on our local Fox affiliate.

The Path To Home Ownership Blueprint™, is the only program of its kind. As a result our average client value has gone from $3,000-$4,000 per client to $15,000-$20,000 per client. We pick and choose the clients we work with, and we are recognized as the go-to experts in our market to help renters become homeowners, even if they have credit issues and limited money for a down payment. I share this to inspire you that it is possible. How would you like to become the most sought after business in your local area or in the country because of your Unique Advantage and proprietary process? Are you ready and willing to put this process to work for you? Let's go!

Now To the Best Part

Here are the action steps you need to take to start implementing The Real Results Now Method™. The entire Real Results Now Method™ is based on a Dream Lifestyle Formula which I will quickly show you:

The Dream Lifestyle Formula

Your Dream Business Model
+
Defining Your Perfect Client
+
Proprietary Process with Premium Pricing
+
Irresistible Marketing to attract Your Perfect Clients
+
Your Perfect Sales Conversation
+
Your Phenomenal Fulfillment Process

These steps have been put in sequential order, and it is important that you take your time completing the exercises below. It is impossible to reach your goal without completing all the necessary steps.

Step 1 - Create Your Dream Business Model

The first step in The Real Results Now Method™ is gaining clarity on what you want. You need to create specific and measurable steps for assessing your progress in creating your dream business. It's important that you not only focus on what you want your business to look like, but also be clear about how your lifestyle will change as a result of hitting these business goals. When you have clarity on what it is you want and why you want it, you will have confidence, and with that confidence you will be able to have the drive necessary to create your dream lifestyle. To complete this process answer the following questions and be as descriptive and specific as possible with your business goals while completing this exercise.

Step 1 Exercise: Creating Your Dream Business Model

1. If we have a conversation 1 year from today, what would have to happen in your business for you to be happy with your progress?
2. It is now 1 year from today, how has your lifestyle changed as a result of the progress you've made in your business?
3. List 3 meaningful reasons for wanting to achieve the business and lifestyle goals you set above.
4. IMPORTANT NOTE: Achieving any business and lifestyle goal takes discipline and hard work. It's important you have a big enough "reason why" you need to accomplish these goals. If you don't, it will be easy to get off track and lose sight of your goal. As Friedrich Nietzsche said, "He who has a strong enough why can bear almost any how."
5. What does your business income have to be in order to live your dream lifestyle?

What did it feel like to complete step 1? If you didn't take your time and thoroughly complete these exercises, go back and do that now. I hear from people all the time that swear they are serious about building a dream business, but the reality is they are NOT committed, they are only interested. I can tell by the answers someone submits from completing the exercises in step 1 just how committed they are. I want you to imagine that I am sitting right next to you now and reviewing your answers. What would I think about your answers? Would I say, "These look good, congratulations!", or would I say, "This is some B.S.!" Why try to move forward if you aren't giving a 110% effort? If you don't know without a shadow of a doubt whether I would congratulate you, then you probably didn't do a thorough job. Remember as your coach I expect nothing less than a 110% effort.

Now that you have a clear idea of what your Dream Business and Dream Lifestyle will look like, it is time to go on to Step 2.

Step 2 – Defining Your Perfect Client

The next step is defining your perfect client. The first step to really understanding the power of working with perfect clients is to understand your Unique Advantage. I talked about Unique Advantage earlier in the chapter but now I'm going to define your Unique Advantage in regards to your perfect client. To your perfect client your Unique Advantage is an immediately recognizable skill, talent, or ability that is superior to your competitors and differentiates you from any other businesses in your market. In addition to your skills, talents, and abilities, your prefect client also recognizes your personal story and past experiences – good and bad – as a major part of your Unique Advantage. The next step in understanding your perfect client is defining your perfect client.

Your perfect client is someone that will pass the following set of filters:

- ✓ They get phenomenal results from working with you. Notice I didn't say they get good results or great results. Your perfect client is the person that gets such a large benefit from working with you that their results will be phenomenal.
- ✓ They can not only afford what you offer, but are willing to cheerfully pay your premium prices and wouldn't even think about negotiating with you to lower it. To them the price is a small fraction of the benefits they get from working with you.
- ✓ They apply the information that you give them.
- ✓ They will see the tangible benefits of working with you very quickly.
- ✓ They can be easily identified and contacted.
- ✓ They will tell other people about you and refer those clients to you.

Step 2 Exercise: Creating Your Dream Business Model

1. Go through your top 25-50 clients and identify the top 5 or 10 that meet all of the perfect client filters.

2. Make a list of all of the biggest problems these clients were experiencing before working with you. Now rank those problems in order of importance with 1 being the biggest problem they were experiencing.

3. Make a list of the Top 5 problems these clients have and make a list of the root causes of each problem.

4. Make a perfect client statement by filling in the following blanks and be as descriptive as possible:
   - My perfect client tends to be _____. (Explain the type of person or business)
   - My perfect client's issues tend to be _____. (Explain their top 5 to 10 issues)
   - What my perfect client needs most now are the following: _____. (Describe the solutions they need)
5. What was your Unique Advantage in getting these clients?
   - If you need help in determining this, don't hesitate to reach out to these clients and get feedback on what they like most about working with you over your competitors.
6. What role did your Unique Advantage play in delivering a phenomenal experience for these clients?
7. How much income do you plan to make per perfect client?
8. How many perfect clients do you need to hit your dream lifestyle income?

This exercise allows you to identify your "cream of the crop" client. By getting a clear idea of what you have done to be successful with these clients you now have a blueprint of what to do to duplicate this client in your business.

It's important to understand that there are three types of clients in business, and they are not at all equal:

1. Problem Clients complain about your prices, don't follow through or implement the strategies you have developed for them, and then they blame you for their lack of success.
2. Average Clients...
3. Perfect Clients on average will account for 25-50% of your profits while giving you fewer headaches and hassles.

How much would your income increase if all you did was work with your perfect clients? When I've done this exercise with business owners, with one small change they were able to increase their incomes on average of 50-100% just by going after perfect clients. Let's go to the next step and look at how you can do even more to create a premium profit model to increase your profits even more.

Step 3 - Develop Your Proprietary Process with Premium Pricing

One of fastest ways to increase your profits is simple: raise your prices. One of the reasons that most businesses face resistance in raising their prices is simply that they don't have a Unique Advantage over their competitors and, as a result, don't stand out in the marketplace. They advertise like most other businesses and have no target market. They are stuck in fierce competition and end up becoming a commodity.

The solution is to develop your proprietary process and focus on solving the problem for the "cream of the crop" clients that are willing to pay a premium for a specialized product or service.

The best way to explain this is to think about buying a steak from local steak house vs. a steak at Morton's Restaurant. They are both 100% beef, but the price at Morton's is 300%-500% higher than the local steak house. The local steak house caters to the local bargain shopper that wants a good steak at a good price, but Morton's sells an experience that is second to none.

This is how you have to look at your products and services. Morton's has developed a proprietary process for giving their perfect clients an experience that they are willing to pay a premium for compared to any of their competitors. What would your client's experience have to be for you to duplicate this in your business?

In the previous section I had you look at the biggest problems you solve for your perfect clients. When you are creating your process, don't get caught up in trying to make it perfect. Understand that just having a proprietary process separates you from most of your competitors, and helps your perfect client feel more comfortable working with you and paying a premium for your service. Your proprietary process will be a living document. It's important to get started by outlining it and advertising it to your clients.

Step 3 Exercise: Creating Your Proprietary Process

1. What are the steps that you lead your perfect clients through that enables them to have an amazing experience and get exceptional results?

2. Brainstorm 5-10 names that reflect the results of your process.

3. Share the name and process with your top 5-10 perfect clients and get feedback.

4. Begin using your proprietary process in all your marketing.

You may not realize it, but you are now in the Top 1% of marketers. Very few businesses have a proprietary process that delivers exceptional results for their perfect clients. It's a terrific way to stand apart from your competition.

Step 4 - Develop Irresistible Marketing to Attract Your Perfect Clients

There are a lot of things you can do to attract your perfect client, and it would take a 5-day workshop for me to thoroughly cover all of those strategies for you. However, I would like to share with you one of the most powerful strategies that almost everyone can use to kick start the process of targeting and acquiring more perfect clients. I'm going to call this the Starbuck's Strategy, as this is a primary strategy that Starbuck's Coffee has used to build their business and capture market share very quickly and efficiently.

Have you been inside of a Target or Barnes & Noble and seen a Starbucks kiosk? Instead of accruing the costs of building an entire location, Starbucks realized they could expand more efficiently by creating kiosks inside of these large retailers, benefiting from their in-store traffic.

When done properly, this strategy can help you grow your business very rapidly. So now you are probably thinking, "I am not a Starbucks, how can I duplicate this strategy?" Complete the following exercise to figure out how you can use the Starbuck's Strategy for your business.

Step 4 Exercise: Creating Your Starbuck's Strategy

1. Make a list of all the businesses that already have your perfect client as one of their clients.

2. Make a list of all the people your personally know that are (a) in this business; or (b) know someone that is in this business and can make an introduction for you.

3. Make a list of how you could create value for these businesses by introducing you to their client base.

   - Be creative with this part. It could be anything from paying them a referral fee to referring clients to their business.

4. Develop a short script to introduce your offer to them.

   - Be sure to keep in mind that you must create an offer that appeals to their self-interest. Before making your offer, read it as if you were the person on the other side. Would you say "Yes" to your offer?

Whether you know it or not, there are companies with access to hundreds of your perfect clients right now, and they are currently not referring them to anyone. This is an opportunity, and I can almost guarantee the results if you go to them and make it clear how they will benefit from this relationship. Don't let the simplicity of this strategy stop you from implementing this as soon as possible.

Step 5 – Your Perfect Sales Conversation

True or false – you love it when someone tries to sell you something? If you're like most people, you hate it. Did you know that negative feelings associated with selling can affect your own ability to sell your products and services?

To combat that, I have created a process to help you have a more authentic sales conversation. This chapter has an abbreviated version of what I teach others, but these 3 steps will help you become more comfortable making sales.

1. Detach yourself from the outcome of the sale. Instead, focus on seeing if their situation is one where you will be able to create a lot of value or solve any significant problems. When your goal shifts from closing the sale to helping others, you are no longer just trying to make a sale.

2. Ask them how their life would be better 12 months from now as a result of solving those problems. Learn more about what it would mean to them to solve these problems. Are there things they will be able to do or accomplish that they can't do now?

3. If appropriate, share how your products and services could help them solve their problem. Explain your services in relation to the problems they shared. When finished, ask them, "Do you think that you could benefit from our product or service?"

This three step process is quite a difference from books that teach 101 ways to close the sale, isn't it? How many times have you bought something when the salesperson simply sounded like they had a conversation with you verses sounding like a used car salesman? That is exactly what today's buyers are looking for – no arm twisting, just a simple conversation. Follow the 3 steps above and I promise you won't make the prospect feel all creepy when it is time to ask for the sale.

Step 6 – Follow Through With Phenomenal Fulfillment

Okay, you've made a sale, and it's time to take your clients through your proprietary process. Now what do you do? Of course the process will be completely customized for your business, but here are some ideas to maximize your profits during the fulfillment stage. The following 3 ideas assume that you are going to do an amazing job for your clients and help you increase lifetime client value.

1. Referrals – Do you know the best time to ask for referrals? Right at the time of purchase. And this is also the best time to set up the expectation with the client that you depend on referrals to expand your business and that you will from time to time ask for introductions to people that could be a good fit for your products and services.

2. What types of systems could you put in place to make sure you are asking every client for referrals and introductions to new clients? Would it be farfetched to believe that you could get 50%-100% rate of referrals that turn into a sale?

3. Case Studies and Testimonials – Case studies and testimonials from satisfied clients are one of the best tools to use in marketing. They help overcome objections that a prospect may have about using your products and services.

4. Take your top 5 objections and create case studies about how you have helped your customers overcome those issues.

Additionally, use stories in your presentation. Stories are one of the most influential and persuasive tools to bypass conditioned responses and defenses that prospects naturally have.

5. If you were effectively and systematically using case studies and testimonials in your marketing how much would your conversion rate increase? What if you included a book of case studies and testimonials in a direct mail package you sent out to new prospects? What if you made new prospects read or look at specific case studies and testimonials prior to your sales conversations- do you think your closing rate would go up? Of course it would!

6. Feedback for Improving & Optimizing Your Process – It's easy to assume that we are doing a great job, but nothing is better than feedback from our clients. A few of the most powerful questions to gain valuable feedback would be:
   - What are the most valuable things we've done for you?
   - If we could improve anything about the experience what would you improve?
   - If someone asked you the top reason why they should do business with us, what would you tell them?

This process will make prospects feel your concern, and it will get them in the habit of giving you feedback rather than keeping complaints to themselves or negatively voicing their opinions about you products, service, and company publicly. The most important thing to remember about this process is that you must be responsive to the feedback your customers share with you or they will stop sharing.

Make these 3 follow through and fulfillment steps a part of your process and you can increase your profits an additional 25%-100% for every sale that you make.

Are You Ready For Real Results Now?

As I told you in the beginning of this chapter, I am not a motivational speaker, just an in-the-trenches business owner and coach. It's ok to say you know what to do to build a successful business if you actually have a written plan to do that. The Real Results Now Method™ is about one thing and one thing only: getting real results NOW. Is there a chance you implement the steps I've outlined for you as the framework of The Real Results Now Method™ and you don't get results? Maybe, but you will just have to implement them to prove me wrong. I am willing to bet on you. I'm willing to bet that with the right steps implemented you will have the business and lifestyle you have always dreamed of. Now the only thing left to do is take action.

The Last Takeaway

The last takeaway from this chapter is to stay in the game. Remember the software consultant I told you about in the beginning of this chapter? He stayed in the game and it paid off in a big way. Within six years of starting his business he made it to the INC 500 list of fastest growing companies, and he stayed there for six straight years. Additionally, his company attracted an investment of over $50 million from the investment banking powerhouse Goldman Sachs.

It took years of trial and error, but he was able to figure it out, create an exceptional business, and is currently blazing a trail as an industry leader. His accomplishments came from staying in the game and discovering the steps for success.

I know you don't want to wait six years, so I have boiled the steps for success down to The Real Results Now Method™. By following these steps you can do the same.

About the Author

Matthew Lee, also known as "America's Home Ownership & Wealth Expert™", is a bestselling author and business growth coach regularly sought by the media for his insight on real estate, credit scoring, business growth, wealth creation, and personal growth. Matthew is Cofounder of The Path To Home Ownership Blueprint™. The Path To Home Ownership Blueprint™ is the only program of its kind to help renters overcome credit & down payment challenges to become homeowners while they build a foundation for wealth creation.

The idea for creating The Path To Home Ownership Blueprint™ was developed using The Real Results Now Method™. The Path To

Home Ownership Blueprint™ is a 5 step proprietary process that uses a multipronged approach to help clients:

- become homeowners
- develop the skills necessary for wealth creation
- gain access to a team of experts to help them in fulfilling on a successful financial plan.

To contact Matthew Lee, America's Home Ownership & Wealth Expert™ and to learn more about how you can customize The Real Results Now Method™ for your business, email matthewlee@thepathtohomeownership.com.

Claim Your Free Bonus Now! $67 Value!

Let me congratulate you for investing in yourself and taking this step in transforming your business. Would you like a plug and play template that walks you step by step through the process of developing a game plan to triple your profits in as little as the next 90 Days? As a reward for your commitment I put together **The Real Results Now Method™ Cheat Sheet** so you can:

Customize a Dream Business Model which allows you to turn your passion into a profit machine.

Attract Your Perfect Client that craves a solution that only your business can provide through your Unique Advantage.

Create a Proprietary Process allowing you to command Premium Pricing.

Create an Irresistible Marketing Plan that helps you to attract an avalanche of your Perfect Clients.

Develop Your Perfect Sales Conversation and close up to 90% of your qualified prospects without sounding like a used car salesman.

Build Your Phenomenal Fulfillment Process to get referrals, testimonials, and to refine and optimize your fulfillment processes.

To Get your Free Bonus **The Real Results Now Method™ Cheat Sheet** please visit **http://tinyurl.com/CheatSheetBonus**

Chapter 3

From Broke to Profit in 21 Days

Nido Abdo

"Good artists copy, great artists steal."

Pablo Picasso

Pablo Picasso, one of the greatest artists the world has ever seen, might have just painted the ultimate formula for success with that simple quote.

This formula could very well determine how you'll live the remainder of your life. More specifically, it will determine the way you conduct business and live your life—independently, in control or controlled—as master or slave. In a moment, I'm going to show you exactly how you can quickly and easily transform your life and your business in 21 days or less.

But first, I have to share one of the scariest ordeals I've ever had to face and, most importantly, the lesson I discovered that shaped the rest of my life. Here's the story...

Two very small, overcrowded fishing boats escaped in the dead of night late July 1991. Twenty-three perished when one of the boats capsized. I was one of only eight who survived my family'x exodus from the barbaric civil war in Africa.

You're probably wondering what my family's tragedy and triumph has to do with your business's profits. It's simple. The answer is…everything.

You see, we were lost in the middle of the Indian Ocean for days and it took us nearly two weeks to arrive at Kenya because we were operating without a real blueprint.

The fishermen in charge found directions for navigating using the stars. Some days, we wandered in the ocean for hours, only to discover that we were heading in the wrong direction because they followed the wrong star. It was absolutely the most miserable time of my life.

As a business consultant and ad writer, I have learned why most companies fail—it's because they follow the wrong direction, too.

For example, I had a client who was operating a restaurant that was on the brink of bankruptcy. He didn't have many customers coming through the doors, profits were declining, and he was living off his credit cards. Certainly not a place you'd want to be as an entrepreneur.

To help solve some of his woes, I asked him this simple question: what are you currently doing about your marketing? He answered, "I mailed out 10,000 menus because it's what the restaurant down the street does all the time".

Shocking answer? Yes. Surprising? No.

Truth is, most people are where they are today because of the road map they followed to get there. It's beyond me how anyone would follow the path of those who have NOT achieved much success… and then expect to get different results.

In the gripping 1992 drama, Glengarry Glenross, Al Pacino plays a smooth real estate salesman named Ricky Roma. While the other salesmen in the office are portrayed as complaining, pessimistic sad sacks who blame the poor quality of the leads for their lack of sales, Ricky is unique.

Ricky is just as hard-boiled and foul-mouthed as the rest, but unlike the others he's optimistic and philosophical. Rather than begging the office manager for new leads like the rest, Ricky sparks up a conversation with a stranger in a bar, eventually getting him to sign a contract and write a check. At one point during the conversation with this stranger, Ricky says, "I subscribe to the law of contrary public opinion. If everyone thinks one thing, then I say bet the other way."

Amen, Ricky.

Rather than join the pity party, Ricky decides to work. Rather than beg for new leads, Ricky goes out and finds his own. Rather than rely on the traditional method of visiting prospects in their homes, Ricky engages in a natural conversation with a guy in a bar. Rather than settle for the poor sales figures of his counterparts, Ricky decides to take matters in his own hands and put himself atop the sales leader board.

Ricky was success because instead of following the crowed, he chose his own path. That's because…

The Majority is ALWAYS Wrong

- 1% of US population will become extremely wealthy
- 4% will achieve financial security
- 95% will live paycheck to paycheck

What does this tell us? It should tell you that 95% (and probably more) of the people around you have the wrong thinking about money, about success, and, in a broader sense, about business, advertising, and marketing. Otherwise the situation would be the reverse and 95% would be wealthy and successful.

You should learn to ignore the well-meaning advice of the 95% who, based on the track record, haven't had much success. Although this sounds easy, believe me when I tell you it's one of the most difficult challenges you'll ever face.

It can be difficult to look at all the people around you - your family, friends, and co-workers - and think, "I will not take advice from these people." However, if you truly want to be a success, you must. How you're going to live the rest of your life is at stake here. You can't let other people make that decision for you.

Earl Nightingale (father of the self-help industry) had some great advice for being a "rebel." Earl said that if you can't find a good role model to follow or if you can't find somebody who's already achieved what you want to achieve, then you should look around at what everyone else is doing and do the opposite.

Or as Ricky Roma put it, "If everyone thinks one thing, I say bet the other way." Now do you see why my restaurant owner client was digging his grave by following the restaurant down the street?

To be different you must think different. Ask yourself these important questions:

- What is unique about you?
- What is unique about your company?
- Your product?
- Your service?
- What are the 'standard operating procedures' in your industry? (Write out as many as you can think of)
  - How many of those 'standards' are you willing to break?

Making Your Advertising Profitable

The truth is, most businesses today are using the same old-fashioned marketing and advertising techniques. But the world today is a much different place and the clients you're trying to attract have grown increasingly immune to these conventional approaches.

In today's over-marketed, over-hyped world, the "same old" techniques for generating response may occasionally work, but not nearly as well as they used to. This is why many businesses are seeing their bottom line numbers decline every year. This will inevitably continue.

The Ultimate Secret to Success

I came to America when I was 11 years old and couldn't write a single word of English.

The language barrier made college difficult; it took me seven years to finish a four year Liberal Arts degree. I couldn't hold on to most jobs I had…the longest one being 2 years and that's because it was seasonal. And I struggled financially for many years. In fact, I had to move my family in with my parents after getting evicted from our apartment.

Yet today, I'm a sought-after copywriter and marketing strategist that lives life on my own terms…working when I want, where I want, and with only the kind of clients who I enjoy working with. What made the difference?

Direct Response Marketing.   Study it.   Understand it, and the keys to the palace are yours.

Direct Response Marketing provides individuals and businesses with a medium to share discounts, promotions, important facts, tips and news on subjects that they are passionate about with people who want to receive that information.

It has long been said that people want to do business with people that they know, like and trust. Direct Response Marketing gives you the opportunity to connect with people through multiple channels.

The utilization of these mediums allows you to have a distinct presence in your industry, which keeps you top-of-mind. By utilizing these optimized channels you build credibility and set your business apart from those using traditional advertising methods.

I've been fortunate enough to learn from some of the "world masters" of Direct Response Marketing and discovered many of their secrets to quickly and clearly laser credible useful "Gems" to solve just about any marketing dilemma – in any business.

Here are some that you can't afford to ignore.

You're In the Relationship Business

Don't get me wrong, your product and service are important…however, if you want to build an Iron Cage around your customers and close the back door forever, then you'll need more than just a great product.

If you open up any yellow pages directory or pay attention to the advertisements that businesses drop into your mail-box every day, 99% of them are all focusing on one thing—themselves.

You'll notice headlines such as "BEST SERVICE IN TOWN." According to whom? Or maybe, "IN BUSINESS FOR 50 YEARS." So What? Or my favorite one, "WE TAKE GOOD CARE OF OUR CUSTOMERS." Well isn't that nice to know.

You'll notice variations of these messages scattered all over the place and small business owners act shocked when their message falls on deaf ears.

To have a great relationship with someone you have to have a great message delivered at the right time, and often.

For example, a letter mailed to a new area resident may be tossed into the trash today, but tomorrow or next week may be the perfect time to reach them. Mrs. Jones, our new neighbor, gets your letter in the mail. She thinks to herself, "Dentist?" No way. I've just barely unpacked the boxes and moved in. I haven't even got a real doctor, never mind a dentist. I've got to find a Chiropractor for my back. It's killing me from all of this unpacking. Dentist? I'm too busy. And then she throws your letter into the trash.

Most business owners would stop right there and say, "Well, I mailed and clearly she wasn't interested, so direct mail doesn't work."

If you want to be a savvy marketer and overpower your competition, then you've got to have a bulletproof self-image. You don't care (nor do you know anyway) what she says about the dentist. You relentlessly mail her another letter and another and another. It's the day your 5th mailing arrives. She's just finished sorting the "A" pile mail from the junk. Mrs. Jones is having a quick bite to eat when her front crown bites the dust! CRACK!

She rushes to the trash bin and starts frantically sifting through until she finds your letter. She picks up the phone and dials your number. "Hello. My name is Mrs. Jones. I just opened my mail and found your lovely invitation to visit your practice… and well, I have a dental emergency and need to be seen right away!"

You'll never know the timing of your marketing message as it relates to your individual prospects... your potential new customer. Today's unwanted pest becomes tomorrow's invited and welcomed guest... depending solely upon the timing of your message's entry into their lives. This is true with any media.

Keep Track of ROI

Very simply, you need to know the costs involved in delivering your marketing message (media independent), and then track your return. Knowing the lifetime value of a customer is also important because it allows you to out-spend your competition in customer acquisition, as they are only focused on the initial cost, not the lifetime value of the customer. On the other hand, you may be willing and financially able to forgo profits on the first transaction. The front end (customer acquisition costs versus short-term gain) may intentionally operate at a loss, but there are handsome profits made through your long-term relationship with the customer.

And once you have a winning campaign, you can simple rinse and repeat. However, I must warn you...

There are scam artists out there trying to sell you advertising based upon an extremely twisted version of the principle of repetition. Many businesses have been like sheep led to slaughter on this one. Yes, as you've heard above, repetition is essential to the maximization of any great marketing message.

In fact, not repeating profitable ads is one of the most common mistakes made in any business. Usually it's from a combination of the absence of sufficient tracking data, combined with perceived lack of time to "get everything done." Hear the message here and now... repetition DOES work... but ONLY with ads that are PROVEN SUCCESSFUL in the first place!

If you run an ad (any media) and it fails to bring much if any response at all, repeating that add will be an enormous waste of money! A bad ad (defined by poor or no response) won't get better with repetition.

I recently ran one incredibly successful ad campaign where a single sales letter brought in 51 new customers in less than three weeks at $500 per person. Four weeks later we ran the same ad, same letter, to the database (only minor changes in the vehicle with which it was mailed), and we enjoyed an additional 24, very profitable new customers. Do you think we're going to run it again? Absolutely! And then we'll run it again... and again... until the return diminishes to the point where the math no longer supports further mailings.

Understand that this is typical. It's not a fluke. You don't get 75 buyers (patients, customers, etc) the first time, then the next time 100 more, and the next time after that 150. If your ad works, it will work quickly, and it can be measured.

Response from subsequent repetition will drop off. Continue to run the ad until you're no longer satisfied with the math. BEWARE of anyone selling you advertising that can't be measured! No type of small business can afford to put precious resources of ad dollars into "image" marketing. Direct response marketing is measurable and trackable marketing, and is the only sane and highly profitable way to go.

About the Author

Nido has been running a seven-figure business since the age of 24. What makes that even more impressive is that he escaped a barbaric civil war and came to the U.S. when he was only eleven years old and without being able to speak a single word of English. Using his direct response expertise, Nido has helped businesses in 9 different industries to get more clients, more profits, and more free time.

Free Resources from Nido Abdo

If you own or operate a profit oriented business, then I would like to extend a special offer to help you understand how you improve every aspect of your business by utilizing direct response marketing. I've created a free video that reveals how to…

- ✓ Quickly and easily maximize your online exposure

- ✓ Automate your business and grow at a rapid pace

- ✓ Create an iconic business that out-markets and out-powers the competition

- ✓ Identify needs that are unfulfilled in your market and become the go to firm

To get your free video presentation, visit my website at www.NidoAbdo.com

Chapter 4

Marketing Psychology: The How & Why of What They Buy

Sam Page, M.Psy, MBA

Psychology is the main driver behind buying behavior. Whether looking to buy a product or a service, consumers do not simply close their eyes and make a random selection from a list of businesses. Instead, they take several factors into account when making decisions. Their brains process different perceptions, emotions, memories, and experiences, which influence their decision to pull out their wallets and spend their money with you. Many scientists and researchers have done studies and gathered information on how and why this happens. It's a field which has come to be known as "neuromarketing". Simply, neuromarketing is using what we understand of psychology to measure the impact of marketing on our decision making processes.

Although neuromarketing is a modern concept, psychology has always been the primary force behind the effectiveness of your marketing and advertising. Think back on some of the most profitable, long-lasting campaigns you know. For example, Marlboro introduced The Marlboro Man in an attempt to create an ideal, appealing, "male" lifestyle around its cigarettes. They knew that their campaign would influence more men to smoke their cigarettes to "feel" like The Marlboro Man. As Cicero the Roman Statesman once said, "if you wish to persuade me, you must think my thoughts, feel my feelings, and speak my words."

There is no doubt that the way peoples' brains work is responsible for the way they make decisions. Cicero knew that the best way to reach people is to get inside of their heads. By studying the human brain, researchers have analyzed how different marketing strategies affect us on a psychological level. To understand the core buying motives, thoughts and feelings of your customer base gives you an almost unfair advantage over your competitors. How could you apply this type of scientific research, on a practical level, in your own marketing and sales efforts? Do you think these insights could increase the overall return on your annual marketing expenditure?

While there are many psychological triggers that play a role in the decision-making of consumers, there are three key triggers that the businesses of today cannot afford to ignore: cognitive friction, conspicuous consumption, and the power of emotion. By understanding these three triggers, businesses can learn how to increase the responsiveness of their customers, how to reach customers through their levels of self-esteem, and how they can use different emotions to influence their customers to identify with their products or services.

Psychological Trigger #1: Cognitive Friction

Research has consistently shown people have a limit on how much cognitive processing their brains can handle. As a result, we take mental shortcuts. Researchers Susan Fiske and Shelley Taylor have found we're predisposed to favor decisions that are instantly gratifying, instead of those which are future-based. They also concluded that consumers will pass up benefits in favor of being able to use less cognitive energy. That is, they prefer the simple option. Furthermore, our brain's processing ability is strained when a consumer knows little or is unfamiliar with our product or service. This conflict is often called cognitive friction.

The number one mistake most businesses make is they put themselves and their product before the customer and their needs. This is the quickest way to promote cognitive friction: instead of spending time on how to make their buying process easy, fast, and preferred they focus on making the selling process easy, fast, and preferred. This forces consumers to use more of their limited cognitive processing. Businesses risk blindness by thinking that if they optimize their selling process, there will be more time to sell more products. However, by focusing on making the buying process easy and optimal, there is potential to attract more consumers and get better results.

Research has proven that by reducing cognitive effort, there will be an increase in response to our marketing efforts and ultimately an increase in sales. In one public policy research study, "Do Defaults Save Lives?", Eric Johnson and Daniel Goldstein researched why only a small number of Americans signed up as an organ donor when 85% of them showed their approval for organ donation as a concept. Daniel and Goldstein conducted an experiment in which they gave participants three options to choose from:

1. An opt-in with a default set to NOT be a donor.
2. An opt-out form with the default set to be a donor.
3. And either an opt-in or opt-out with no default.

Their findings showed the form of the question had a big impact on the results. By having donor selected as the default, the number of donors increased by 100%.

Case Study: How Amazon.com Reduces Cognitive Friction

A great business application of Johnson and Goldstein's findings can be seen with the way Amazon structures their online shopping experience. Consumers view Amazon as a default shopping website because it already has their personal information, such as credit card numbers and address, already punched in. They make it easy!

There are two more ways Amazon reduces cognitive friction:

1. Through their shipping options. One of the options is to award free shipping with a purchase of $25 or more - which will often

drive consumers to add one more item to their checkout cart just to get out of paying shipping costs.

2. Amazon also offer free, two-day shipping for an upfront payment of $79 a year. By getting customers to choose this option, there is an increased chance they will exclusively shop on Amazon.com and more often, because they have already made an investment in the site. Again, the ease of the shopping experience reduces their cognitive effort.

Other companies, such as Zynga and Groupon, also take advantage of reduced cognitive effort and friction. For example, Zynga has monetized their addicting online game, FarmVille, because they know a significant portion of their 40 million users will spend money simply because they're already so invested. Groupon has capitalized on the basis of group approval. For example, they only offer deals that a large number of users have utilized, which provides social proof, and makes the decision to join the ranks that much easier. By recognizing the level of cognitive friction and effort in their marketing strategies, businesses can easily find ways to make improvements.

It is important to understand how the human brain makes decisions and processes thoughts about buying behavior. By reducing how much a person has to think, businesses can see a drastic change in their customer perception, whether it is through ease of options, time investment, or social acceptance.

Psychological Trigger #2: Conspicuous Consumption

Conspicuous consumption is a term that Norwegian-American economist Thorstein Veblan coined in 1899. It describes consumers who buy expensive, luxurious items in an effort to show off their wealth and to climb the ranks of the social ladder. They want to be better than others or prove that they are of the same status of a social group. The Constitution of the United States claims that all men are created equal but conspicuous consumption can very well widen the gap.

Two of the underlying psychological driving factors behind conspicuous consumption are power and control. Conspicuous

Consumption can also boost self-esteem and have a direct impact on a consumer's buying behavior. For example, consumers looking to achieve a high social status choose to buy expensive, high-end brands and services as opposed to brands and services that do not have an expensive reputation or are of low-quality. This can sometimes be achieved through literal consumption. For example, there has been a general social stigma between Dunkin Donuts and Starbucks coffee. People often view those who drink Starbucks coffee as opposed to Dunkin Donuts coffee as more "high-end" because the prices at Starbucks are higher. In addition to achieving conspicuous consumption through food and beverages, researchers Hupfer and Gardner concluded that different consumers can have different perceptions about personal possessions as well. They found that cars were one of the top most important personal possessions, especially among middle-aged people. Researcher Mason concluded that people use their cars to communicate their status and social class to others. For other generations, conspicuous consumption is achieved through clothing, accessories, or technology.

Self-esteem is one of the biggest internal, psychological, driving factors behind conspicuous consumption. As the famous psychologist Abraham Maslow suggested in his paper, "A Theory of Human Motivation," all people have a need for respect and acceptance. It is no doubt that people will most often do anything, including pay high prices, to impress others and usually it involves the purchase of certain products. Younger generations often try to impress each other through clothing and personal accessories and older generations often do it through expensive cars, homes, and other types of personal property. They do this in an attempt to become, or be perceived as "the best-of-the-best" among their peers. When businesses leverage this psychological trigger, not only will they capitalize on unrealized revenue from those who already live a life of high status, but also from those who are willing to spend more money to be able to join them.

The key to taking advantage of conspicuous consumption is for businesses to market their products and services in a way that will show their customers how it will make them more appear reputable. Marketers must get into the heads of their audience. It is important to understand how consumers think. Many of them believe that if something is very costly, it means that it is of high-quality and it will help them achieve their desired results. Also, many of them will want something that is unique and exclusive. If a high-end product or service is scarce and consumers are under the impression that businesses are only offering limited quantities, their desire for that product will increase. Their desire will also increase if businesses market a product using the words "new," "improved," or "latest," because they will believe that if they are among the first to have it, they will set a trend. Finally, not all consumers are alike. By finding out the specific reasons as to why consumers want a certain product or service, businesses will be able to market it in a way that relates to them.

Conspicuous Consumption is one of the many ways in which businesses can capitalize on the emotions of their audience. Since power, control and self-esteem are some of the strongest psychological triggers every human experiences, businesses can analyze how they can utilize conspicuous consumption through their products or services. It can influence their marketing campaigns and how they reach out to consumers. It also leads to the third most important psychological trigger, emotional connection.

Psychological Trigger #3: The Power of Emotion

Emotions are one of the biggest internal, psychological driving factors for making purchasing decisions. Research has shown that emotions create certain chemical reactions in our brains, which cause us to process and memorize information. Similar to how businesses can attract more customers by figuring out how to boost their customers' self-esteem, emotions of all kind are a big, internal driving factor in making buying decisions. Businesses can utilize the mood, morality, and overall happiness of their customers in order to boost sales.

The biggest key to attracting more customers is to be able to connect with them emotionally. If your target audience is not moved by, or attracted to your message, that means less sales. Before you can connect with your audience, you must first understand them. By understanding your audience, you will know what types of words, images, messages, etc., attract them. For example, some businesses will want their audience to feel attractive, adventurous, healthy, financially secure, independent or in control. By knowing how your audience wants to feel, you'll be able to connect on a more powerful level.

Businesses often make the mistake of advertising their product or service instead of advertising a solution that their product or service can provide. For example, the founder of Kodak, George Eastman, once asked his sales team what they were selling. Most of them answered with a product, such as cameras or films. They were all wrong. They were selling memories.

In his book, *Neuromarketing: Understanding the Buy Buttons in Your Customer's Brain*, Patrick Renvoise explains how powerful memories, such as driving a car for the first time or living though a national tragedy can cause the brain to react in a way in which it creates intense emotions that are hard to forget. Researchers call this emotional marketing, which all businesses should utilize. If businesses advertise their product or service with nothing else but the hopes that people will buy it, they will most likely end up with little success. However, if businesses know the needs and desires of their audience and advertise in a way that addresses them, they will most likely find themselves with more loyal customers.

Emotions play an important role in the decision-making process. If a business offends a customer or if a customer does not agree with the message that a business is sending out, they will not be able to identify with the products or services being offered and will most likely not patronize that business. If a customer agrees with the messages a business sends out, they will more likely be influenced to patronize them. The mood of the audience plays a huge part in the area of emotions and decision-making. According to Walter Dill Scott, author of *The Psychology of Advertising*, feelings such as joy, love, and happiness will cause the feelings of the heart to enhance while feelings such as fear, hate, and jealousy will cause more negative effects on the body, such the breathing rhythm. Pleasurable feelings will cause a customer to act quicker and more on an impulse than non-pleasurable feelings.

Finally, business owners who have physical stores can manipulate their environment to appeal to the emotions of their customers. For example, think back to the Starbucks versus Dunkin Donuts example.

While a typical Dunkin Donut store dons a drive-thru, bright colors, and a fast-paced, fast-food restaurant-like environment, a typical Starbucks location is more relaxed, often with no drive-thru, couches and lounge chairs in a dim-lighted environment, and always some kind of music playing over the loudspeaker. Although both businesses serve coffee, the two environments are a sharp contrast with each other and can appeal to different types of people. For example, a group of college students working on a project would most likely chose to meet at Starbucks because the space is more comfortable and relaxed and there is plenty of work space. The environment of a business can play an important role in identifying with the emotions of the customers. Businesses who know that their customers want to feel a certain way will be able to give them those feelings through their unique business environment.

There is no right way for businesses to emotionally connect with their customers. Every method depends on the target audience, the product or service, and the business. By knowing how to get inside of the heads of their customers, businesses can customize their messages and marketing strategies to become more appealing and to evoke more emotions that will make customers want to buy. Businesses that can figure out how to make their customers happy will always hold a distinct advantage.

Conclusion

By ignoring these three psychological triggers, you could be inadvertently cannibalizing leads, sales, and revenue. Marketing isn't a choice. You have do it, so why not do it with the greatest leverage and greatest possibility for return? Integrating the science of consumer psychology into your business development strategies will give you a head start in climbing to the top.

First, prioritize the ease of the buying process over the selling process and decrease the amount of cognitive friction put on your customers.

Next, take advantage of conspicuous consumption. Through understanding how self-esteem affects the buying behavior of your customers, you'll be better positioned to appeal to the intangible value attributable to elevated status.

Finally, by knowing how to emotionally connect with customers, you can structure your marketing efforts around the thoughts, wants, desires, and frustrations of your customers, better placing you as the provider of choice. You can utilize each of these triggers separately or combine them for a more powerful effect.

<u>**Self-Assessment:**</u>

How to Best Leverage Consumer Psychology in Your Business

In terms of thinking about your business, ask yourself these questions:

- What is my buying process like and how can I make it easier for customers as a means to reduce cognitive friction?
- How will it be easier over other similar businesses?
- Is my business more about my customers or my products/services?
- Are there ways for my products or services to take advantage of the conspicuous consumption affect? What would appeal to my target audience?
- What messages does my business send to my customers? What kind of emotions should I be evoking from them?

By reflecting on these questions, business owners will be on their way to making great improvements in their marketing strategies and will see a greater response from their customers.

About the Author

Sam Page is the CEO and founder of NeuroTriggers, the world's only full service neuromarketing firm.

With a Master's degree in Psychology, coupled with an MBA, Sam recognizes better than most that effective business development hinges on the science of human behavior. His company develops campaigns which directly tap into to the thoughts, feelings, and beliefs of his clients' target market. This is reflected in his three step Profit Engineering formula:

Understand - Connect - Grow

Sam's philosophy is that marketing's greatest battles aren't won or lost in your store, in the street, or on the web… they're won or lost inside the mind of your customer.

With 10 years "in the trenches" experience with direct sales and marketing, he's been responsible for generating millions in revenue for some of the world's most successful owner-operated businesses.

Born and raised in Australia, he takes a no-holds barred approach to re-engineering business development systems.

Free Resources from Sam Page and the NeuroTriggers Team

As an expression of gratitude for reading my chapter, I would like to offer you two FREE gifts so you can leverage the power of marketing psychology in your own business.

- Visual Impact Map. How well does your website engage your users' reptilian brain? Using predictive analysis, we'll present a full color map outlining your website's primary engagement points. (Normally $129).

- Follow-up consultation and discovery session (with a licensed consumer psychologist) to review your neuromarketing score – which can be accessed at www.NeuroTriggers.com/Score. (Normally $250).

To claim these FREE gifts, just head on over to our website at www.NeuroTriggers.com or shoot me an email at Sam@NeuroTriggers.com.

Chapter 5

Selling from the Heart

DISCOVER YOUR R.E.A.L. BOSS AND A RENEWED SPIRIT FOR SALES

Jennifer Villarreal

As soon as I collapsed, I was trapped and didn't know how I could free myself. The screams of tortured souls were relentless and deafening. I would have given everything I had to get rid of that pain, anguish, and sorrow. But there I was without any clue how to release it. The fact that I am writing this proves that I'm alive and well but, in that moment, I didn't know if I would ever make it back.

Would You Like the Uncensored Version?

I'd like to share the R.E.A.L. and uncensored version of my story in this book, but unfortunately I've been told people can get easily offended by this topic, and I also keep things real, authentic and transparent. Plus we are told there are certain things that don't mix with business and we should keep them separate.

If you want the uncensored version of my story, make sure to grab your free copy at www.SalesFromTheHeart.com/RealStory.

Now, I'll come back to being trapped and not knowing how I could free myself in a moment, but first I want you to take a hard look at yourself. I want you to think about your life and how it has been thus far. Think about your relationships with other people, about the things you've done throughout your life or what others have done to you. Now, turning to your working life, I want you to ask yourself a simple question: *Who do I work for?*

Who do you work for? It might be a question you are not accustomed to asking yourself, especially if you are an entrepreneur or business owner. "That's a question I would expect my staff to answer with no problems," you might say, sidestepping the question a bit. And you might continue: "Surely, they would say they work for me!"

But, upon reflection, you know that you have not answered the question. Why would such a simple question be so difficult to answer? Perhaps you come to the conclusion that it's about working so that your family can afford the type of lifestyle you've set up for them, or you may say that you work because it fills a need for your customers.

That's all well and good. But are you really going to be satisfied with that answer? What about you? Where do your health, happiness, and well-being fit into this equation? Are you merely selling a product to your customers, or is the selling process—your relationship with staff members, management, and your customers—really a reflection of how you feel about yourself?

I have come to believe that sales is not just about profits. It's really about serving other people. As you'll see in a minute, this aspect of service goes on to an even higher level.

In this chapter, I am really going to challenge some of your core beliefs. And I am going to leave you with a renewed spirit for sales that will not only improve your business, but also inspire you to improve the lives of your clients.

So, what is sales? What does it mean to be in sales? Sales is not so much about how well you know your product or service. It's more about who you are. That's right, who you are. I know you may be scratching your head right about now, but please bear with me.

When you can really understand that very key concept, you will change your relationship to your business. And you'll know what types of energy, enthusiasm, and inspiration you can bring to your organization that will lead to greater profits and more unique opportunities to grow. And, because your genuine self will shine through, you'll also attract the types of workers who will be inspired by your example and produce phenomenal results. You do have access to that power. Access to that type of power comes easily by acknowledging its presence and inviting it within. It's not the typical approach sales professionals and business owners take when trying to improve their bottom line, attract new business, or build a great team. But I am here to tell you that impacting your true bottom line—your emotional and spiritual health and well-being—requires a great deal of patience, perseverance, and the determination to release any parts of you that may be subconsciously affecting your performance.

Most sales professionals may be aware of some of the philosophies circulating in business circles. Many of them are designed to reorient workers toward what really drives them or to align them in such a way that they become a living embodiment of a company's mission or vision. There are countless seminars, webinars, and books available to the general public about the art of selling, the importance of attaching oneself to an emotional connection, and shaking off some of the fears that may be associated with contacting complete strangers. They're all designed to provide a participant better access to the fundamentals of human connection. And, let's face it: after a while, they start to sound like a bunch of boring rules that just go in one ear and right out the other. There might be a slight bump in your performance. But, without constant focus on what is really driving you, you are likely to fall back into old habits.

I've been through some of those seminars myself, and I've even read some of the self-help books that try to train people to think and act differently. But it wasn't until I started searching within myself that I reached the great epiphany with regard to my personal and professional life. That involved a reassessment of what was going on inside me.

There are many who would gladly state, upon learning of such an approach, that spirituality has very little to do with the day-to-day tasks of running and growing a business. However, in order to affect positive change and generate that free-flowing, ongoing, everlasting spirit of innovation and steady progress, it's important to lay some sort of solid foundation. In fact, your foundation is what propels you to do great things in the first place. When that foundation is firmly established you can make sound business decisions, attract the types of clients who will enjoy what you are selling, and bring that much-needed confidence and enthusiasm to the selling process.

I work with clients from every background imaginable—yes even self-proclaimed atheists. It doesn't matter what faith tradition my clients come from. I respect where everyone is coming from. My job is not to convince others that I know more about how the inner self works, or convert others to a particular faith tradition; rather, as a coach, I encourage my clients to dig deep within themselves and develop a solid foundation, such that it becomes a critical component of the dreams they were destined to turn into a reality.

My Story

I wasn't always so keen on acknowledging my personal life in my professional life. I always thought that the two were separate: I worked so that I could have a fruitful personal life. It took me a while to see the light. Before that could occur, however, I faced my own internal demons and asked, who am I?

You see, I used to be a bit of a control freak, neurotic, and depressive; I was filled with arrogance and a ton of fear. My feisty Latina temperament wouldn't allow anyone to get in my way. And I thought I had to do everything on my own. But I established a new beginning that was built on a solid foundation that won't crack because it's righteous, everlasting, authentic, and loving (R.E.A.L.). I chose a new life and underwent a rebirth. I finally realized how important this personal relationship was in my life; it was filled with many blessings and fruits.

I was then able to truly embrace my unique gifts and have been serving others as a speaker, coach, and author who trains business owners and professionals. I inspire others to achieve victory by advancing their skill sets, releasing excuses, and soaring with wings of purpose, power, and prosperity.

Up until just a few short years ago, I thought I had a pretty good life. In terms of the goals I had set for myself earlier in life, I was proceeding along a steady path toward attaining the things I really wanted. I had gone to college and established a good career. I was making good money and I had relationships with family, friends, and significant others. But I was filled with a lot of pain, anxiety, depression, frustration, and resentment. I couldn't figure out why I was so unhappy.

Just like other people who attempt to deal with deep-seated emotional wounds, I self-medicated. I masked my heart through alcohol, marijuana, sex, work, and the pursuit of money. I thought that this was a normal way of relaxing or taking the edge off. But it ended up leaving me more depleted, and I felt emptier inside. I finally reached the point a few years ago when I really wanted to know what was going on with me. So I did some digging. I demanded to know what was going on with me.

On Labor Day 2011 I had received the answer from my demands just a few days prior. I was hanging out with three other friends and I decided to take a few hits of marijuana. Unbeknownst to me, my body had had enough; I was sitting on a couch and I knew that I didn't feel very well. Then, upon getting up to go to the bathroom, my knees buckled and my body collapsed to the floor. I hit my head and I started going into convulsions. My eyes rolled back into my head. I was still conscious at the time; I could hear my friends. Suddenly, I was able to see my body lying helplessly on the floor with my friends surrounding me in a worried state of fear and confusion.

Some conscious part of me left the area. I was transported through time and space. It was so unusual that I can't really describe what it was like. But, unlike the stories you hear of other people who have seen a light at the end of a dark tunnel, or visions of angels, or being in the presence of loved ones who have passed away, I ended up travelling through a very sinister, dark, and uncomfortably demonic place. I could hear blood-curdling screams, like what you might expect from someone who was being tortured. I was surely in my own personal hell.

I had never felt so vulnerable. When I had finally stopped travelling I was surrounded by a collection of dark, hooded beings that were tugging violently at me. As they continued to pull me, I felt like I was battling for my soul. It felt like this lasted for a few hours. Can you imagine having to go through something like that for a few hours? Every fear, doubt, and sinister thought buried deep within me suddenly erupted like a volcano. I screamed as loud as I could. I didn't know I could feel so much pain.

I said a short prayer. At that precise moment, I was instantly transported from the evil surrounding me, and I had returned once again to my body, where it had continued to lay, lifeless and surrounded by my friends. The top half of my body shot straight up off the floor in an instant and I opened my eyes. The horrid looks on my friends' faces said more than I ever could.

You can probably imagine that I had some sort of afterglow following that experience. You can't stare death squarely in the eyes and not be deeply affected by it, right? Actually, I was in a bit of denial for a few days and figured it would just pass with time, but I felt a calling to get to the bottom of this. Four days passed and I only had brief conversations with many unanswered questions about what happened. My sense of a clear direction was still blurred.

But I was drawn to strike up a conversation with a woman who had been taking care of my three dogs while I was in an intense period of transition. I went to visit her and the dogs at the amazing dog retreat facility located on her property. Tiny little gnats were out buzzing around and soaking up the sun's rays along with the dogs. As the minutes ticked by I had developed a lump in my throat that kept building; I had to tell the story of what happened just a few days prior.

All of a sudden a swarm of dragonflies surrounded us. There must have been forty of fifty of them! This prompted me to reveal my experience and we talked for several hours. We talked about every block that was in my heart. Out of that one conversation with her, I received the best gift ever: I renewed my faith, first and foremost, and I developed a greater understanding of my purpose in life and how I was meant to serve others.

What Having No Center Costs Us

"Yes, but what does this have to do with sales?" you might wonder. I'm getting to that! But, since you're so eager, here's the short answer: it has everything to do with sales! Sales professionals are disproportionately predisposed toward highly addictive personality traits. The same is true for business owners and entrepreneurs. The pursuit of the sale, the pursuit of the next big contract, can consume sales professionals to such an extent that they end up beating themselves up when they don't make projected quotas. The initial addiction may be to the power, prestige, or status—the perks, if you will, of having money and bringing in revenue.

There can be an egotistical element, whereby a sales professional measures his or her own personal worth by performance levels in job functions. Workaholics fall into this category. These types of behaviors can lead to health complications, drug overdoses, or death.

The Five Business Success Pillars

As I stated in the beginning of this chapter, sales is more about *who you are* than about any knowledge you have of products or selling. I work with my clients by establishing what I call the 5 Business Success Pillars. These include:

1. clarify your direction
2. strategize your actions
3. upgrade your skill sets
4. enhance your environment
5. master your psychology

Clarify Your Direction

"Those who are successful in business increasingly and continuously offer value to their customers; part of that value offering is who you are." That's what one of my clients, Demetrio Garcia, realized after working with me. Demetrio is a business owner who works in the food industry. He's an engineer by trade, but got into sales and business development, something he says he enjoys. He discovered some time ago that he needed to change his perception of the sales process and about selling in general. This is what I mean by *clarify your direction*.

Most of my clients already have a pretty clear idea of what clarity of direction means. Most of them just need a little help refining that singular and critical vision. By putting a personal perspective on the sales process, Demetrio was able to have a breakthrough in his relationship to selling.

"I like to consider myself a high-energy person," he said. "I consider myself a person who likes to be around other people who are excited and enthusiastic about what they do and about who they are.

"I consider myself *to be that type of a person*, but I wanted more. I wanted that to translate into results for my business, my activities, my friends, my influence, and my clients. So it was more of a kind of a quest for continued learning but, more importantly, it was also about self-learning, self-development. I knew that I needed to learn more and discover more of who I am; I needed to learn about my purpose and my mission in life."

Demetrio had already considered himself to be a high-energy person, the type of person who is enthusiastic, likeable, and approachable. He believed that he aligned with other high-energy, enthusiastic people. But there was a disconnect between how he saw himself personally and professionally. "I would ask myself questions like, 'Why aren't things going my way?' and 'Why aren't things like they used to be?' But then I realized that I never lost that spark; I never lost that energy. I always had it. It was re-tweaking my thoughts, re-believing, and understanding who I am and who we know."

As a result of clarifying his direction, Demetrio now states, "I'm learning, I'm growing, and I'm having wins in my business—wins in my relationships. I'm hitting home runs in everything I do now."

Strategize Your Actions

It's really important for business professionals to have a very specific action plan so they know exactly what they need to do and how to get there. What many people don't realize is that this is a very personal, customized aspect of business. By strategizing your actions, business professionals know what resonates with them, what works for them, and they know exactly what they need to be doing to focus on their growth—both professionally and personally.

I remember some fifteen years ago coming up with the idea to be a coach when I was a copier sales representative. Upon telling one of my peers about my big plan, she said to me, "Well, you can do that." But what was missing was confidence. Several years later I began to study coaching, and I even began selling coaching services for some pretty prominent people in the industry: Robert Kiyosaki of *Rich Dad, Poor Dad*; Carleton Sheets of the longest-running real estate infomercial; Jack Canfield, author of *Success Principles* and *Chicken Soup for the Soul*; and Dale Carnegie Training. Pretty soon, however, all this emphasis on coaching became a bit too overwhelming.

We all have these unique and specific gifts that we have been given. When we are ready to surrender and acknowledge these gifts, they will flow through us more easily. And it makes strategizing your actions much easier. Action is where we build the momentum for the dreams our creator wants to turn into a reality for us. But, without clear determination of your strengths, and without someone who believes in you and who is willing to guide you along in your progress, it can be the same as spinning your wheels in a muddy field. The actions are clear: you know you have somewhere to go. But, if you can't understand why you aren't moving, you might require the assistance of someone who can see the big picture and keep you on task without wasting precious time and energy.

Upgrade Your Skill Sets

When I first thought about going into business for myself, I believed the process to be quite simple. I already knew what I wanted to do, and I figured all I really had to do to be "in business" was to set it up. So long as I had come up with a nice company name, a logo, and some business cards, I deemed myself ready to go. Looking back now, I can see that I had this process all backward.

While these seemed to be tangible aspects of setting up a business, they were not actually preparing me to do business. The skill sets required to do my line of work were certainly something I had developed for a period of time, but there was something missing. It wasn't until I started working with a personal coach that the answers came to me. I was not including among the skills necessary to succeed three that were vital to the success and survival of my business: sales, marketing, and communication.

First I had to realize I was trying to control aspects of my business that I really had no control over. We all believe that we need some level of control over the things we are doing, but how much control we seek and how well we resign ourselves, opens ourselves to our human frailties, and determines our success. This is where upgrading your skill sets comes in handy. You look for opportunities to strengthen those skills necessary to enhance your business. Most often, that comes in the way of taking a good, hard look at yourself in the mirror and asking, "What am I doing right now to prevent business?" Note that this question is the opposite of what most business owners ask themselves.

One of the most important skills I had to learn early on was how to be humble. Have you ever thought about what you might be doing to prevent business from coming in? Perhaps you have an attitude that turns people away from you. Or you may have had a disagreement with a particularly needy client who shut you down emotionally. This may have limited the amount of enthusiasm you bring to your work and your brand. In this case, taking a hard look at what lies beneath the surface could mean the difference between a highly successful year and one in which you are barely scraping by.

Also, a lot of times we try to do everything we can in our business because we don't want to release that control or resign ourselves to the fact that there are other people in our social and business circles who are better equipped to handle a specific work function. By tapping into your authentic self, you can begin to understand how to look for the types of people who can fill in the missing pieces. Outsource the things you are not very good at.

Enhance Your Environment

We can learn how to speak to other people's interests when we can tap in to our heart space and speak on a loving level. By allowing your heart to come through in your interactions with other people, you invite them to approach you from a heart-centered place as well. And the connections you build, simply by changing the place from which your communication emerges, will lead to fruitful and rewarding professional relationships.

This is what I mean by *enhance your environment*. Oftentimes we may think too much about how to get to where we want to go. But we all know that too much thinking and not enough action won't get us very far. Through training, we can learn to turn off or ignore the continual process of thinking things through, of wrestling over and over again with a decision. And, when we come from the heart, our decisions can be clearer and more authentic.

Enhancing your environment is about attracting the team of talented individuals who will be inspired by your company mission or who will be turned on by your enthusiasm and confident spirit. The energy you project from inside transfers to every client and potential client who is making a decision about whether to do business with you. If our focus is narrow and comes from our heart space, we invite others into the circle of relationship. It becomes less about what type of product or service you are offering. It doesn't matter all that much where your services rank as opposed to similar products. It really comes down to the experience you create for the customer. I think the following quote sums it up well…

"I've learned that people will forget what you said, people will forget what you did, but people will never forget how you made them feel."

Maya Angelou

I encourage my clients to answer a very simple question: why are you doing what you are doing? It may seem simple enough at the outset, but when my clients really think about that question, many of them are shocked when they discover the true purpose of all their labors. "Without purpose, you're always walking around with a rock in your shoe," one of my clients, Gustavo Mendoza, said.

Master Your Psychology

Oftentimes we need a little push to help us recognize limiting beliefs, doubts, and fears. All of these negative emotions can stand in the way of you achieving the type of success you have always imagined. Here are some of the limiting beliefs my clients have conveyed to me:

- I'm not good enough.
- My sales aren't where they need to be.
- My bank account isn't where it needs to be.
- I don't know who I am anymore.

I have other clients who are very successful in their businesses yet, personally, they are going through a divorce, seeing their kids every other weekend, hanging out with the wrong crowd, or hiding behind deep-seated emotional issues by self-medicating.

When we *master our psychology*, we get to the root of problems we may have avoided in other aspects of life—things that may have emerged due to the loss of a loved one, an abusive parent or spouse, or when we have suffered a personal or professional setback to a goal we set out to achieve.

Recently one of my clients revealed to me the extent of the emotional trauma she had been dealing with for most of her life. At age fifteen she was raped and nearly left for dead. For ten years she suffered from post-traumatic stress disorder, depression, low self-esteem and suicidal thoughts. She resorted to cutting and experimented with drugs and alcohol to help her deal with the pain. She ended up being involuntarily committed to a mental health facility and placed on a steady diet of antidepressants and anti-anxiety medication. After several years of therapy, she turned to coaching to not only affect her outlook on business, but also her personal life.

"I've broken away from having jobs that don't have to do with my career, which is in the performing arts, and now I am working as an instructor in group fitness and doing performing arts. You have helped me organize my time and get away from a lot of the negative energy that was constantly consuming me," she said after working with me for a couple of months.

She also said that, through coaching, she was able to get away from some very simple but utterly damaging belief systems. She learned to relinquish control. She feels that her self-confidence and passion have grown considerably, which has directly affected the number of clients she now serves. She is ready to invite new possibilities into her life—ones that she could not see because she was desperately trying to hold on to an image that didn't quite match up with her spirit. At the time of this writing, Kelly Good is in the process of opening up a performing arts studio to serve the youth of Chicago.

Conclusion

There are three main points that I want you to take from this chapter. They are intended to serve as a guide for you as you get to the heart of your business and begin the task of attracting new clients.

First, I want you to remember that you can find more clients when you allow them to actually contact you. That seems pretty simple, right? Position yourself in the marketplace as an authority and expert in your field. This comes from a deep understanding of knowing exactly who you work for and who you really are. Then, the service you provide, the products you offer, will be clear for your very specific, targeted market.

Second, I would like you to keep in mind that the number one thing preventing people from saying yes is how you connect with them. Ask questions, listen, be of service and, most importantly, speak from the heart. I have a couple of clients who say people just do not call them back, but they also realize those patterns exist within themselves; they have a pattern of avoiding. They would rather connect via email as opposed to picking up the phone and really truly engaging with someone on the other end.

Finally, learn how to make the entire sales process feel like you are helping your client instead of merely selling a product or service to him or her. Again, sell from the heart; communicate from the heart. **Keep the process R.E.A.L. Remember what this stands for? Righteous, Everlasting, Authentic, and Loving. And S.A.L.E.S. is about Serving, being Authentic, Listening, being Engaged, and Spiritual.**

Many blessings to you on your journey toward real sales!

About the Author

Jennifer Villarreal is a speaker, coach, and author who has coached and trained prominent business professionals. She is the founder of Sales from the Heart, Inc., a non-traditional coaching program that transforms the heart and soul of a business by teaching the core principle, "Serve to Sell." Her methodology combines spirituality and sales to lay a solid foundation that builds solid relationships and business systems that last a lifetime.

Sales from the Heart teaches how being victorious means unlocking R.E.A.L. potential, using unique talents, incorporating a sense of humor, and nurturing the body and spirit to live life with intent and on purpose. Jennifer's coaching style is warm, direct and humorous. She inspires people to take ownership of their victory by advancing their sales skills, releasing excuses from their mindset, and propelling themselves with wings of purpose, power, and prosperity.

To find out more about Sales from the Heart workshops, coaching, books, audio and video training programs or to inquire about Jennifer's availability as a speaker or coach, contact (773) 614-SALE.

For your uncensored version of this story make sure to grab your free copy at www.SalesFromTheHeart.com/RealStory.

Connect with Jennifer Villarreal on Social Media:

www.LinkedIn.com/in/jennifervillarreal

www.Facebook.com/JennyV.JV

www.Facebook.com/SalesFromTheHeart

Bonus Gift

To be one of the first to receive a copy of *Sales from the Heart: Removing the Unknown to Reveal the Unlimited*, message me directly.

I will also include an extra bonus gift as a thank you for reading this chapter.   I look forward to hearing from you...

Jennifer@SalesFromTheHeart.com

Let's connect on Facebook and LinkedIn. The links are provided above.

With Love and Many Blessings to You,

Jennifer Villarreal
Author / Speaker / Coach
Sales from the Heart, Inc.
www.SalesFromTheHeart.com
(847) 903-3983

Chapter 6

Empowered Mom:
Achieving Success at Business and Home.

LaShonda Steele Allen

"I tapped into a part of my existence that had never been explored. I discovered an underutilized energy, and knew I could do more amazing things."

"I love your life," a friend said to me. Two things went through my mind.

One. I'm making "my life" look too easy.

Two. My friend didn't understand how hard it is to have "my life."

Was it a compliment? Sure, I think that was the intent. At that point, I realized it wasn't about me. This was about her. Why isn't she saying this about her own life? I think her overtly vocal admiration was an outcry for help on how to manage her own life as a busy executive mom. This chapter is dedicated to my beloved friend and fellow moms out there trying to conquer the balancing act of family and business. I hope my advice and techniques can help you as much as they have helped me successfully manage my family and business.

Say it, "Put me first."

Being a mom of two children and a wife who runs her own business, "put me first" was difficult to roll off my tongue. I had to wonder why it was a complicated task for me to accomplish. I'm a taskmaster, the queen of multi-tasking. I should be able to make time for me. However, "me" was often the uncompleted task dangling at the bottom of my own to-do list, continuously getting bumped to the next day. I thought of everything and everyone but myself. I thought of my children's needs, husband, parents, family and my business—all the things I value most. Then I realized I'm just as important to them as they are to me. I learned that the same reasons I needed to put myself first were the same reasons I wasn't. Since grasping that concept, I no longer feel guilty when I schedule a spa day or spend a couple of hours at the gym. It makes me feel better. The better I am, the better I perform. The better I am, the better my family performs. The better I am, the better my business performs. Of course, as moms and career women we all make sacrifices or what I like to call prioritize, based on life demands. If I wanted to continue to be a loving mom and wife as well as a successful businesswoman, I had to put myself first—and feel good about it. Yes, you can be a mom, wife and career woman and still put yourself first. It's okay.

"I learned that the same reasons I needed to put myself first were the same reasons I wasn't."

Make time for late nights.

No, I'm not talking about the office. One night my husband came into our bedroom. He said, "You think you can make room for me?" I looked up at him and then followed his eyes as they stared at his side of the bed, which was buried with papers, spreadsheets, briefs and my laptop. At that moment, I knew he felt my work was taking his spot— literally. Of course, late nights come with being a career woman. Sometimes after leaving the office, picking up the kids, preparing dinner, doing homework and bath time, late evening is the only time you may have for your significant other.

After kissing the children goodnight, we're exhausted. To help us recharge, we created "Breathers." For fifteen minutes, we turn the lights out and do nothing but listen to each other breathe—not talk, just breathe. When I lay on his chest, I could literally hear the anxiety in his heartbeat dissipate into a calm state of relaxation. After our "Breather" we lightly talk about our ideas, our family goals for the next day, and where we need each other's help to get things done. This allows us to slow down our day and focus on one another—not work, not our phones or emails. It may not be a lot of time, but for me it's the small things. Of course, the Friday night dinner reservations, weekend movie nights and vacations are also wonderful times. For us, the "Breathers" can deflect a potentially tension-filled evening (with an argument on the horizon) into an evening of understanding, open communication, and my husband even asking what he can do to help me get my work done. This allows us to have more time together. We've realized, sometimes it's best to join the work than to compete with it.

Find small windows.

The every day can put wear and tear on even the strongest relationships. I believe the workweek can be brutal and turn a loving couple into robotic roommates. Here's a tip. Think about what little things can be done to make each of you feel each other's presence. I schedule my husband into my alerts on my smartphone. This may sound rigid, but it works. If I can remind myself to call a business contact or to pick up the dry cleaning, why not include one of the most important people in my life—my husband. He loves head massages. So guess what reminder pops up on my phone? Every night at 10:00 p.m. my phone reminds me to brush my husband's hair. The point is not about "penciling in" your loved one, but more about realizing what they like and making time for it. Using the reminder feature on my phone, I'm sure is the last thing on his mind—if he even cares at all. I believe, at the end of the day, all that matters is the head massage. Think about the little things. A small detail can add years to a relationship.

One evening, I was on a business call and my husband said something to me. I asked the person on the phone to hold and gave my husband immediate attention. Even though he offered to wait, I let him know he didn't have to and inquired about his need. After all, I was at home and in our home anything other than home life is intruding on our time—our family's time. To me, that is just what's fair and respectful. It may have been minor, but it didn't go unnoticed. Making your relationship a priority makes the person you love feel ... well, loved.

Own your weekends.

I am not my mom. I am not my grandmother. My family does not wake up to a hot breakfast with homemade biscuits, fresh out the oven before going to school. I'm tossing my children a cereal bar, a piece of fruit and a reusable travel cup filled with orange juice before heading out the door. I'm not alone. A lot of working moms are racing the clock trying to perfect the morning rush. Evenings feel like coming home to a second job—hustling to get the family ready for the next day. Every day the family sees Mom shouting out orders and racing the clock. Here's what helps me make up for the "Bossy Weekday Mom."

Show your weekend face. On the weekends, bring the fun. I remember my parents' personalities on weekends and family vacations. They were . . . nice, actually. The kind of people I could live with. I believe it is vital for children to see their parents' fun side.

On Friday evenings, my family does not see my computer. If I do need to wrap up a few things, I do it while everyone is sleeping.

Swap Saturday morning emails with big, fluffy pancakes. The kids wake up to their favorite cartoons blasting on the television. The air is filled with pancakes, syrup, eggs, turkey bacon—and, of course, coffee for the hubby and me. After everyone is stuffed with all-you-can-eat pancakes, the fun continues. Stop 1: Practice. Followed by the park, shopping, movies and dinner out topped off with the biggest sundae the restaurant can make. Yes, the Allen Family rocks on Saturdays. By the time 8:30 in the evening rolls around, the kids are pooped from fun-overload, and I'm proud because I didn't miss one second of it checking my email. I've also learned to allow the weekend face to linger into the weekday. It helps to reinforce good behavior and I let my children decide when the "Bossy Weekday Mommy" should reappear.

Equity ever after.

Equity. One of the most important statements I can express about relationships. My husband works his tail off for his family. We both do. It's about working together. When I'm working late with my team preparing for a client presentation, he is home helping with homework and cooking the only dish he knows how to prepare – spaghetti. By the time I arrive, the children have been bathed, put to bed, and my plate of spaghetti is in the microwave ready and waiting. We are willing to jump right into any role necessary to keep our home in order.

I don't expect things from my husband that I am not willing to do for myself. I don't expect things from my staff that I am not willing to do for my own business. I don't expect things out of my life that I'm not willing to put into it. That's my belief for everything I do. For a successful household or business, there is no room for non-essential members. To reach the goals as a team or individually, there has to be a willingness to work together and just as hard.

Of course, there are times when all things are not equal. For a whole month, when I was starting my business, I did not do one domestic duty. First, I acknowledged it. I expressed to my husband that I recognized he was carrying a lot of the household burden, and I appreciated his patience and help. Acknowledging someone's hard work helps lessen the potential feeling of resentment and increases the feeling of appreciation.

"The every day can put wear and tear on even the strongest relationships. I believe the workweek can be brutal and turn a loving couple into robotic roommates. Here's a tip. Find small windows of time to recognize each other's presence. Every little bit can add years to a marriage.

Empathy. Another essential attribute the most successful relationships possess. What is helpful for us is removing assigned responsibilities from the household and our marriage. Everyone just does what it takes. We rely on each other. However, just because we're a couple, does not mean we get to be over-dependent on one another. If I return home first and I notice the garbage can needs to be pulled around back, I do it. If my husband is hungry, he cooks (or reheats). Setting realistic expectations for one another sets us both up for success.

Don't be a Superwoman. Save time, instead.

Even the "Superwoman" types can't truly do it all—have a successful career and do everything that a full-time homemaker would be able to accomplish. Some things will get neglected. Rather than being a superwoman, I'm a sharing woman. When my husband and I share in the household responsibilities we structure them by our strengths, not by our gender. Just like in business, it all comes down to who is better and most efficient at each task. My husband does the washing. He is just better at it. He realized what took me days to do, he could accomplish in a few hours. Initially, a couple of my sweaters fit a little tighter and my son wore pinkish color socks for a while, but once he mastered the art of color separation, the whole house flowed better. The art of folding, neither one of us has the time to master. And that's okay. My family may be wearing wrinkled clothes, but we're wearing clean clothes. With running a business and maintaining a family, I had to learn early how to separate what's essential and what can wait.

I am not a superwoman, and my husband is not superman. However, we do like to think of ourselves as super-supportive.

> "Running one less errand could mean an extra fifteen minutes on the treadmill, one more bedtime story or a few extra minutes of sleep. In my life, saving time offers the bigger reward."

Velcro—and go.

Like any executive mom, my schedule is packed. With managing a household, I'm often left to make a decision that can help me save time or save a dollar. I always choose time. I see it with moms when grocery shopping all the time. One day while waiting to check out, this sweet lady whispered to me that the paper towels I had in my buggy were on sale, and offered me a coupon to save $1.50 at another store. The other market was fifteen minutes away. We're all doing the best we can for our families and our budgets. I'm the first to admit sales are attractive. However, choosing to save money could potentially cost you more. Convenient circumstances where I can achieve saving time and money are a win, such as shopping for my organic vegetables and finding them on sale—score one for me.

For years, I only purchased shoes with Velcro closures for my daughter—still do for my son. My ongoing joke is shoes with laces are out to sabotage my morning rhythm, and are not allowed in my home. It's all about Velcro—and go. My daughter did not learn to tie her shoes until she was 5-years-old. However, she was reading at the age of two, speaking two different languages, and doing 4th grade math in preschool. I had other priorities for her, and quite frankly, the shoe-tying thing did not fit into her schedule. Velcro is my best friend. At times, it may cost me more, but seamless mornings have led to more timely arrivals— which led to happy teachers and happy clients.

When you're running a business and have a family, every minute counts. Running one less errand could mean an extra fifteen minutes on the treadmill, one more bedtime story or a few extra minutes of sleep. In my life, saving time offers the bigger reward. Value for me does not equate to savings. I believe value is an important factor when it comes to relationships. I may need to go out of my way to help family, close friends or clients. For me, the reward comes from the gratification of being around a loved one or helping someone who needs me. At times, those situations are not always convenient, but are worth the time spent. The decision comes down to what's more meaningful to you, your priorities and how it aligns with your goals.

Can we talk later?

Marriage can be great, but it's not perfect. When there is a "glitch" in the system, address it. Take the time to talk about it. Know that every time may not be the best time. Ask first if it is a good time, and express the topic (let them know of the minefield they could be walking into) to help ease curiosity. If it is not convenient for your loved one, allow them to suggest a time that's better for them. I've learned, most of the time we will drop everything we're doing to talk. It may not be the case every time, and we respect that. It's okay to say, "Can we talk later?" With my career, inspiration is key. Depending on what we have going on, the conversation can be distracting or change my mood. The result may not leave me feeling inspired.

Most of the time we will drop everything we're doing to talk. It may not the case every time and we respect that. It's okay to say, "Can we talk later?"

If you decide to take the talk later route, my advice is to initiate the discussion within 24 hours or at the time you requested. If you don't, watch your step. You may be walking onto a landmine.

There are times when the "Can we talk later?" can be interpreted as disrespectful, especially when used to greet a caller, and even more especially when the caller is a loved one. When my husband calls, I answer the phone every time I can. I believe it makes the caller feel important. Secondly, when taking the call—no matter how busy I am, I ask if there is something pressing. When you ask if everything is okay, it's easier to accept that you're not available to talk. This way, you appear more engaging to the caller even if you are ending the conversation. I make sure to return the call as promised after the meeting or upon completing the task.

From Ms. to Mrs. to Mom.

When I became a mom I felt more empowered than ever. Every chromosome in my body evolved, and I knew I would never again be the person I was 9 months before. I am Mom now, and forever. The delivery process requires a deep connection between mind, body, soul and baby. I tapped into a part of my existence that had never been explored. I discovered an underutilized energy, and knew I could do more amazing things. Giving birth to my child meant I could accomplish anything in this world. My spirit was elevated to a greater sense of existence. Mentally, I was transformed. Physically, I was dealing with a moderate identity crisis. Standing in the mirror, looking back at me was a body I didn't recognize and a whole new world of experiences. Motherhood. No matter how many books we read, and the research we do, you can't prepare for it—you just have to go through it.

For some, having children and running a business is a full and exciting life. Others may feel overwhelmed with having so much to do. A friend of mine, a successful accountant, shared with me that she always wanted to open a bakery. But with children and a husband, she couldn't seem to find room for her own dreams. The clutter of life and a busy routine can muffle our internal compass. Being one with yourself becomes less of an option when you wish you were more than one person.

I'm here to tell you that you can do anything in the world—and having a baby is just the beginning.

About the Author

LaShonda Steele Allen is a loving, devoted wife, mother and President of Words of Steele Creative Services. She balances her home and work life as if it were a well-choreographed dance. The mother of two seems to stretch her days past the 24-hour limit, as she works countless hours with her professional teams and juggles product launches, family time and meetings. LaShonda has become the go-to for friends, family and business associates on career and personal advice.

Professionally, she is an advertising powerhouse. Her talent involves developing advertising campaigns with some of the top agencies in the world and major Fortune 500 companies. Her achievements, which are great and varied, include copywriting and spearheading some of the most successful television commercials and most memorable taglines. In addition to her work with major corporations, LaShonda has lent her expertise to national non-profit organizations. She is a philanthropist at heart and works with organizations for children and families, and volunteers her time to women-owned start-ups. In her personal life, LaShonda also volunteers her time at her children's schools.

LaShonda is launching a time-saving baby product in 2014. Her invention will revolutionize mealtime and is sure to become an essential household appliance.

Keep up with LaShonda at:

- Website: www.LaShondaSAllen.com
- Email: info@LaShondaSAllen.com
- Facebook: LaShonda Steele Allen
- Twitter: @lsteeleallen

More Resources from LaShonda Steele Allen

Thank you for taking the time to read my chapter. As a token of my appreciation, I would like to give you free tips, techniques, and updates on:

✓ Mastering the juggle: Career, family and home life without dropping your dream™.

✓ My new product: Designed to revolutionize mealtime, it will certainly become an essential household appliance. Sign up today and be the first to know when it is available to you at a special introductory price.

To get free information and updates about how to manage life as a busy mom and executive, along with information on my new product visit www.LaShondaSAllen.com

Chapter 7

China: How to Successfully Do Business with an Eastern Superpower

Nicholas Cooper

Understanding the Eastern Opportunity

Right now, the business landscape has opened in the East with both American companies and entrepreneurs rushing to get their fill of the Pacific Rim. The biggest draw for such business relationships is that the Pacific Rim boasts of having the most vibrant economy and entrepreneurs can leverage their personal expertise and expect top monetary value for their services. However as fabulous as that sounds, working in China is not easy. There are several facets to consider such as cultural nuances, the Eastern business ethic, and a jittery government notorious for stepping in and pushing back on what should have been sealed deals. Other aspects that have proven difficult include a lengthy brokerage process, legitimizing the business opportunity, establishing the credibility of possible Chinese business partners, and understanding the most effective way to vet those with whom you want to do business. The best way I've found to weed through such confusion is to connect with either a Chinese affiliate or an ex pat who thoroughly understands the cultural and business ethic nuances of the Chinese company with whom you are trying to do business.

Having been the only American, let alone African American, in most of my meetings in China, I can't tell you the number of times I've sat through five-hour dinners with no one speaking English. And after each meeting, my Chinese hosts would leave astonished that I was able to translate occasional gestures and words especially since I spoke less than 15 percent of the language. I learned to really listen in those meetings. And the more I listened, the more my Chinese hosts would share. Soon, we began to understand one another, form genuine connections, and do great business.

Over the course of the next 17 years, I discovered that this and changing the way I saw obstacles were the secrets to experiencing long-lasting and lucrative business in the East. Wayne Dyer, author and motivational speaker, once said, "If you change the way you look at things, the things you look at change" (Dyer). Understand this, I easily could have become frustrated and given up instead of enduring meetings of foreign language conversation, lots of smiling faces, and no true understanding. But instead of throwing in the towel, I decided to do like Dyer suggested—change how I see. That meant I had to give up my Western style of business and communication and wholeheartedly embrace doing things the Eastern way.

True Connection Takes Selflessness

In the East, intuition and gut reactions govern the Chinese people; therefore if I wanted to do business in China, I had to be willing to meet them on their communication terms. I couldn't bulldoze my way using Western tactics because I would leave the negotiating tables exasperated like Facebook, Twitter, YouTube, and Microsoft. Even Apple recently bumped its head and had to bend to the Eastern way of business. Although they are strong companies, each recently have been rebuffed by the prevailing governing powers. Why? They did not tap into the secret I stumbled across: respect a heritage and culture beyond the push to forge a "business deal." My willingness to let go of my "business comfort zone" in order to embrace the Eastern unknown cracked the Eastern universal code that unlocked the business doors for my American partner and I to experience several years of record-breaking success. Never before had any American forged a joint venture with Hunan Television Broadcasting System, which is the Fox TV of China, and made money in the process! Since, I have secured deals for A-list talent, purchased the license for *America's Best Dance Crew* (to broadcast in China), become the first American creative director for a show on Hunan TV, and brokered technology deals with one of the most powerful families in the country. All of this because I chose to put my potential Chinese business partners' needs above my own. I chose to be selfless.

As someone who has worked, and continues to work, throughout the Pacific Rim and other European countries, my intention is to share my hard-learned lessons, the failures I've overcome, and unveil China's current business needs that could unlock financial doors for those willing to open their eyes to global possibilities. So, if you're ready to embark upon an Eastern adventure that could broaden your financial futures, let's get started.

Awaking the Dragon

With China's communist rule and government that beats to the sound of its own drum, it's no wonder why companies like Facebook, YouTube, Twitter, Microsoft, and many other entrepreneurs who want entrance into the country have often left empty handed. Much of this, I have discovered, is due to those businesses' reluctance to acclimate to cultural values and nuances able to sustain a multinational's existence within the proposed new territory. By refusing to acquiesce and adapt to the new culture and its business norms, no one wins at the negotiating table. With so much new interest in doing business in the East, many companies there are now opening their eyes to the possible new power they wield. Many call this new awareness the awakening of the sleeping dragon. Now fully aware and awake, China emerges with fresh resources, new ideas, and a world of infinite business possibilities.

Awake and Hungry

Part of China's business awakening includes an economic evolution tied to the country's burgeoning middle and upper classes. According to a McKinsey Quarterly report in 2013, it is estimated that by 2022, 75 percent of China's urban consumers will be in this bracket (Barton et al. 2013). It goes on to say that the expansion is due to "…labor-market and policy initiatives that push wages up, financial reforms that stimulate employment and income growth, and the rising role of private enterprise…" (Barton et al. 2013). Because of this, this nouveau riche are becoming aware of what they want and the type of life they want to live, which includes better services, education, and technology. As they aspire to more, they lust after the perceived decadent Western lifestyle where bigger is better and more is never enough. However, many of the companies outside of China that do see this wealth of opportunity have not been able to capitalize on the open window. Why? The answer is simple: they have not figured out that the Chinese will not do a deal without forming a real relationship. Most companies take the Western approach to business: get to the bottom line where money talks and all else walks. In the East, it's all about getting to know the person and the company. But on the flip side, there have been companies like LVMH, YUM Brands, Audi, and Proctor and Gamble that have decided to change their tactics to one that benefited both them and the East. In doing so, these companies have all found abundant favor with both the young and older generations in China. Business for them has flourished.

Taking a Deeper Plunge

In 2012, the Hunan Television Broadcasting System, China's top entertainment TV network, contracted me to be the creative director of a new show called 'Up Junior'. As I researched the company, I noticed that other countries, primarily America, had purchased all of the licenses for most of the flagship shows. Digging deeper, I discovered that much of the advertising on these shows promoted Western products, services, and lifestyle brands. With 200 million viewers per episode, I realized the window of opportunity: advertising. If I could broker product placement and integration deals using this entertainment show as my platform, I could position myself for greater influence and opportunities within China, offer American companies a way to advertise their goods and services to a hungry Chinese market, and experience greater financial gain using a syndicated show. Ultimately, my partner (Daniel You) and I purchased a license for the hit show America's Best Dance Crew believing that both online and offline advertising will offer the next surge of economic growth. Because we have just begun this adventure, only time will tell if we gambled right.

The Cultural Exchange

I often ask why would any American travel to another country and expect the communication style, business protocol, and social etiquette to be that of which they are accustomed to in the States? Sounds basic, right? However, I can't tell you how many of my cohorts have done just this. China not only is one of the oldest countries in the world, but it has a culture deeply entrenched in the philosophies of many of the greatest minds to shape modern thinking. Because of these philosophies, the Chinese have developed business practices that have nothing to do with the bottom line but everything to do with who they are as people, which includes the art of patience.

Patience Is More Than a Virtue

It's critical when engaging in business in this region to first understand the cultural nuances of the marketplace. Upon your initial introduction, the Chinese host typically will gauge your understanding of the culture by first testing your patience by NOT discussing business. That's right. No business. Instead, they want to know about you, your upbringing, your background, and your reasons for coming into the country. Then, they talk about their vision, their needs, hopes, and desires for a long-term engagement. This is the Chinese host's way of discovering your true motives for wanting to do business with them. Are you going to be selfless and discover how you can meet the Chinese businesses' needs, or will you be selfish and only discuss your own personal agenda? Oftentimes, talks with the Chinese executives will feel more like a game of high-class chess than a simple game of checkers as the host meticulously assesses your every move. Please understand that this chess game is a test of your business endurance and your personal patience—both of which are prized among Chinese executives. Remember, the one still standing gets to sign on the dotted line.

Although I, and several like me, have taken the Eastern plunge, there are many who are overwhelmed by the idea of doing business in China. From language and physical distance barriers to even experiencing breached contracts and over-embellished opportunities because of the governmental structure and lack of federal business laws like the ones enforced in the U.S., the result for most American entrepreneurs seeking entrance into this market has fared with less than stellar reports. However, this doesn't have to be you.

Save Face, Give Respect

I believe that one of the reasons many companies have not been successful in the East has to do with something called saving face. Saving face, which is a cultural nuance that must be mastered, means giving and showing respect. Culturally, the Chinese are a very shy and private people. Letting strangers into the center of their worlds takes a lot of trust, which is why business is never conducted without first creating a relationship. Part of their cultural slant means never being seen as foolish in front of family, friends, and definitely not potential business partners.

In business, it is preferable to allow the Chinese host's conversation to be viewed as valuable no matter what. According to Tom Doctoroff of J. Walter Thompson advertising, "You need to take whatever people are saying, whether it's a creative idea or a strategy idea, and you need to find that kernel of wisdom in there. Usually there is something that is relevant. And they need to build on that" (The International Herald Tribune 2010). But if you do just the opposite, or cause them to "lose face," your Chinese host's embarrassment will bar you from ever doing business with them. Historically, foreign countries wanting to colonize China exploited the country for business purposes. Now, the Chinese have no desire to go back to that posture.

7 Keys to Successful Business in China

Over the years, I've come to understand that true successful business follows an open mind. Having such has allowed me to experience infinite business opportunities that have stretched my imagination and allowed me to create a legacy far beyond what I previously had deemed possible. The key to such success lay in seven principles: as business executives, we must learn to establish a solid relationship, appreciate karaoke, watch our conversation, wait for the real meetings, respect the business card, don't expect much eye contact, and speak slowly. These seemingly simple values mean the difference between an abundance of business or going home with none.

Establish a Solid Relationship

If you want to snag a deal in China, first solidify a positive and mutually beneficial working relationship. The Chinese—in business and in friendships—are relational people; thus they are quite partial to those with whom they have connections beyond dollar signs. Doing business in China is like conducting a courtship for marriage. On the first date, bring a gift. Although not expected, the Chinese will consider your gesture respectful. Respect, to the Chinese, is given and not earned. Children learn to respect their elders just as subordinates learn to respect their superiors. China is a country that runs on the principles of deference. Understanding these cultural and business nuances is the cornerstone to experiencing successful long-term business with the East.

In addition, the best way to begin to build a solid relationship is by not asking for too much too soon. Remember, you cannot conduct business with a Western mindset. That means you can't rush toward a business closure. It's like going for the kiss on the first date without having wined, dined, and laughed with your partner until the restaurant closes. Potential Chinese partners will perceive this move as possibly selfish, self-centered, or just rude. These are not the types of people with whom the Chinese executives want to be connected. If this happens, you can kiss your business idea with the East goodbye. Remember while it may be true that you are the king in your land, you are on someone else's turf. So, let them RULE!

Appreciate the Power of Karaoke

The next thing to do in order to do great business in China is learn to sing. No, really. I mean it. If you happen to be a great at-home shower singer, you rock along to your favorite tunes while driving and don't care who watches, or you won a singing contest back in the sixth grade, dust off your singing chops and let go of all stage fright. The Chinese love karaoke. But even more importantly, the Chinese love to do business after a few rousing rounds of the singing game. Karaoke to Chinese business is like golf for American business. Both are conducted before signing on the dotted line. Understand this: Karaoke is not about singing when it comes to closing the deal. Karaoke is about your character and the character of your business. So, pay attention to what you do during and after the karaoke experience. Remember, you are not there to just party. You are on display and being judged. So, sing well, stay sober, and show the Chinese executives that your head and heart are in the connection and the deal.

Watch Your Conversation

The Chinese are masterful listeners. Although it may not seem like they understand your random banter during interactions, such feigned ignorance is a ploy to allow you to continue to reveal your true business motives through too much conversation on your part. The Chinese constantly utilize the arts of observation and listening to determine whether you and your business will be an asset or a liability. They want to know if you understand your own authority and know how to responsibly wield it. They are taught in business and life to perceive those who talk too much as subordinates and to realize that those who chose their words carefully to prove but a simple point are more like kings. In your conversations with the Chinese, they try to determine where you fit.

I once met with the Minister of Culture in Shanghai, China. My partner and I snagged the meeting with him because of a relationship the Minister shared with my partner's uncle, who at the time was a two-star general in the Chinese military. Upon introduction, the Minister of Culture's assistant shared that the Minister did not speak English. However for some reason, I just didn't buy it. So, I told my partner at the time to be careful with his words because I believed the leader understood everything we said.

This meeting was quite interesting because my partner and I were slated to provide all of the talent for Olympic Village in Beijing in the 2008 Summer Olympics. At first, everything flowed smoothly. When I spoke, the leader's eyes glazed with anticipation, so I knew he at least had a cursory understanding of our conversation. All went well until the last night of our meetings. After a fabulous meal, we rode back to the hotel in a taxi with the Minister of Culture. During the ride, my partner turned to me and ranted several grievances in English about how the Minister of Culture conducted business. Shocked and dismayed, I knew in my gut this was not going to turn out well. Sure enough, once we arrived back at the hotel the Minister of Culture excused himself to go to the men's room. Upon return, he informed us that we were not the "right fit" for the venture he had in mind. He thanked us for our time and promptly left us holding our hats in our hands. What should have been a $30,000 deal became a distant memory and a lasting lesson.

That night I learned to respect relationships. The first mistake was my partner not respecting the boundaries of business and personal relationship. He forgot that it was his uncle who put us together with the Minster in the first place. That alone should have forced my partner to bite his tongue. The next thing is that my partner should have respected the Minister enough not to talk about him negatively. My partner caused the Minister to lose face. Ergo, we lost business.

The next valuable lesson I learned was to appreciate the art of connection. This trip taught me that despite your efforts or intention those with whom you join your vision determine your outcome. Long before the meeting, I had glimpsed that my partner was not the man of integrity he claimed, but I did not listen to my gut. My mistake was not listening. Had I done so, I might have snagged the deal alone. Needless to say, the lesson was learned…and my partner and I parted ways never doing business together again.

Wait for the Real Meeting

The one guaranteed way to garner great information from the Chinese is when they are alone with you. Over the course of my career in the East, I've learned the wisdom of not rushing to leave after meetings or presentations. Oftentimes, many executives will insist on scheduling private appointments with you once the crowd departs. It is here that the Chinese host will feel more comfortable to let you in on the heart of their business venture. To get the invite, engage the executives in light banter until the Chinese host executive initiates further discussion. Once initiated, allow the Chinese host to guide the discussions. Don't be in a hurry to share your vision. Instead, listen and remember you are in that room because of your specialized skill set. Your Chinese host will ask for your expert advice and seek your counsel in their venture. At this point, speak boldly and with confidence. You will be rewarded.

Respect the Business Card

The Chinese place a great deal of emphasis on the formality of exchanging business cards. Make sure that you have plenty of your own before going to China. Translate your name and title into Chinese. Everything else can remain in English. When the Chinese offer their business card, it's typically given with both hands. To be courteous, you should receive the card in the same manner. At that point, place the card before you and read it. Don't be in a rush to put the card away. By reading the card at that moment, you show greater respect for the person and a desire to recall his/her name and title if needed. The Chinese are a very status-conscious people; hence your effort to recognize people's ranks may win a little influence as well as favor.

Don't Expect Much Eye Contact

Americans expect steady eye contact when talking with people. This customary behavior is considered basic and essential for effective communication whether in business or life. Direct eye contact shows respect and that the listener is engaged in the conversation. However, this is not the case for the Chinese. Steady eye contact for them is not a lack of interest or respect; however, steady eye contact is considered inappropriate. The Chinese are an authoritarian culture, which means the demonstration of deference is preferred. For example when subordinates speak with their superiors, you will often see them speak while looking downward. In fact, steady eye contact is occasionally viewed as a gesture of challenge or defiance. Although some Chinese executives are accustomed to American interaction, it is best to gauge their personal temperaments. So, pay attention to visual and cultural cues while being yourself.

Speak Slowly

Because English is the international language of commerce, Americans often forget how hard it is for non-English speakers to fully understand us. Sometimes we don't even realize that we speak a mile a minute. As a result, we lose our audience and potential business. Remember no matter how brilliant the idea or expertise, your plans must be conveyed in ways your audience understands.

Culturally, the Chinese do not ask people to repeat themselves because it is considered impolite. So if they don't understand something, they will continue looking engaged in the conversation though they have mentally checked out. Therefore, all of your well-laid business plans go over their heads and out of the window. This is also true of Chinese interpreters. If you speak too quickly, interpreters will miss the core of your intention and will often choose not to translate those segments. So to help bridge the communication gap, speak slowly.

I encountered this dilemma while being interviewed on the Day Day Up Show in Changsha, China. It was my interpreter's first time on a major television program. Besides her obvious nervousness, she just didn't know how to capture the nuances of what I shared with the audience. Midway through the interview, she removed herself from my side. I later learned that she did so because I was talking too fast. Fortunately, my business partner sat in the front row miming my responses (in real time) as the lead interviewer hurled question after question. Somehow, we managed to it pull off. But, I learned a valuable lesson that day. To carry on effective communication with Chinese business people, I must slow my conversation pace, simplify my answers, and look at the interpreter to ensure the nuances of what I share are understood. Bottom line: keep the language simple in conversations, and you will do just fine.

Benefits of Simple Principles

What I learned by following these simple principles has led me to a long and lucrative career. I have been able to work with Nicki Minaj, Beyonce, Jennifer Lopez, Zendaya, Katy Perry, the hit TV show *American Idol,* and set designer Anton Goss. In addition, I have worked with EE-Media, a C-Pop record label founded under the parent company—Hunan TV. For 10 years, I worked with Rock Records as an arranger and singer with hit producer Johnny Bug Chen. My work with him helped shaped the sound of Pop and Pop music throughout China. I am the first American judge for a Hunan TV show called *Up Junior*, and I'm the first American to have a one-hour TV special of my life. That one-hour special was rated No. 2 in the 8 p.m. time slot and seen by more than 200 million viewers. As a result of these experiences, my sphere of influence is far beyond what I could have even considered and has opened global doors of business.

In addition, I have become a more business savvy entrepreneur and a better man. My dealings in the East forced me to concentrate not just on what my business could offer, but also what I offer as a person. I learned it's not enough to be lucrative. I must be engaged in the person-to-person connection. This is where all business dealings are hard won. Who you are when you come to the business table will determine what you walk away with when the moment is over.

Innovation: China's Deficiency, but America's Expertise

Can I let you in on a little secret? The Chinese like to "borrow" innovation, which includes companies, business operation styles, and intellectual property. In various meetings, I've discovered that most of those conversations had been devoid of fresh ideas and innovative strategies. Here is the key to American business success. We are bred to create the next greatest thing; we thrive from the thrill of innovation. Over the next decade, the Chinese are open to the exposure of proven concepts able to advance their growth in areas from the food and beverage industry to technology. It's incumbent upon every multinational business entrepreneur exploring the Chinese market to evaluate their core strengths and strategically align themselves with companies seeking innovation. Once connected, the mutually beneficial relationship you establish will lend itself to new opportunities and possibly in other industry markets once closed to you.

Look for Business Market Holes

As you evaluate your core strengths, begin looking for holes in the Chinese market where you can add your pioneering approach to create economic, social, and technological change. For example, Finland air carrier Finnair began offering direct-flight services to Chongqing in 2012 becoming the first European carrier to promote the new route as a gateway to Europe. With about 32 million people—about six times the population of Finland—Chongqing is the largest and fastest growing city in China. According to a recent report in Bloomberg News, Dariusz Kowalczyk, senior economist and strategist at Credit Agricole CIB in Hong Kong, confirmed that after a seasonal adjustment imports in China rose 4.3 percent from a year earlier and exports gained 3.3 percent (Pi et al. 2014). In addition, Western and European companies push to expand their global operations. According to recent reports, those in the electronic, chemical, and automotive industries have fared exceptionally well as Chongqing continues to open its commerce to the world.

But Chongqing is not alone. Other of China's second-tier cities like Wuhan, Dalian, and Chengdu are poised to offer Western and European businesses open doors to commerce. No more are Shanghai and Beijing the only "go-to" cities. Over the next decade, I believe that because of the growth of these second-tier cities and others like it, China will emerge as the premier market in the world. This is evident in the current prevalence of global real estate acquisitions, shifting governmental policies, economic solvency, and expedient growth in industries that American and other countries once dominated.

With growth comes new wealth. Now surfacing in China are strong new middle and upper classes yearning to acclimate to Western culture and lifestyle. To appease their appetites, China's malls burst with major designers and luxury brands. But the major difference between China and America's malls is that no one is window-shopping. China is a buyer's market where more is never too much, and the companies stocking China's product shelves are reaping huge benefits. But, they are not the only ones. Industries willing to help push the products—marketing, advertising, and branding—will experience financial boons as well once they jump aboard the fast moving economic train.

In order to keep the wealth in the family, the entire family must be educated to do so. Many of the nouveau riche sends their children to top Ivy League schools in the U.S. to be educated. Harvard, Princeton, and Yale graduate many of those born in generations Y and Next. However upon graduation, many of these young people return to their homelands bringing with them all of the innovation taught to them by their American instructors.

If American business executives were serious about broadening their global reach in the East, it would behoove American human resource professionals to lure these young people into various State side companies before they depart. These educated young people are the budding executives who could possibly become the bridge between the East and West. While they are clearly immersed in American business culture, strategies, and innovation, they also are a product of China's cultural mores and business etiquette.

Emerging Industries in China

As long as China continues to expand, the country will experience growing pains that cannot be answered within China's borders. Executives will be forced to look globally to fulfill their needs. Below is a list of areas in which American businesses can become the answers to Eastern economic prayers.

Food and Beverage

There are about 1.34 billion mouths to feed in China, and that means big opportunity in a country where some local brands have suffered a series of food scares. Currently, foreign restaurateurs and specialty food retailers have cashed in on the economic growth by targeting their premium products to expats as well as China's growing middle and upper classes. As long as the consumers keep buying, the food and beverage industries will continue growing.

Private Education

In order for the nouveau riche to have their children prepared to enter Ivy League schools, there must be a competitive educational foundation. To make this happen, many are demanding better schools and teachers. In 2012, Deloitte estimated that China's private education sector—pre-school education, after-school tutoring, private universities, test prep, and continuing education—will reach a market size of $102 billion by 2015 (Chou et al. 2012). In the same report, it states that the English-language training alone has reached a market size of $4.8 billion (Chou et al. 2012). Those in America planning to enter the educational system might want to look to the East for teaching opportunities.

Clean Technology

Right now, the Chinese government looks for ways to boost energy sustainability and create clean air technology. While China is home to some of the world's most polluted cities, its residents speak out daily in great numbers about choking air pollution, contaminated food, and unsafe drinking water. Chinese journalists have zeroed in on the problem and raised people's awareness through various newscasts and reports. To show how much this is a priority, CNN Money reported in 2013 that China invested $67.7 billion in 2012 to its clean-energy efforts, which included solar and turbine technologies, (Yan 2013).

E Commerce

One of the upsides of a burgeoning middle and upper class is the formation of Internet businesses able to provide for these new consumers' shopping preferences. Going digital for the Chinese market may indeed be the way to go. According to a recent report by independent consulting firm McKinsey, the Chinese market is projected to top $650 billion by 2020 (Dobbs et al. 2013). The report also stated that online sales, or "e-tailing," totaled more than $120 billion in 2011, which beat Japan's online sales at $107 billion and the U.K.'s at $56 billion (Dobbs et al. 2013). And, all this will be supported by the current 130 million residential broadband accounts, which are expected to only increase over the next five to 10 years.

Cloud Computing

As businesses in China look for ways to move filing, accounting, and sale systems off physical servers, cloud computing will become more attractive. Internet giants IBM and Microsoft are heavily moving into the China market, competing against the local company Alibaba, which currently has a cloud service in the primary Chinese province.

Given the sheer number of companies adapting to this new system, I believe this will quickly become a multibillion-dollar industry.

Let China Lead the Business Dance

If I have learned nothing in my 17-year business dealings with the East, I have learned to let China lead. It's their country and their businesses; I am just someone with some new ideas to help them get to their next level in my area of expertise. Therefore, I cannot be arrogant nor can I be in a rush to get the ink dried on the dotted line. That's a Western mindset. Being successful in the East means that one must accept and engage in an Eastern mindset. So, I've learned to embrace their culture and adhere to their rigid protocols. I understand that patience is not just a virtue; it's their way of life. And I acknowledge that relationships—above all else—must be established before there is any engagement on any level.

Real success in China takes place when respect, honor, and relationship have been established. Once these principles are securely in place, you will be able to connect, engage, and experience a level of business success only once dreamed about but never truly tasted. The experience I shared above — my successes and failures — I hope demonstrate not just what I've been able to accomplish, but also inspire you to go out and do the same. What I've experienced does not have to be an isolated case. In fact, I believe that many can join me and become bridges of peace, goodwill, and fresh ideas that can change a world one country at a time.

My advice to anyone choosing to do business in China is to first find a trusted advisor or mentor with proven success. Make sure the person has experienced failures as well as major successes, for you will glean valuable lessons understanding how they navigated from their setbacks to triumphs. Always remember, winning is a game of patience, and should you not know how to wait...do not board the plane!! If you'd like help navigating your way through a possible business opportunity in the East, I can: Help you through the vetting process; broker a deal; serve as a liaison between you and the Chinese company in question; facilitate potential ideas and turn them into possible revenue generating avenues, open doors for brands seeking product placement in

TV, digital media, and other platforms; be the face for your brand in that region; and finally generate advertising and entertainment content geared toward this region for your company.

About the Author

Nick Cooper is a world renowned creative director, artist development expert and innovation strategist. From co-staring with Nigel Lythgoe on the hit how Opening Act, to forging the first joint venture with China's top entertainment network Hunan Television, he is certainly one that eludes the ordinary.

Ask Beyonce' about Nick the musician and she will boast of him arranging her highly acclaimed Oscars' performance. Watch American Idol and you'll see him arranging songs for contestants on season 12.

Nick is also a leading authority on creating strategic alliances with established companies throughout China and the Pacific Rim, with over 18 years of high-level experience. He is the first American to have a one-hour special about his life on Hunan Television's premier show Day Day Up, the first American to be a creative director and judge on a major network show for Hunan Broadcasting System.

From Jamba Juice to Jennifer Lopez, Nick's diverse background and commitment to excellence make him the first call for many exclusive businesses and artists alike.

Contact Nick Cooper:

For information about doing business in China and other countries throughout the Pacific Rim, contact Nick via email at Nick@WesternDragon.tv.

For information about bookings and artist development, contact Nick at www.TheVocalCornerStore.com, or via email at Nick@HeliumTV.com, or by phone at (213) 747-1614.

To see a web video about Nick Cooper and his work in China, visit http://vimeo.com/84705814

Chapter 8

How to Sell to the Public Sector

Niki Papazoglakis

"Failing to plan is planning to fail."

Alan Lakein

The public sector is one of the largest industries in the United States, and government spending accounts for a significant portion of our nation's Gross Domestic Product (GDP) according to the Bureau of Economic Analysis. While the public sector provides ample opportunities for businesses to sell their products and services, there are unique advantages and disadvantages relative to other industries.

Government provides a stable market and is largely immune to market fluctuations experienced by many other industries. In fact, government spending can have an inverse relationship to private markets. An example of this was the American Recovery and Reinvestment Act (ARRA) of 2009 where the government invested over $800 million in infrastructure improvements to stimulate the economy during the recession. While government contracting is often more stable and predictable than other industries, profit margins are typically lower and do not offer significant upside potential.

Beyond the financial benefits, selling to the government can provide personal satisfaction from providing solutions that aid in the health, safety and welfare of the people and communities served. However, some companies and sales professionals are deterred by the long sales cycles and bureaucratic hurdles which must be overcome.

Certain key factors should be considered when determining whether or not to pursue public sector opportunities. Many companies that choose to venture into the public sector abandon the efforts after wasting significant time and resources – a situation that can be avoided through proper planning and setting realistic expectations. The most important factors are:

1. Make sure to have the contract mechanisms in place to sell
2. Patience and incentive structure to endure long sales cycles

Procurement Rules & Regulations

One of the biggest factors in public sector sales efforts is the complex set of procurement rules and regulations that must be followed. Purchasing guidelines are governed by law and vary by jurisdiction, so care must be taken in understanding the rules for each account. Over the last decade, we have seen a significant effort by the National Association of State Purchasing Officers (NASPO) and other organizations to develop best practices for government contracting. This has led to more consistency in rules and regulations, procurement processes and terms and conditions across jurisdictions. These efforts have greatly simplified and streamlined the legal aspects of government procurement for both agencies and contractors.

Most jurisdictions require some form of registration in order to be eligible to do business. There is typically a cost associated with registering. The complexity of the process and the time associated can vary significantly; however, there are companies that provide this service. In many cases, vendors must be registered in advance of any formal procurement activities (e.g. responding to a bid) and must always be registered before a contract can be awarded.

Governments leverage two primary mechanisms for purchasing: convenience contracts and competitive bids. Convenience contracts are contract vehicles designed to reduce the time and effort required for government entities to competitively procure certain types of goods and services. These contracts vary in how they are executed and how they can be used. The important thing to understand is whether your products and services are eligible to be purchased through an existing contract. This is almost always the preferred procurement mechanism, and you will be at a significant disadvantage if you are not on the contract. Before embarking on a sales pursuit, understand whether or not the solution you are selling can be purchased through a convenience contract. If so, determine if the solution is already on the contract or if it can be added. If not, you could end up putting in a lot of effort to have the customer ultimately purchase from your competitor. This information is available on each government's website, and you can always call the purchasing division if you have questions.

Some contracts are open, meaning that vendors can get added to the contract at any time by simply following the designated process. Others are for specific terms. For these contracts, the purchasing division will release a bid asking for vendors to respond with specific products and/or services and associated prices. Some jurisdictions allow any qualified respondents to become authorized on the contract while others limit the number of vendors in each category.

One strategy for reducing the time and effort for getting on a contract or for being able to sell your products and services when you are ineligible to get on the contract is to partner with a vendor authorized on the contract in the category(s) that you are selling. This approach not only provides a tactical means for selling without directly holding a contract, but it can provide a mechanism for quickly engaging with public sector clients before making a strategic decision to pursue this space. The downside is that you must comply with the pricing guidelines of the prime contractor which may or may not support healthy profit margins, particularly when you account for the prime contractor's markup.

The other procurement mechanism is the competitive bid which is usually called a Request for Proposal (RFP) or a Request for Quote

(RFQ). RFPs are generally reserved for large, complex solutions where the customer does not have the exact technical requirements. They will outline the project goals and objectives along with any functional requirements and ask vendors to propose their own solutions. While RFPs are sometimes awarded strictly based on price, it is becoming more common to award to the vendor that provides the best value. RFQs are typically product-oriented and often used when the agency has a specific solution in mind. The RFQ will usually provide detailed product specifications and be awarded based on price.

One thing to keep in mind with competitive procurements is that most jurisdictions have open records laws. In some jurisdictions, only the winning proposal is subject to these laws. In others, all proposals submitted are subject. This can put you at a significant disadvantage when your competitors can see your proposal, so it is essential to separate confidential information/trade secrets from your main proposal in order to protect your intellectual property. Most jurisdictions have pretty clear guidelines as to what can be considered confidential/trade secret. The flip side is that you can obtain your competitors' previous proposals to gain a competitive advantage.

Navigating the Bureaucracy

The inefficiency of government bureaucracy is one of the biggest deterrents keeping many organizations and individuals from pursuing business in the public sector. The very nature of bureaucracy is to resist change. This is particularly challenging for those trying to enter public sector accounts, but it offers a tremendous advantage to those businesses that successfully break in.

In order to penetrate the public sector, it is important to understand the role of bureaucracy in government. Our Founding Fathers intentionally structured a system where policy was developed by politicians with frequent elections, and those policies were administered by bureaucracies inherently resistant to change. Government agencies were designed so that bureaucratic inertia would protect the country from radical or short-term shifts in political sentiment that could produce long-term consequences.

Government agencies are designed as bureaucracies in order to prevent corruption and the consolidation of too much power by a single individual or small group. So while it is often frustrating to deal with the inefficiencies and complexities of a bureaucracy, it is helpful to understand that the design is intentional and serves a valuable purpose in protecting the foundation on which this nation was built.

Understanding and appreciating the principles and purpose of bureaucracy is tremendously helpful in tolerating the intrinsic challenges.

So what are the inefficiencies and complexities? They come in a variety of shapes and sizes, but there are some key elements that are virtually universal.

Complex Approval Processes

Unlike many private businesses where executives are often empowered to make purchasing decisions unilaterally for their business unit as long as the budget is available, government executives must follow rigid procurement processes. The procurement process typically gets more complicated as the size of the purchase increases.

Below is a sample of tiered procurement authority; however, keep in mind that the thresholds can vary significantly across jurisdictions, so it is necessary to understand the procurement guidelines of each account:

Line manager	Up to $5,000
Agency head	$5,001 - $15,000
Mayor	$15,001 - $25,000
City Council	$25,001 & above

Regardless of the level of approval required, there are a number of other individuals involved in the process. Some agencies have internal purchasing divisions, whereas many jurisdictions have a central purchasing department.

For example, say you are trying to sell an anti-virus solution to a state Department of Transportation (DOT) worth $250,000. You will have sold the IT staff at DOT on the value of your product. You have either identified a contract vehicle or convinced them that they need to put out an RFP (as opposed to buying your competitor's product off the state contract). In either instance, DOT must obtain approval from the state CIOs office to ensure that the product meets statewide standards. Once the CIO's approval is obtained, the IT manager must obtain authorization from the agency CFO to use the funds. The IT staff is working closely with the procurement manager at DOT to obtain the necessary approvals. Due to the size of the order, DOT must also get authorization from the State Purchasing Officer who typically resides within the Office of Management and Budget. At some point in the process, there must also be a legal review of the contract. In this scenario, at least six approvals are necessary to order your product. And unfortunately, the process is typically a little more complicated than this – especially if they have to issue an RFP.

As a taxpayer, you appreciate the processes and controls designed to prevent corruption and the frivolous use of taxpayer money. As a sales rep trying to close a deal with DOT, you see the time and expense associated with the process as inefficient and a waste of taxpayers' dollars.

While the approval process is complex and time consuming, the first contract is always the most difficult. Once you understand the process and have built relationships with the approvers in the various departments, it becomes much easier to shepherd your contracts through the process. One word of caution: do not expect your customer to handle it alone. There are strict hierarchies in every bureaucracy, and folks who have been around a while know better than to break the chain of command.

Annual Appropriation Cycle

All organizations have budgets, but the budgeting process in state and local government is much less flexible than in private industry.

Unlike the federal government, many states and municipalities have balanced budget laws which prohibit them from operating at a deficit. Government purchasing is extremely cyclical and centers around the beginning and end of the fiscal year (some governments use bi-annual budgeting but the process is the same). Many departments have pent up demand, so they have a flurry of spending at the beginning of each fiscal year when their funding becomes available. For example, most subscriptions have their renewals at this time.

There is sometimes a second wave of spending at the end of the fiscal year. Often departments have excess money that they must spend or run the risk of having that amount reduced from the next year's appropriation. This is known as the "use it or lose it" mentality. There are never enough funds to go around, and legislators often believe that if a department did not need all of the money appropriated in the previous year, they should reallocate those funds to more needy departments.

Because the budgeting process is lengthy and requires legislative approval, most states start planning for the next year's budget shortly after the beginning of the fiscal year. Agencies are required to submit their budget requests by a specific date so that the Governor's office can develop a budget to propose at the start of the legislative session. The process is similar, albeit often simpler and shorter, for most municipalities. Regardless of the level of government, it is important to have your project included in the department's budget request. Without the appropriation, it is usually difficult to find additional funding for new projects.

Due to the budgeting process and depending on the size of the deal, sales cycles in the public sector often exceed 12 months.

Removing the Barriers to Entry

Politics

One reality of the public sector is that it is highly political. And the larger the contracts get, the more politics will influence the sales process. If you have committed to penetrating the public sector, one of the fastest ways to do it is by hiring a well-connected lobbyist. Most lobbyists have relationships in the legislative and executive branches of government, both of which are important as administrators usually make contracting decisions while legislators approve the appropriations and sometimes contractor selection.

Due to the hierarchical nature of government, it is beneficial to have relationships at the top, but it is difficult to gain direct access to these individuals. Having a lobbyist who can get you in front of the decision makers can significantly accelerate the time it takes to penetrate the account.

Another unfortunate reality is that money influences politics. I am not saying that campaign contributions are absolutely necessary for securing government contracts, but they certainly don't hurt. Very few politicians engage directly in corrupt activities, but they do pay attention to who supported them during their campaigns (and sometimes more importantly who supported their competitors). The ugly truth is that it has gotten so expensive to obtain public office, politicians are dependent on campaign contributions to maintain their seat. While political donations should never be used to try and buy contracts (trying would probably land you in jail rather than with a contract), they can help you gain visibility with key decision makers which can possibly help tilt the scales in your favor in a highly competitive procurement.

If you are serious about penetrating this market, it would be wise to have a budget for campaign contributions if possible, although some companies strictly prohibit political donations. A good lobbyist can help you develop a donation strategy to maximize the benefit. I strongly recommend that contributions be reserved for fundraisers where you will have the opportunity to network with government officials and monitor your competitors, rather than simply sending a check.

Leverage Public Information to Identify Buying Criteria

Depending on the sales methodology that you learned, this list may vary slightly, but most sales training teaches you to qualify opportunities early by identifying the following key elements:

- Knowing the budget
- Having access to the decision makers
- Validating the need for your product or service
- Understanding the timing and urgency of the procurement

A significant benefit to selling in the public sector is that much of this information is publicly available, including budget documents. While they typically do not drill down to the project level or sometimes even the department level, a lot of information can be gleaned from budgets.

For example, knowing whether an agency's budget increased or decreased from the previous year can be extremely valuable.

Some jurisdictions publish their organizational charts and employee directories, making it easy to identify the decision makers and staff responsible for buying your product or service.

Many governments publish strategic plans outlining where they are today, their goals and priorities for the future and how they plan to get there. For tactical product sales, it is likely not necessary to conduct this level of research. However, any strategic sales pursuit should begin with a review of the strategic plan and any other relevant materials published by that account.

Conclusion

As discussed, there are a variety or pros and cons of selling to the public sector. If often takes a significant investment of time and money to penetrate this space; but once in, it can produce a steady stream of business for a very long time.

About the Author

Niki Papazoglakis has fifteen years' experience working in the public, private, and nonprofit sectors. She has spent the majority of her career as a sales executive with technology giants IBM, Unisys and Hewlett-Packard selling to public sector accounts across the nation before becoming General Manager for the Louisiana branch of a regional IT company.

Ms. Papazoglakis is currently the Vice President of Sales and Marketing for The Digital Decision, a technology consulting firm specializing in public safety communications.

Niki Papazoglakis holds a Bachelor's degree in International Trade & Finance and a Masters in Public Administration.

You can connect with Niki via the LinkedIn network at: http://www.linkedin.com/in/nikipapazoglakis.

Chapter 9

How to Get the WOW in Your Brand

Julie Trotter Clark

We all know how many times you get to make a first impression, right?

That is why brand design and application is of the utmost importance to a company. It is the face of your company to the public, the first point of communication to the people who will support your business and make it grow. This first impression should be the result of a carefully planned brand design strategy. In this chapter, I will share with you valuable information, tips and current ideologies of the brand design world.

The Top Three Things You Need to Know About Branding:

1. Make it a single point of distinction.
2. Make it memorable.
3. Be consistent.

I have been a professional designer for over 30 years. My expertise is in strategic, creative marketing design. "Creative thinking for design" is a strategic process that I've developed and honed for the last 10 years, drawing on experience with my extensive client list, my teachings and my published writings. This process involves developing ideas from the initial brainstorming stage, through the refining and revamping process, and into actual execution. These ideas then represent your company in the marketplace and will differentiate your company from the competition. We help companies, products and services create and establish their name, logo, POS or positioning statements, and identity as the proper foundation to build a brand.

Often it is best to check with the experts, so when you are building your own brand, you can work smart!

"Good design is order out of chaos." – Julie Trotter Clark

First, I would like to emphasize the importance of creating an effective marketing strategy. Then we will get into the "how."

The goal of any successful branding design is to make the product or service POP! You want to create an emotional connection to your customers that will ultimately increase your market share. Effective branding is all about creating a buzz among both existing clients and potential new ones; you want your brand to communicate that your product, service or even yourself is the ULTIMATE in a field of ho-hums. Successful brand design creates a lasting and memorable connection with your customer.

The top three things you need to establish your brand would be the following:

1. Name
2. Logo (or icon), and
3. The Visual/Verbal Presentation

Things They Never Tell You!

One of the first pointers I can give you about brand design is **protect it!** By this I mean that once you have a logo, name or tagline, you need to register it as a trademark/service mark, use a copyright notice, and then establish the '.com.' I will discuss this topic in more detail when we get to naming, but make sure you do the proper paperwork in order to protect your business!

•••

In today's market, with so many new companies being started every day, it is imperative to develop a strong brand foundation. This is my area of expertise; I help companies build their businesses so they can grow and flourish. Establishing a strong brand provides your company with intellectual property, which can be worth as much in this marketplace as brick-and-mortar. Think of McDonald's golden arches, or the Nike "Just Do It" slogan. These brands have been protected under the trademark laws, and are highly valuable intellectual property for their respective companies.

So now that we know the importance of brand design, let's explore the different levels. There are five key levels to establishing a successful brand marketing strategy. This is what I call "The Brand Ladder."

The Brand Ladder refers to the levels of branding and how effective your brand is in the market. You can use this ladder in your marketing plan to target growth and measure awareness with one BIG goal in mind… GET TO THE TOP!

These are the ladder descriptions for each step:

The First Step: BRAND ABSENCE

Think of this level as the beginning, the blank piece of paper. This is the start and the initial design development phase of the process. Once your name, icon, identity, and initial development are done, you are at the bottom of the ladder. Now you need to tell the world that you are a BRAND and your customers should take notice! So, be diligent about getting it right. Later on, I will share some tips on how to get the proper foundation in place.

The Second Step: BRAND AWARENESS

This is when a customer recognizes your name, logo or tagline (which is the same as your verbal presentation). They see it, recognize it, identify your company by it, and thus it becomes familiar. This is the start of your relationship with your customers; you are letting them know why your brand is unique. It is critical that the message is consistent. Make sure you present the same image, tagline and positioning every time you have a brand touch point. Unfortunately, I know of great advertising campaigns that garnered much attention, but no one can remember the name of the company or the product after the ad has appeared. Another branding failure occurs when the ad campaign is confusing and tries to make too many points, thus clouding the issue. Be sure to make one single point of distinction. Keep it simple and be consistent throughout all the channels and touch points of Brand Awareness. From the person that answers the phone and takes an order to the person thanking someone for their business, be consistent with the name, the logo and the message.

The Third Step: BRAND PREFERENCE

When Brand Preference is in proper order, your customers will drive that extra mile, make a consistent effort to use **your** product or service, and be happy they are doing so because they PREFER your brand over any others in the market.

This is, of course, where we start getting into **Brand Loyalty** and customers that actually choose one brand over another. Price plays a role here, but interestingly, this is where charging more money because of the brand is acceptable. Even when ultimately a product is the same as a competitor's, customers are willing to pay more because you have established yourself as the premier brand.

The Fourth Step: BRAND ADVOCACY

Brand Advocacy is when your customer starts telling other people about your product and recommending it. Your customers become the best kind of advertising there is: word of mouth. This is a goal for all companies to reach: when your family or friends tell you that you should use this brand of kitchen appliances, or that kind of hair gel, or that this accountant helped me with my taxes, or that school was the best place to learn that information. This is loyalty marketing at work and shows that you have achieved Brand Advocacy. Companies pay large sums of money to get people to make brand decisions. Remember, when you have a happy customer, they will tell their friends, typically three or four. BUT, when a customer has a bad experience, a person will tell ten to twelve people **NOT** to use your brand. There is nothing more damaging than bad, loudmouthed customers, regardless of whether they are right or wrong. Often the damage they cause is irreversible.

So, Brand Advocacy, when someone is actually telling people that they prefer your product or service, is wonderful; however, there is still room at the top for the most important level and the highest step on the Brand Ladder...

The Fifth Step: BRAND INSISTENCE

YOU HAVE REACHED THE TOP! Now your customers are your brand leaders, talking, teaching and telling everyone about your brand! It is the best possible scenario when your customers insist only on your brand AND spread the good news!

Your customers now make a conscious decision to pick your brand and no other brand will do. This is the top of the ladder and explains why we will pay more for a certain product or service. We tell our friends, share our discoveries, and teach our compadres what this brand stands for and what it means to us personally. We have made a personal, emotional connection with a particular brand, even if the competition has exactly the same product or service. This is the ultimate goal!

Favorite Brand Moments

Coco Chanel went on the map with one product. Do you know what that was? She was well into her career as a couture fashion designer and happened to be in a lab with scientists when she was introduced to test tube no. 5. To hear more, check my blog and search 'chanel,' but you probably guessed what was in the tube... CHANEL No. 5

•••

Putting It All Together

You need to have the marketing plan prior to any design; I call it a "brand tool kit." What do you need in your brand tool kit?

First, get the plan in place... your marketing plan, that is. I don't claim to be a marketer, but with all my experience I am well acquainted with many industries and have created numerous customized marketing strategic designs. Let's now concentrate on the design and development side of a brand.

Remember, "plan your work & work your plan."

Things They Never Tell You

Microsoft is NOT a layout program! Layout programs are all forms of software designed specifically for final art. You need to know how to enable proper formatting for printing, digital and video electronic files. Know what these are and how they work.

Last time I checked, these programs were over $1,000. Depending on your budget, it may be more desirable to hire a designer.

•••

The first step in designing and developing a brand is to... CREATE YOUR PLAN, GOALS AND MARKETING VISION.

As clear, straightforward communication is the cornerstone of any successful project, begin with an extensive analysis of your competitive strengths and weaknesses. At this stage, learn everything you can about your target market, your competitors and your risks – set your goals, define your unique assets, and begin to plot a forward marketing strategy for your business.

This is typically in your marketing plan and is a strategic piece of your overall business plan. It is an overview of your business today and where are you planning to go in a month, a year, five years, and beyond. What are the steps that will take you there?

The list below features the must-have items for every business' brand development:

Marketing Overview:

- Scope & Methodology

Brand Strategy

- Name
- Logo
- Identity

Multichannel Marketing Plan

- Traditional media, Print & Digital

Measurement Tools:

- Feedback test
- Results test

A solid plan will consist of both digital and traditional media, and a way to track spending. Your tracking should include a way to measure how each tactic performed.

The beginning is a testing period. Large companies spend huge amounts of money on tests prior to getting a new product into the market. However, over the last several years, the onset of the web has changed everything, and a small business operation with only several people can blossom overnight and become a serious brand. Make sure you are ready and the blossom does not turn into a bust. Be prepared for the growth or you could lose your business before you even get started.

Basic items in the tool kit would be the name, the logo and the positioning statement. This also includes decisions around color and typography... altogether, this will determine the essence of what the company needs to communicate about its product or service.

Depending on whether your company is offering a product or service, the items will differ on the list of what you need. For instance, a product needs packaging and labels, etc., whereas a service may need a brochure explaining the process or service offered.

The next step is to create the identity package. This may consist of a business card, an electronic letterhead, a note card, a brochure, a folder or press kit, a label, an initial web home page, and a template for the type of digital presence that best suits your business goals. This digital presence includes items such as mobile applications, e-mail marketing, social media campaigns and blogging. Also, consider direct mail, publication ads, billboards and/or YouTube commercials.

I like to say that a business card is your billboard, so make it stand out and make it memorable! People will appreciate an unusual look and they will hang on to something that speaks to them.

When I work with clients, I like to start with the basics. What I am sharing in this book will hopefully help you understand naming and design basics and how they work. My goal is to help you think of how your brand presents itself in the marketplace and help you build a solid foundation for your brand design strategy.

Favorite Brand Moments: Make a "Brewski Run"

I was hired to design a winter campaign for Corona Beer. The brand positioning at that time was "Miles away from ordinary." Excited about this unique concept, I consulted with the client and then presented three creative ideas for the campaign. The brand team at Corona decided upon the concept that used their mascot (a parrot) on a snowboard, with the headline "Make a Brewski Run." During our client meetings I suggested that the corporate attorneys check the headline to confirm their ability to use the term 'Brewski' and, if possible, to protect it. Much to our surprise, the tagline and the word had no previous trademark registration or application protecting it, and Corona Beer was successful in protecting the trademark on that tagline. A sample of this campaign is on my website in the *portfolio* section.

•••

Naming

There are five different types of naming categories that you may or may not be able to protect with legal registration, thereby starting the process of building intellectual property. This can ultimately be the MOST valuable marketing solution you own, your BRAND. Names are evaluated in terms of the goods or services offered under them.

The first and most distinctive names to protect are **FANCIFUL NAMES.** They are the easiest to protect because they are made up, and do not exist until you put an identity to them. What are a Kodak, an Exxon, and a Xerox? We all know and identify with those names because the companies they represent have spent significant time and money establishing the identity and the BRAND essence.

The next would be **ARBITRARY NAMES.** This is a word that exists, but the BRAND has given it a different meaning from what it actually is. Examples are brands like Apple and Macintosh. We all know what a piece of fruit is, but a new meaning has been established from the BRAND identity and we therefore understand now that Apple can refer to a computer.

Next are the **SUGGESTIVE NAMES**. The name suggests what we are to understand for the BRAND essence and communicates the BRAND properties. Examples of this type of naming are common in new product launches, like Radiance, Edge, or Tilex. The name actually partially describes what the product's attributes do or mean.

Next would be **DESCRIPTIVE NAMES**. This is a description of the way the product performs and behaves. Names and examples would be Edward Jones, or JT Clark. They are the description of who or what the product or service is. Soft for a fabric softener or Computer Store for a computer store would be descriptive names. They are not able to be protected as trademarks unless the owner establishes a long period of exclusive use… The last would be **GENERIC NAMES**. These types of names are things, which you cannot really protect with trademarks.

They are what we actually refer to as the item or product when we communicate about it, such as an Umbrella for umbrellas or Slipper for slippers.

The laws for trademarks are established for clarity and protection and to avoid consumer confusion. It is important to check the legal status of the name and get it properly registered when you start.

It would be a big mistake to start a product or service and not get the proper paperwork in order to operate your business. The first to use a name for a particular product or service has the strongest rights in it. That owner could object to your use and demand that you stop using it. This could result in damages such as losing your name and/or a lot of hard work because someone else did the proper legal homework. They could potentially send you a "cease and desist" letter, take you to court, close your business or force you to change your name. A very costly mistake!

•••

Things They Never Tell You

When it comes to naming, do it RIGHT - GET the .COM

If you are thinking of a great name, do a trademark search, check to see if it is available and then be prepared to spend the few dollars that it takes to pay for the name online. This is very easy to do and is a fundamental first step. When the name comes up as available, be ready to purchase it immediately. If you do not, it will not be there the next time you search. Web crawlers see the search and the next time you check for it, it will be hundreds or even thousands of dollars. You will want a name that is your business and easy to remember because that's how people are going to find you on the web.

•••

So, how and where do we start? Consider two things, the written message and the visual message. This is the essence of your BRAND, with a UNIQUE STRATEGIC POSITIONING statement, often referred to as the USP or the POS. This is the supporting copy that describes exactly how you want to communicate what makes your product or service different or unique.

The WRITTEN message is the NAME and the USP. (UNIQUE STRATEGIC POSITIONING)

The VISUAL message is the ICON or LOGO.

Let's Discuss Logo Design

I think of the actual name and logo as what Aristotle would refer to as 'logos,' the LOGIC, the why. It is the logic that is the written message with a visual that will establish the brand essence. Remember, make it different. It is your unique identity with a unique selling proposition and it communicates clearly why your product or service is different from anybody else's.

•••

Things They Never Tell You

Many different needs must be met when a final design goes to be produced. If you're creating art files, make sure you know what your final format should be. For instance, many color logos don't translate across multi-platforms, such as web, print, video, fabric, packaging, signage and screen printing. Final art files that can be included are: eps, pdf, jpeg, png, and psd, in cmyk, rgb and even b&w. Always tell your printer what your client wants in order to be sure you get the best results.

•••

Design Theory

Gestalt is a psychology term which means "unified whole." It refers to theories of visual perception developed by German psychologists in the 1920's. These theories attempt to describe how people tend to organize visual elements into groups or unified wholes when certain principles are applied.*

These principles are:

- Continuation
- Similarity
- Anomaly

- Closure

- Proximity

- Figure and Ground

* "The Gestalt Principles," accessed September 17, 2013, http://graphicdesign.spokanefalls.edu/tutorials/process/gestaltprinciples/gestaltprinc.htm.

The following examples are logos that I have designed for clients over the years, as well as designs that I have selected to help you understand the concepts.

Continuity or Continuation: This occurs when the eye is compelled to move through one object and continue to another object. Continuation is often used in web design because the viewer's eye will naturally follow a line or curve. The smooth, flowing crossbar of a design leads the eye directly through what is being communicated.

The first example: Chip Nine. I created this logo for a new product that will launch this fall. A fun family game.

Similarity occurs when objects look similar to one another. People often perceive them as a group or pattern. When similarity occurs, an object can be emphasized if it is dissimilar to the others; this is called **Anomaly**. If one in a series is different, that makes it stand out visually.

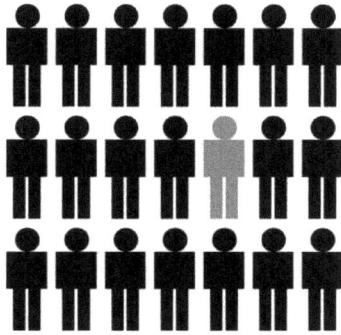

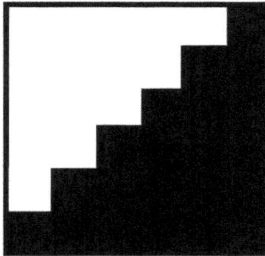

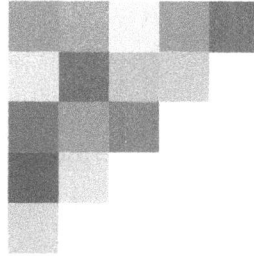

Closure occurs when an object is incomplete or a space is not completely enclosed. If enough of the shape is indicated, people perceive the whole by filling in the missing information. The design itself is not complete, but enough is present for the eye to complete the shape. When the viewer's perception completes a shape, closure occurs.

A logo I designed with Lady Gaga in mind. When I look at it, I can hear her sing.

Proximity occurs when elements are placed close together. They tend to be perceived as a group. When the squares below are given close proximity, for instance, unity occurs. While they continue to be separate shapes, they are now perceived as one.

Examples: The title for my book and my website, and a logo I created for CVS Caremark to represent Supplier Diversity.

Figure and Ground is when the eye differentiates an object from its surrounding area. A form, silhouette, or shape is naturally perceived as figure (object), while the surrounding area is perceived as ground (background). Balancing figure and ground can make the perceived image clearer. Using unusual figure/ground relationships can add interest and subtlety to an image.

A classic example

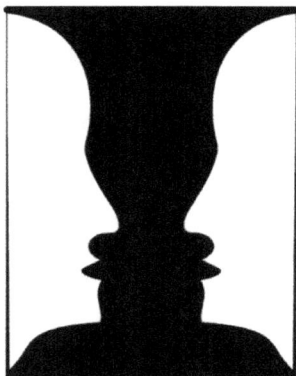

My JT Clark Logo:

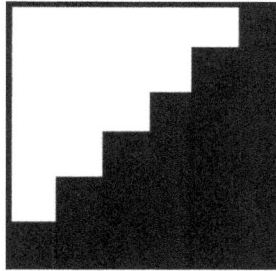

Anyone can design a logo, but if you're just starting out, consider hiring a professional to get it right!

•••

Favorite Brand Moments

I had the pleasure of studying under Milton Glaser while he was at the School of Visual Arts in New York. You may not recognize his name, but I am positive that you'll recognize his work. Known as the "Grandfather of Graphic Design," Milton is famous for the logo he designed as a gift to New York City: "I ♥ New York." Interestingly, Milton was never paid for the design and never put his copyright on it. Thus, it has been used as a public symbol and a design that we've all enjoyed.

•••

Putting It All Together

Remember that a strong brand makes an emotional connection with your audience. You need to communicate your brand's distinct advantages, so tell your story in a creative way with unusual typography, color and design. Plan your work and work your plan. Today's business environment is like never before; one day you can be a startup, and the next, your business can be off the charts.

JT Clark can help you with *working smart* and getting the *proper foundation* for your brand to enter the market without breaking the bank. Connect with me on LinkedIn and we can discuss the details.

For more information on how to get the WOW into your brand, call or e-mail me and I'd be happy to talk with you about how we can help.

•••

About the Author

As an innovator, and entrepreneur, published author, speaker, guest judge, and graphic design expert, Julie Trotter Clark is a sought after "Business Branding" visionary. She has guided the introduction and re-invention of countless brands through her use of strategic planning and implementation of intelligent marketing and creative design solutions. Daily she is the creative "heart" of JT Clark Design, a 27 year-old design agency on the north shore of Chicago.

An established branding and design boutique with a reputation for excellence, JT Clark Design focuses primarily on exclusive, high-end products and services. Leading her team of seasoned professionals, Julie provides inspiration and insights gained from over two decades years in marketing, design and communications. Her business is based on her core principle of "Marketing Solutions by Design."

After earning a degree in Fine Arts from Kansas University, she had the honor of studying with the world-renowned designer and mentor, Milton Glazer, at the SVA (School of Visual Arts) in New York. Her years at St. Louis-based Anheuser Busch and Maritz Motivation helped her build a solid foundation in branding principles and established her as a creative designer with a fundamental understanding of business needs and processes.

Among many others, her awards from the Chicago Business Marketing Association (BMA) for outstanding work are especially appreciated since they represent not only design excellence but also measurable success for her clients. She is proud of her participation over the past fifteen years in the Women's Business Enterprise (WBE). She is an active board member of the Chicago Inventors Organization.

Staying involved with her family, community and profession keeps the creative focus her passion, not just her job.

•••

The following are a few websites that I find very useful. Check them out and maybe they can help you too. Thank you for reading my chapter and connecting with me.

Visit my blog and website for more information: www.JTClarkDesign.com

Connect with me on LinkedIn

Julie Trotter Clark

JT Clark Design LLC

Lake Bluff, IL 60044

The best way to reach me is to call my cell, at 847-409-7170. If I don't answer, leave a message and I will call you back.

RECOMMENDED links and RESOURCES

- http://forwardprogress.com
- https://www.youtube.com/user/JTClarkAgency
- http://www.hubspot.com
- http://JTClarkDesign.com blog on wordpress.com
- http://www.brandchannel.com
- http://www.uspto.gov/trademarks/search/
- http://www.uspto.gov/trademarks/search/

Step Up Your Image

Call me if you need a logo, a brand image or a re-fresh of a current brand product or service. I take on two new clients per month! Ask about my design audit to find out what you should keep and what to change. I can help you step up your brand to be the absolute best!

For the first 50 people to take advantage of this offer, I will extend a 20% discount on your next logo, identity, design project, or a review and update of your Brand Image!

I schedule two new clients per month, call me!

E-mail me at Julie@JTClarkDesign.com

Call on my cell 847-409-7170

NOTE: We are in Chicago, IL.

Chapter 10

The Importance of Managing Your Brand Using Social Media

Shannon Allen

It's 3 a.m. in the morning on a Sunday night and you've just learned via multiple texts, tweets, emails, and frantic voicemails that a past client's social media manager has just tweeted a pornographic photo of a toy airplane inside of a woman to half a million followers, mostly business travelers and frequent fliers. What would you do? This scenario sounds like it was made for TV but for a major US airline and their social media department, it was a reality. To some people social media might seem like all fun and games, similar to Candy Crush, but in this day of business, social media must be taken very seriously.

Social media is one of the hottest topics in all of business right now, and it should be. Unfortunately, most companies are still in the dark on how to use it as a productive business development tool. As a result, it often seems like a waste of time.

The world has fully embraced the digital age and social networks have been internationally connecting individuals and bringing society up to speed. With over 1.4 billion members at the time of this writing, Facebook is the current social media leader, allowing people to easily communicate with each other across time zones and oceans. Social media provides businesses with many unique opportunities but it can also be very harmful if not managed properly. Many businesses have lost credibility and market share through negative attention that has gone "viral" on social media.

This chapter will show you how to use social media platforms as a vehicle to propel your business forward in this new technological age.

Social Media Points to Consider:

Facebook:

- 98% of 18-24 year olds use Facebook.
- Humans spend 700 billion minutes on Facebook every month.
- 250 million access this social network with their phone.

YouTube:

- 490 million unique users log onto YouTube each month.
- They spend 2.9 billion hours watching 90 billion videos monthly.

With these statistics in mind, all business need to develop their social media platforms in a way that is designed to target their desired audiences. Mobile phone use has skyrocketed along with Internet speeds. Mobile phones help support social media growth. Many companies have learned to leverage the incredible power of this, and social media has become the backbone of their marketing and business growth strategies. This chapter is not for people who want to get more Twitter or Facebook friends to flood their inbox with "selfies." The world is moving from a desktop/laptop world to an instant/mobile world. Is your business prepared? There is a worldwide movement toward the mobile way. This mobile uprising is revolutionizing both the Internet and social media.

Social Media & Brand Building

Future decisions will hinge on how you handle your brand with social media in the present. Individuals and corporations must take great care in maintaining their best foot forward in regards to social media. It is now the primary means by which most people in this new technological world get from one person to the next. The whisper of information from one person to the next has become the retweet and hashtag of the social media generation. Perhaps you are a social media manager responsible for getting the world to know about your company's brand online, using the right tools with social media. Maybe you are the future executive business owner who wants to establish your own online brand. If you are doing any form of business in this current day, it is a must that you develop a proper plan for your social media marketing strategy.

For entrepreneurs, branding is the most critical aspect of the job. A respectable social presence gives you the credibility to attract clients, partners, and investors. You can make yourself available while also demonstrating your personality and experience. The amazing part is that you can do this from anywhere in the world. With the power of the Internet and even mobile phones, branding can be done 24/7 from the palm of your hand. For the first time ever in the U.S., time spent on mobile phones has overtaken the time that people had normally spent on a desktop computer. The times are changing. Mobile phones and social media are driving the next set of innovations.

The key to developing thriving and successful brands is to adapt to the migration away from desktop computers. Branding will help a client think of a specific company first when he or she thinks of their specific niche in the market.

Building your online brand in a meaningful way is no easy task but there are many tools available to get you on the right path. Over the years, I have watched some exceptional brands gain momentum in a crowded online marketplace. People should remember this mantra: the web is written in ink, definitely not in pencil. Mistakes are seldom forgotten. Building your brand online should be handled with care. Anything you do can be stuck in the pages of Google for an eternity. It is up to you how you want the redundant servers of the world's search engines to remember you. People should keep in mind that we are ALL brands in this day and age. All human beings that go on the Internet are microcosmic brands. People have to realize this when they open their social networking accounts.

Certain bloggers become famous for no reason except for the fact that people enjoy consuming their concepts and the content they create. My fiancé is addicted to reading some bloggers, websites, and social feeds. Either they interest her or she finds them amusing. It is interesting that part of human nature is to be curious about what other humans are doing. Of course, we also want to know how and why they are doing it. Social media takes this thought process to a whole new level. You can see what almost anyone is doing as they post their lives in real-time on the Internet.

I know many people reading this might not think they have the time to really manage their online brand. Who has the time to post on Facebook, Twitter, Instagram, LinkedIn, & Pinterest while also staying productive? I totally understand that you may encounter some people in the social feeds who might be as interesting as watching paint dry. My first piece of advice is to make sure that you follow the right people. If you follow the wrong people, it can seriously affect your disposition. I am a positive person, and, in general, I only post information in a positive light. I even had someone send me a message telling me that they were un-following me because I was too positive. It is important to understand where you are now and then make a plan for where you want to go. It is a good practice to utilize deductive reasoning when planning your brand. Think with the end goal in mind and work backwards.

Building Your Brand with Social Media

To become a leader in your field you need to be someone that people go to for professional advice. They may not actually come to your office or have extensive meetings with you, but you can interact with them through social media. This way, your customers can know a lot about your brand. Social media is about sharing. Share your knowledge as much as you can without losing advantage over your competitors. Keep in mind to not "over-share" as well. Clogging up peoples' timelines with messages can be annoying.

Well-timed messages where key people remember your updates are critical. Today's consumer speaks the language of Social Media. If you do not have an active Twitter or Facebook account, people start to perceive you as untrusting. It is unprecedented how credibility is now not only how you act offline in real life, but how your online brand acts as well. When building your online brand, planning and sticking to your script is key. Storyboard your brand's voice so you do not seem scattered with your content. For example, if you are a fashion blogger, you should not be random and post something about the inside gaskets of a Bugatti.

Boosting Your Klout

The key question people in many companies ask is, "How do you quantify it?" How do you increase sales and get more clients and leads for your company using social networking? People want to know: is it the quantity of followers or quality of followers? I would suggest that it is about the quality. If you have great people in your social feed that are engaging with your brand, they will be happy people who will share your content as you share it. I have seen many people with multiple thousands of followers who just sit there and do not engage. I am sure that some of those followers are purchased. That is another trend that people are utilizing— most of the purchased followers are profiles that are either fake or people who are prompted to follow you from another country. This makes the quality go down.

You want engagement. Engagement is key. It is not the bottom line. Your posts must have the right effect on people for you to achieve your ultimate marketing goals. If you are not creating the desired effect, you are not using your energy correctly. There are a few tools available on the Internet to help you understand your level of social influence. Klout is an example of a website/portal that does a quick and easy assessment of your social media influence. It also helps you with ways to enhance it. Klout evaluates your overall Twitter impact by calculating the "true reach" you have in the social sphere. Klout looks at your brand's most influential topics as well as the ratio of actively engaged followers.

The cool thing about Klout is that you can compare your scores with your competition. Peer Index, which is similar to Klout, is another great free tool. These days, the Internet has terrific analytics as far as social media is concerned. These are just two to put on your radar. These kinds of tools are useful for checking the competitive difference between you and your peer brands. Let me give you a great example of how Klout works. Mya, a Grammy-winning artist, retweeted a post of mine and ever since, she has had a high Klout score. Additionally, it gave me extra points for that. If you happen to have certain individuals that have a lot of followers take interest in your posts, it always looks good for your Klout score and credibility in general.

As I write about this concept, I have to reflect on my own experiences. I am just in the process of establishing the KingCreative social media space on Klout. I signed up and my score is currently 15. I intend to utilize their network and drive my Klout score up. If you and your business sign up, be sure to connect with me so we can assist each other in building Klout. Make sure that you are a real person. I am not going to engage any spammers trying to get their score up by leveraging my Klout scores.

Purchasing Power in Social Media

One-third of all purchases could be influenced by socialism because we are in such a social media age. According to the McKinsey Global Institute, social media has a current potential value of over $1.3 trillion dollars. Unfortunately, only 20% of marketers found a real, quantifiable ROI from social media (source: eMarketer). That being said, there is room for a new framework to achieve results through social media. One thing to remember with your brand and social media is that you must facilitate the consumer's journey. Take them on a trip they will remember. As they discover new things through your page, casual fans can be converted into loyal fans by building and increasing the awareness of your brand. Experts estimate that half of all web sales will come from social media and mobile platforms. Since only 20% of marketers are currently taking advantage of this opportunity, your business needs to know what it's doing with social marketing.

Most people get into social networking with the mindset that it is just for fun. However, it is important to remember that what you post will stay with you forever. Even children have to get into the habit of thinking about their branding on social media and parents should help with that. I am thankful that I do not have the traces of my childhood on the Internet to such extremities. I just have to worry about a random college acquaintance, colleague, or high school friend trying to post something old. On the bright side, in order for them to do that, they would have to get out a scanner for it to be of high quality. These days, everything is instant. When you are young, you tend to not really think about how you will feel about sharing irresponsible or immature things in 10 years or more.

The YOLO generation will be the DOH generation in a few years, hitting their hands on their heads like Homer Simpson. Parents will have to advise their children on this, especially if they would like them to have successful careers in the future. The wrong photo lasts forever on Google. I have assisted numerous friends in trying to help get photos off of search engines. Sad to say, those efforts are numbered, as it is harder than ever to get photos off of the Internet with the viral capability that the Internet has.

What's the Best First Step?

In my humble opinion, when it comes to branding your business on social media, the first thing that you need to conquer is your visual esthetics. When you first make a profile for a social media website, it usually asks for a bit of personal information and a photo. The profile picture is what people usually remember you by, especially if they do not know you personally. What are you showing people in your profile photo? What is this piece of branding saying about you, what you do, and how you do it? Does it show that you are serious or that you have a sense of humor? No matter what, people will first resonate with your profile photo and then they will read the rest. You can get creative with your profile photo, but try to keep it focused around your brand. Also keep in mind that your profile photo will now be the basis of peoples' memories of you for a while, even after you might decide to change it. Try to choose one that represents you and what you stand for.

An example of a great profile photo comes from my friend and business associate Douglas Diggle. Doug is a great entrepreneur that has worked for several major entities including Lufthansa Systems and the Federal Reserve. Doug gets to travel a lot with his own company, Across Oceans Group. He consults with cruise ship companies worldwide. Doug has a great LinkedIn profile photo. It depicts him on a beach with his suit and tie, sitting with his legs crossed in a peaceful, meditative way with a smile on his face. He replicated the photo in many iconic places like the Great Wall of China and the Taj Mahal. Anyone that sees Doug and his photos will get the idea that Doug is a great and friendly professional who has traveled the world. His photos are so fun and interesting that it makes people want to engage in a conversation with him just to learn more about him and his experiences. He told me that he has random executives connect with him just because of his profile photos. I know everyone has not had the chance to travel the world like Doug, but this shows that you can still use creativity to show off yourself and your brand.

On the other hand, you do not want to put up photos that you will be embarrassed about later. Use discretion when taking photos or videos and even when allowing other people to take photos or videos of you that they intend to place on social media. I am kind of glad that I did not have Facebook accessible in my college days. When you are young, you have to use as much discretion as possible. What might seem like a funny thing to do today might be something that your future client or employer finds on the Internet when doing a search on you. You want only the best and most positive look for yourself and your brand. Keep that in mind at all times no matter how old you are.

What about the rest of your profile information? That part depends on what network you are using and how much information you plan on sharing with the world. Keep in mind that whatever you put on the Internet is going to be there forever and will be indexed by Google and other search engines. You have to remember that, with the Internet, less is more. Some people go overboard with content. If you have to ask a mentor or colleague as a barometer, feel free to do that. You want to make sure that you get a second opinion to make sure that you are staying in the realm of your branding goals if you are using to Internet to build it.

How do I find the right people to follow?

You are the average of the five people you spend the most time with. Think about that for a moment. If you think that the people you are spending your time with on the Internet does not work in this case then you are dead wrong. Their effect on you is subtle but it is there. Who you follow matters, because it changes you. Think about the fact that your followers affect your thoughts. The root of everything begins with a thought. You move from thoughts to feelings, from feelings to words, and from words to actions. If your thoughts are plagued with things that make you envious, it can either be motivating or cause you to go crazy. In the same way that television has shaped our culture in the past, social media is in the forefront of the present. The difference is that you have more choices of whom you tune into. Sometimes it's good to prune your Facebook or Twitter list. Sometimes because of people who post too much. Sometimes because of the things that they say. A general rule for me is that I do not follow negative or crude people.

Remember: garbage in, garbage out. If your social media feeds are a constant stream of negativity or inflammatory comments, you will live the same and emulate those thoughts. Surrounding yourself with inspiring people is very important. Taking in content that moves you and your brand forward is key. It is just as important as being talented or hardworking. If you allow it, social media is like a forced injection of outside interests.

Choose what you want to fill your day with. Be honest with things that you don't care to see or read if you notice that they are setting you or your day on its side.

- **Be Selective.** Make sure that you take advantage of the different levels of content control that most social networks offer. Content controls help keep the content that you do not want to see out of your feed. If you do not want it in your view, tune it out, and continue to be selective.

- **Having New "Friends" is Up to You.** You don't have to friend everyone and you can always un-follow people later. I pride myself on asking someone that I do not know or whom I am skeptical of, who he or she is, and how he or she found me. Some people like to collect friends like trading cards but the key to remember is quality over quantity. It isn't a personal statement on you, nor on the person whom you chose to un-follow. Take control of what you continuously allow yourself to be exposed to. Some people are into drama. However, you do not need drama in your life. Some people do not have the same goals or viewpoints as you. **Sometimes you have to prune the friends.** Pick your friends in cyberspace like you would pick them in real life. In theory, you can possibly pick them better online if you use the right discernment.

- **Scale back your availability.** Locking down some privacy settings and using customized audience features allows you to control who sees your content and, in return, who will respond with feedback. When I scaled back my availability I noticed that the quality of my content and knowledge went up. People felt like I got information ahead of time as if I was in some secret spy network. I love having great people in my network. You will feel the same if your network is very selective. For some of us, allowing in too much without being selective has a negative effect. It can cause distraction, unsettled emotions, twisted perspectives, and skewed priorities. You don't need to have the full fire-hose of commentary, opinions, and shared posts from every person you've ever known each time you login to Facebook or Twitter. It can become abrasive and wearing at times. Take control over how you interact on your social networks. The networks may seem unimportant but they have an impact on you and your real day-to-day life.

- **Sometimes Your Tastes May Evolve with Social Media.** I had people in my Twitter feed that I have not spoken too since 2009, so one day I had to go back and un-follow all of the useless feeds. If you are taking in the right information, you are going to grow. Some people do not grow at the same rate that you do. If you outgrow people, it is safe to un-follow them on your social media feed. You must maintain your sanity, and you want to stay focused. It is always business, never personal.

- **Strategically Align Yourself With Movers and Shakers.** 53% of Americans aged 12 and older who follow brands on social media are more loyal to those brands. Knowing that fact, you should apply it to yourself as well. If people are used to getting their trusted information from you, then they will continue to do so and see you in a positive manner. Think about it this way: if you keep your composure and build your brand according to plan, without going off on tangents, you should be able to build a nice space for yourself online. Social media is now and forever at this point. Everyone should know and behave as they are their own brand, whether they are a business or not.

Which Social Network Should You Focus on First?

I would pick a couple of social media platforms to focus on and create some reminders for posting in other areas just to maintain visibility. We only have so much time in the day, so social networking and using social media does not have to happen all day, every day. I set different reminders to help me remember to post on each of my profiles during the week. Even if I do not post every time I get the reminder, it is just a subtle encouragement to post something to maintain activity.

Special tips for industry branding includes being ambitious, but understand that ambition isn't about age. You have to set your plan and consistently plug away at it. Another one of the things that I do is set random reminders to keep myself in the right zone where everything flows through me and I do not veer off focus. I customize the messages for each reminder. Be passionate and assertive when making personal or professional statements. When making social media statements, think tactically. This will be a representation of you when people decide to take a trip down your social feed. You want to have them thinking about you in the most positive light, so managing the information you share is something you should think about all of the time.

Why You Should Not Follow Everyone!

If you simply follow everyone you will find that you are just wasting your time. Social media is like an ultimate convention that you create. If you are on Facebook and you want to just follow your family and friends, then your social media feed will be a family reunion. If you choose to follow scientists, then you will have a science-based social media feed. You get the idea. If you have a specific clientele that you want to target, you must get into the mindset and networks of that target market. It will keep you up to date on information as well as give you ideas, tips, and tricks from the network that you would like to affiliate yourself with.

Targeted individuals with the right information is ultimately the best way for you to build your information base as well as collaborate with the best and brightest in your realm of influence. With strategic responses, you can gain the trust of the network you would like to work in and infiltrate. Over time you will be seen as a peer within the network. Pace yourself. You should not just try to jump in and take over. Use some form of social media etiquette.

Social Media Etiquette

What works on one platform does not work on all platforms. You have to approach each one with the mindset that you are going to engage that particular audience and get the most out of its users. Social media is great because you can connect internationally and with people who you'd otherwise have to go out of your way to call or physically see. Plus, it allows you to connect quickly and creatively. You can also see what others are doing at the moment to learn something new. Many people do not realize that there is etiquette to this online experience. Many put their cowboy hat on and just do what they want but then cry when they do not get the results that they desire. According to a USA Today, a new study of the Chinese social network Weibo — a platform that resembles Twitter and boasts twice as many users — concluded that anger is the most influential emotion in online interactions. What does this tell us about social media and why is it so much easier to rage at a screen than at a person?

11 Questions to Ask Yourself before Posting:

1. Is there a specific group I should target with this message?
2. Will anyone really care about this content besides me?
3. Will this content offend anyone? If so, who? Does it matter?
4. How many times have I already posted something today? (More than three times can be excessive.)
5. Did I check the spelling?

6. What is the rating of this message? G/PG/R/X?

7. Am I posting something vague and useless? Will everyone understand what I'm saying?

8. Is this my emotional dumping ground? If so, why? Is a different outlet better for these purposes?

9. Do I use too many abbreviations in this post? Am I starting to sound like a teenager?

10. Is this Reactive Communication or is it well thought out?

11. Is this really something I want to share?

Think about these 11 questions before clicking "post." This might help save you some challenges in the future and help you make sure that your brand stays in the best light.

Revenue into Branding Opportunities

There are hindrances that are keeping marketers from putting in more dollars, mainly because it is especially difficult to measure a return on investment (ROI). This is a new area of communication and much of this is just getting started. Mobility is just beginning to take shape and the industry is always adapting to the fast moving state of the mobile Internet. According to eMarketer, 69% percent of marketers said they would increase online brand ad spending if there was an improved clarity around ROI, and similarly, 68% said they wanted to be able to measure the impact of the advertising. It seems that marketers are somewhat more confident in their ability to measure offline ROI vs. online. A lesser but still notable one-third of respondents sought the ability to evaluate online brand advertising according to the metrics used for offline brand advertising.

EMarketer estimates that branding will grow its share of digital ad spending during the next few years. This year, US advertisers will spend $17.46 billion on branding, or 41.6% of the total digital budget. By 2017, branding will grow to $29.33 billion, or a 48.5% share. If large corporations are placing that much emphasis on brand spending, entrepreneurs should definitely pay attention and follow suit in growing their brands.

Top brands recognize that consumers care about what other consumers think. Now marketers are reaching out to online influencers, such as bloggers or users with a greater than average reader base, to increase brand recognition and promote online customer interactions.

Brands Leverage Influencers

Thinking that just having a Facebook or Twitter page will not cut it. Branding in this digital age will require some targeted focus to get the most out of the time you spend online working on your digital brand. The key is to become an influencer. Become an influencer within your target audience as well as with your closest friends and allies in your network. The more people who spread the word of your social network, the higher your level of influence will be. The gift and the curse of online branding is that you can spend a lot of your time online and feel like you are spinning your wheels. You have to work through the influence network, see what has worked for you and your audience, and apply repetition. A little information at a time goes a long way.

6 Degrees of Separation is now a Myth

With the advent of social media, I would say that the 6 degrees of separation is now at least half that these days. I would say the 6 degrees of separation are closer to 3 or less. Some people follow their favorite celebrities or business moguls online. With social media, if someone sends a message to a person, they may or may not answer back. In some specific cases, the degree of separation is only one. A friend of mine that is a very big Los Angeles Lakers fan was angry about Dwight Howard's choice to leave the team. He was so angry that he decided to send him a message on Instagram.

Most people would think that Dwight would not respond, as he has millions of fans all around the world. You would not think that he would answer a random fan that choses to speak his or her mind using social media. My friend made the post, which was a joke to him, but he shared the message and hit him with the @DwightHoward. Most celebrities, athletes, or personalities do not answer back, especially if they have millions of people following them. To his surprise, Dwight ended up answering him back with a less-than-thrilled comeback. My friend will forever be able to tell the story of him vs. Dwight Howard on

Instagram. This is just one example of how the theory of 6 degrees of separation is now over.

Branding on Facebook, Twitter, and Google+

Facebook has 1.1 billion users, Twitter over 500 million, and Google+ is at 400 million. The demographics of each network have their primary and dominant focus. Facebook users spend an average of 6 hours a month on the website. Twitter users spend 21 minutes per month, and Google+ users only spend 3 minutes on social networking.

I am sure that Google+ users will learn to adapt to their service but I am quite surprised that the number is so small. Twitter and Google + are great for real-time updates from people, news outlets, and websites. If you want to take in a myriad of opinions quickly, jump on Twitter. As you see current news that is relevant to you and your brand, do not hesitate to share it. Be sure to check its accuracy, though. There are a lot of random hoaxes that go around and you do not want to be caught in the latest Jackie Chan or Jim Carrey death hoax share.

The Other Social Media Outlets

There are other great networks that you can leverage to enhance your brand online. The hidden jewel of the bunch is LinkedIn. This is the place where all of the professionals hang out and tout their resumes and skill sets. They also network, network, and network. Using LinkedIn, I have done well with not only making great business associates, but also great friends. Since LinkedIn is a very professional social network, you can leverage it in the most professional fashion to make you look as serious as you can about what it is that you do. LinkedIn etiquette is a lot different from Facebook, Twitter, or the others. It is a place where you should be on your best business behavior.

You do not want to toss up photos of you at the beach or vent about your political feelings. As long as you demonstrate value to your followers, results will follow. You can create a LinkedIn Company page and provide value to your target audience through a stream of well thought out content. In doing so you will build engagement and the relationship with your customers will be built on trust. Post statuses with substance and talk about more than just your company. Provide value in the midst of your followers and you will have them checking to see what you are selling because of the relationship that you have forged with them, using your online branding position. With LinkedIn, you are leveraging your networks to the extreme. Business contacts, past colleagues, friends, alumni, and even your family can be leveraged.

Get the right profile image with a great headline that says why your brand is the way to go and then tell your brand story. Once you have done those two steps, you will be off to the races. You can showcase all of the great accolades you have won along with the experience you have gained with LinkedIn's professional layout. If you are not on LinkedIn with at least a profile page set up for yourself, make sure this is next on our to-do list. It could be the entrepreneurial task that makes you stand out in this global economy.

After you have created a LinkedIn profile, you should network and create a systematic approach to building your brand through testimonials. Many people like to see professionals vouch for your work at the different positions you have held. If you have other colleagues that are also on LinkedIn, one idea is to exchange recommendations.

Instagram is another great social network that you can use to show people what you do. Pictures are a great way to make people see, feel and understand your brand. Recently, Instagram introduced 15-second videos. Vine is another community that is focused on (7 second) videos. You can build your brand there by creating mini commercials to let people know about you. Since Instagram and Vine are all about photos and videos respectively, you must use discretion when you post.

Make sure that when you approve the picture or video going up online you believe that it represents your brand well. Humans are visual creatures. For example, Instagram focuses on imagery. There are pictures and now small 15-second video clips. Following the right people on Instagram can either be motivating or outright depressing, depending on the type of people that you follow.

Reputation Management

External websites and search engines can have a tremendous impact on your business and your bottom line. A strong online reputation requires happy customers, honesty, engaging content, and proactive work on your end. There is now a term called ORM or Online Reputation Management, that many people are now using because of the growth of social media. You have to maintain control of your personal brand as well as your corporate brand. You want to have people speaking in the most positive ways of you and your brand. You have to keep an eye on your reputation at all times.

A great example is if you owned a restaurant. Restaurant owners have to be aware of great resources like Yelp, which allows clients or customers to rate their experience. If the food is great, you hope that they tell the world. If the food is not great on the other hand, it is something that you might want to manage. People are going to speak their mind and you want to give them the best experience possible. Just know that there are tools like Yelp that give a lot of the power to the consumer who then use social media to tell their friends, family, and network whether they loved or hated your food. All businesses should keep an eye on their reputation and even use it as a gauge for what the clients want and need. To keep your service as well as your reputation at the highest level possible, you have to monitor any and all feedback.

Tangible Facts

94% of clicked search results are organic, not paid. This means that businesses must focus on making and maintaining an organic footprint in their online business arena.

Most people in the US do a search on someone before doing business with them. In most cases, consumers can discover things online that will potentially change their mind about doing business with those people.

Every month, consumers using social media are hearing about other peoples' experiences and learning about brands, products, and/or services. They are complementing brands as well as expressing concerns or complaints about brands. Most small businesses are not equipped to handle crisis if a bad brand buzz occurs.

Social media is about your brand's voice first and your products second. Proactively build a positive online reputation to get happy customers. Foster brand advocates and positive online reviews and mentions. Your reputation across social media will affect search results. Every online user has power so don't be quick to ignore anyone.

Continuously monitor the online mentions of your brand. Always engage with your audience. Keep in mind that 99% of US online specialty retailers use YouTube.

Execution Ideas

- Consider Facebook advertising for targeting.
- Create an affiliate program to extend your reach.
- There are more than 5 billion mobile phone users worldwide and 1.1 billion smartphone subscribers. Develop smartphone/mobile apps for your brand.
- Share links with and advertise on websites that rank highest against the search terms most important to your brand.
- Monitor what people are saying about your brand on social media (Facebook, LinkedIn, etc.) and on websites such as Epinions.com and Amazon.com.
- Make sure to include your brand's signature and web link in each email. People should be able to know your story in a matter of a few clicks. You need a consistent image.

Your online presence needs to be crisp, clean, and memorable. It always looks more professional if you have a custom Twitter background/Facebook cover and YouTube Channel Design. Your online brand should stand out.

One client that I currently work with, a South Florida marine shipyard for mega yachts over 100 feet, started working with my company from the beginning of their re-branding stage. Going into the project they wanted to focus on targeting mega yacht captains and crew for upgrading and repair of their client's yachts through their corporate website and various social media channels.

Networking with mega yacht captains and crew is a highly focused marketing task, so my team devised a targeted social networking strategy using LinkedIn, Instagram and Facebook. Utilizing various techniques such as targeted keyword posts and advertising, we were able to micro-target the niche rather than going after the masses.

Tastemakers with huge niche followings on the internet like @TheYachtGuy, with his over 200,000 loyal yacht feed followers, empowered my client with additional social push by tapping his network. Quality over quantity was the assignment in this case, and micro-targeting through social media can be one of the most cost effective ways to reach a niche market.

We completed the branding overhaul with revamped visual web concepts and full-scale high-definition commercials with footage captured by drone helicopters. My marina client is building great connections in a very tough and targeted industry, mega yacht captains and crews.

A successful social media strategy isn't always about getting lots of random people to like your pages, as that can water-down a company's true engagement from their real market. Very often quality is more important than quantity.

Survey your network

While preparing the piece that you are reading now, I decided to ask some of the people in my network about what worked for them when utilizing social networking and social media. I was surprised at some of the great feedback that I received. Much of the feedback that was entrepreneurial in nature came from LinkedIn. From stories of new deals to new jobs, LinkedIn is the best place that has gotten the people in my network the best opportunities.

Facebook is a grand social network, but at the end of the day, it tends to trend more socially than anything. I am sure that there are lots of great business opportunities going on in regards to Facebook, but when surveying my business network, the best business success seemed to come from LinkedIn. When discussing Facebook, my network mostly used the platform to keep up with friends. Those that used Facebook to do business had more leisurely or social businesses. The bright side to what I have found with Facebook branding and business that I have noticed is, once a person has gained someone's trust on Facebook, they are very open to doing business. Gaining trust might take a bit, but once it is earned, it is priceless.

Network Testimonials

Below are a few testimonials from the random surveys that I did on my network. I received some interesting responses. I would love to know what your network has to say if you survey them in a similar way. If you do a survey like this about your network and you get some interesting responses, I would love to hear them.

My Questions: I asked my network two questions:

1. What benefits does Social Media provide to you?
2. Do you have any significant stories to share about Social Media and your brand?

•••

I landed my position with the Celtics through LinkedIn. A recruiter contacted me when I was working with the Houston Texans, through LinkedIn. I am originally from Boston and never thought that I would have the chance to move back home and back to the east coast. After about a 6-month interview process I landed the gig. I also use LinkedIn as a source to find qualified leads when developing new business through my network of qualified contacts, aka referral business. - Chris

•••

Facebook has connected me to so many people from yesteryear. Even to say hello. It has brought me business just by connecting. I don't spend as much time on LinkedIn, because of TIME. I don't want to live my life totally connected, as there is the personal connection hand-to-hand that works with a heart. - Nancy

•••

The survey even prompted someone to say this:

Wow you inspired me to develop my LinkedIn profile page. Glad that you sent me a message. Hope you had a wonderful holiday! - Catherine

•••

Thank you for reaching out. Branding is so important for any industry. Name recognition and logo identification are both part of branding a company. I have had some success using LinkedIn and Facebook. I think the key is to target all forms of Social Media in a consistent manner. Stick to one logo...use a phrase over and over again...post consistently. - Daniela

•••

Yes, I have had some good experiences on LinkedIn. When it comes to connecting with the VIP's of the industry your business has to be promoted like a blockbuster movie!!! That is what branding and marketing is all about. For the mass audience, the consumers of your product, it's about the hook in the story, either in the music, the video, or just the text. If your audience can feel that message and sparks that emotion then that's what's up. It all starts with a Spark! - Borris

•••

Social media is about sharing! TRUE! So much to learn but I understand the concept. It's really about sacrifice. You can place yourself in conversations that you would never be able to have and network with people from around the globe. Never has there been a time like this where information is instantly at your fingertips. - Elias

•••

Shannon's points are some of the most valid in regards the importance of social media to an Entrepreneur. Dealing with social media is the way to go, a company doesn't even have to invest in advertising if they have a strong social media presence. I have worked to take many of his social media principles and put them into my BadAssVegan.com movement. - John

•••

Thanks for reaching out and using connections as I consider proprieties as a means of sharing ideas and collaborating to gain insight for mutual benefit.

One of the benefits of the great construction depression is the strengthened resolve and resilience that our company has experienced as well as my own personal growth. We continue to improve our business practices, customer communications and outreach through social media and public relations.

We recently hired a PR firm to augment our marketing companies' efforts. I am far more upbeat about our business and the economy in general. As my father that is a disciple of W Clement Stone, Napoleon Hill, and Norman Vincent Peal would say, "With every adversity there is a seed of equivalent or greater benefit, but first you must look for the seed." - Rick

•••

A Fun Branding Exercise

I have a fun and simple exercise that I would like for you to try. Everyone has a favorite movie or comic book character. I grew up loving comics and enjoyed the story lines while growing up. Now the rage is comic book movies like Avengers, Ironman, Batman and others. The exercise is to think about your favorite movie or comic character and how they branded the character in your mind. Now, apply the same concept to yourself. If you were featured in a movie how would you be seen? What would your character breakdown be?

My love for comic book characters and drawing comic books has helped me evolve the way I think of branding. When thinking about branding yourself or a company ask yourself, if this brand was depicted in a James Bond film, what would it look like? This is an interactive exercise if you actually write this down and it can also help you in moving your brand forward.

With millions of people on the Internet embracing social media now, what makes you stand out from the crowd? Long ago, when Twitter first started, if you were an early adopter you could end up getting a bunch of followers just because of being there early. Now you have to connect with the right people and get the right ones to follow you back for being there to make sense.

My concept is for you look at yourself from the 3rd person perspective and view your brand as if you were a character in a comic book or movie. Taking a step outside of your box and looking at your brand like this will help you approach your plan in a new way. Now you can see yourself like the great comic book creator Stan Lee sees when developing his various, timeless characters.

If you approach the concept of branding from this perspective, you will be able to highlight your strengths and be aware of your potential perceived weaknesses. People might be able to discern these ahead of time and you will do well to plan a great strategic attack of your target audience and their minds. The first thing they will think of when they think about your brand are the best aspects because you planned for them to be remembered.

Is there a character that you think epitomizes what branding is about? What stands out about the character? Is there a story behind your love for this character?

Put this branding exercise to action and you will have a fun time building your brand from a different perspective. If you try this and get some good results out of it, send me a tweet on twitter with your positive results at @NextWorldLeader.

Anyone with determination can make their mark using social media. Remember: it is not too early to start branding yourself online. I had a great friend of that started his brand at 50 years old. His name was Andrew Gallop. Andrew did not know how to use a computer very well when we first started doing business but he was determined to learn and start his own business online.

I am proud to say that he ended up learning how to use a computer and was able to run his own business online. Andrew is not here with us today, but when he left us, he had learned to manage his brand online and build a business. He even learned to make his own YouTube channel where he gave business advice. All of this is to say, it is never too late to create your brand, manage it, or start your business. Make sure that you use the techniques that have been articulated in this article. It will only help to give a great primer for kick starting and establishing your brand online.

There's way too much competition out there so slacking isn't an option when you're aiming for success! If Mr. Gallop could do it, you can do it too. As you read this chapter, think about how you are branding online and how you and your business are presented in the social media landscape. You may have to rethink your social media strategy after reading this, but do not let that scare you!

Embrace your brand and keep it fresh. It will give your clients and users something to hold on to and remember when thinking about products and services that are in your realm. You have to remember that you have one time to make an impression with a potential networking client. You must put your best foot forward with your brand.

I appreciate you reading this chapter. If you want to contact me with ideas about business and social media, do not hesitate to send me an email at info@kingcreative.tv, or a tweet to @NextWorldLeader.

About the Author

Shannon Allen, also known by his secret code name, NextWorldLeader, is a seasoned entrepreneur that has worked in the internet space since the first browser, Mosaic. Primarily focused on empowering brands by enhancing their corporate online branding strategies, Shannon has over 11 years of using the internet to help clients connect with their current and future customers.

Are you ready to take your brand or business to the next level using social media? Contact Shannon Allen today:

To contact Shannon Allen about Social media strategies and consulting for web and mobile applications, email info@kingcreative.tv.

Connect with Shannon Allen:

- Email: info@KingCreative.tv
- Web: http://www.kingcreative.tv
- Facebook: https://www.facebook.com/nextworldleader?fref=ts
- Linkedin: http://www.linkedin.com/in/nextworldleader
- Instagram: http://www.instagram.com/nextworldleader
- Twitter: http://www.twitter.com/nextworldleader
- Klout: http://klout.com/nextworldleader

Chapter 11

Cause Marketing

HOW TO PRODUCE A $35.71 RETURN FOR EVERY $1 INVESTED IN MARKETING YOUR BUSINESS

Aaron Davis

"Customers have changed forever and their voices carry far more clout than they have in the past. In order to standout in a crowd of me-too competitors, you must be open to new ideas."

Aaron Davis

Customer loyalty contributes immensely to bottom-line profitability in business. Consider the finding of several recent studies:

- Repeat customers average 33% more spending and are 2x more likely to refer new customers.

- Word of Mouth (W.O.M.) 'promoters' of restaurant/retail businesses are worth an average of $1,700.00 per customer and account for over 50% of new customer acquisitions.

- 66% of customers would be influenced to visit restaurant and retail businesses more often if they received at least 10% cash-back on their bill.

- Businesses that reward their customers' purchase behavior show W.O.M. promoters are 70% more likely to refer a business than one without a rewards program.

- A working database nearly doubles the value of a business.

- 87% of U.S. adults find a recognition and rewards program 'very appealing' with 79% of the 87% indicating they preferred instant cash-back rewards verses points.

- 80% of customers said they would be influenced to switch brands, receive less quality, and pay more for a brand that supports a cause they believe in.

Putting your business on the map with your current and potential customers is critical if you wish to thrive and grow. Of course, one way to increase your profitability (with lower costs) is as simple as rewarding your customers for their loyalty and patronage. But chances are you're probably missing out on one of the most profitable and little known strategies you can implement.

You may already donate to local charities and have a gift card or rewards program in place...yet you may not be using them for maximum business-building effect. It's also possible you don't participate in fundraising or offer a gift card or loyalty program because you're not aware of their profit pulling potential. Regardless of which category you fit into you now have these solutions for your business.

In this chapter, I'll share with you some of my favorite and most powerful strategies for integrating Cause Marketing (fundraising) with a gift card and customer loyalty cash-back rewards program to produce a business-booming marketing machine that runs automatically 24/7/365. The best part is, at the end of this chapter you'll find an "offer you simply can't refuse" so be sure to take full advantage and see exactly how to put these profit-producing ideas in place with little or no extra effort on your part!

But first, allow me to introduce myself, define some grounding information on Cause Marketing, and how to measure its beneficial effects on your business.

How I Discovered the "Holy Grail" of Marketing

Since 2006 I've helped business owners and entrepreneurs save a fortune on their merchant account and credit card transactions. I work with large and small businesses to get more out of their payment processing systems, often with a simple tweak or a small adjustment to the things they're already doing.

But in 2009, when one of my longtime clients (and closest friends) called and asked me about the best practices for marketing her gift card program, to increase sales and bring customers back to her business, I had no idea what to say.

At the time I knew that gift cards improved her cash flow through "breakage" and "the float" (two profit-producing concepts I'll cover a bit later in the chapter), but until then I hadn't really thought of a merchant account as a marketing tool. Usually my clients would simply place their gift cards next to the register and let them sell themselves. During the holiday rush this seemed to work quite well, however, the rest of the year card sales were stagnant. How could I change that to provide more value to my friend's business?

Delving into the strategic approaches that worked best with the regional businesses, national franchises and even mom-and-pop-style small businesses I've served, I've found they all had one thing in common...

Every one of those businesses could benefit just as much by adding a few income-generating features to their merchant services, along with the money-saving features I usually emphasized with my clients. Some of them stood to gain thousands of dollars in monthly revenue they were leaving on the table, with just a few simple tweaks.

Then it dawned on me: an important source of consistent popularity for your business – plus a significant portion of your monthly revenue -- comes from making it easy for your local community to deal with you. And keeping them coming back to buy from you, again and again. And that's when I discovered Cause Marketing, the "Holy Grail" of customer loyalty and profit-producing marketing strategies!

What is Cause Marketing?

Cause Marketing is one of the most advanced and innovative topics in loyalty today and when used properly it can deepen engagement with your customers. It's often defined as a cooperative business relationship where a for-profit business and a non-profit organization work together for mutual benefit.

One very successful example is Yoplait's Save Lids to Save Lives® program where the yogurt company donates $0.10 per lid (a trackable customer purchase) to the Susan G. Komen® breast cancer foundation. It's a win for the charity which has received millions of dollars in donations, a win for the customer who feels their life is enhanced by their contribution, and that goodwill is transferred to how they feel about the product they purchased…a win for the Yoplait brand.

In the past, when you wanted to support a non-profit organization it meant little more than writing a check to the charity with no way to quantify or guarantee the return on investment (ROI). However, increasingly business owners are incorporating Cause Marketing tied to the transaction into their marketing plans.

In this chapter I'll introduce you to a proprietary program which seamlessly blends a properly designed Cause Marketing program with a full suite of gift card, membership, rewards and loyalty solution.

A Little Fundraising History

Fundraising in the past played an important role in developing community goodwill and growing business through word-of-mouth publicity.

For example, in the restaurant industry, fundraising events and parties are planned on a regular basis. Schools, religious institutions, and other charitable organizations often approach restaurants to help raise donations for their cause and support the community. There are numerous examples of how this is done, but almost every strategy has been a 'one-off' campaign designed to raise money based on a particular one-time promotion.

Currently you might turn down some of the donation requests from community groups, viewing it more of an expense or 'civic duty' during these tough economic times.

However, when you put the Cause Marketing strategies I'm about to present in this chapter into your business, I guarantee you'll actually go out of your way to search for additional charitable organizations to support. And that's because each organization you donate to becomes a full-time marketing team for your business.

That's good news if you desire to support your local community and by doing so sell your products and services more profitably, create goodwill, and reap all the other warm-fuzzies that go along with helping!

A properly designed Cause Marketing plan eliminates the costly old-school fundraising mindset and replaces it with one that converts your donations into an automated revenue generating, new customer acquisition, and database building powerhouse.

For these reasons, and more, Cause Marketing is completely replacing the old outdated approach to fundraising.

Side Note: The business principles I'm about to share are the same whether you're a dentist helping patients, a personal trainer working with clients, or a restaurant serving customers. Therefore, just to save time and eliminate confusion, I'll refer to all patrons as customers for the remainder of the chapter.

How is Cause Marketing Different than Fundraising?

Cause Marketing is one of the hottest trends in restaurant and retail for good reason. Before we jump too far into our discussion, remember the term 'Cause Marketing' is different than the word fundraising. I may use the terms interchangeably since Cause Marketing involves fundraising but it's a much different approach.

The key difference between fundraising and Cause Marketing is *how* the donations are accrued. Rather than the use of flyers, cereal box tops, freebies, discounts, and all the other old ways, Cause Marketing is tied to every transaction at your business with real time tracking.

For an effective Cause Marketing strategy to be in place, the donation needs to take place *after* the customer has visited your location and paid full price for their purchase. A cash-back reward for the customer, in addition to the donation to the cause, should also occur. By triggering *both* a donation and a reward you tap into the **two most powerful emotions in your customer**:

1. Satisfying the need to feel appreciated and get a good deal
2. The desire to support the community or cause (goodwill)

Proper Cause Marketing puts an end to donating without a ROI. Notice the word "marketing" in Cause Marketing with no such implication in the word "fundraising".

Now you can put a solution in place that funds local churches, schools, and little leagues, et al, but does so ONLY when a member is purchasing from you and <u>paying full price</u>!

No advertising expense, no discounting, and no advance donations until after the non-profit group or individual within the group <u>supports your business first</u>!

The non-profit organizations prefer this solution more than any other because now they can participate without any upfront cost, selling, planning, or volunteering, with 100% accountability and transparency tied to 24/7/365 donations.

A properly designed Cause Marketing solution is a win-win-win for everyone involved. The customer wins, the non-profit wins, and the business owner wins. No more one way street for anyone involved, this is pure and effective Cause Marketing and the solutions are available to put into your business now!

How to Spot Cause Marketing

Cause Marketing helps you connect with local non-profits while increasing sales and reducing traditional advertising expenses. When you're looking to implement a Cause Marketing program into your business, keep in mind the differences between fundraising programs and real Cause Marketing strategies.

Ask yourself the following:

1. Do donations accrue only AFTER a sale takes place, where my customer pays full price?

2. Is my customer database built automatically (without paper forms) and can I segment the data to track visitation and spending so I know who my best and most profitable customers are?

3. Is my customer database integrated with the communication tools to make sure I'm sending only relevant and targeted messages to bring them back over and over again without additional advertising expenses?

4. Does the fundraising administrator have the ability to check sales and donation activity online in real time? (This accountability and transparency gives everyone involved the peace of mind to frequent and spend with confidence.)

5. Does the fundraising program also reward customers on an individual basis with transparent cash-back rewards to satisfy the consumer's desire for a good deal in addition to helping their charitable organization?

6. Is there an automated follow-up message to the customer verifying their visit, donation, and reward balance so all the emotions are cemented for maximum benefit?

7. Does the fundraising program actively build my business every day, or does it run just once in a blue moon?

If you answered "Yes" to all these questions, then you know you've got a quality Cause Marketing solution designed to increase profitability, attract new customers, and keep existing customers coming back to your business more often for the long haul!

Now that you understand the difference between the typical outdated fundraising models, compared to Cause Marketing (which generates donations on an ongoing basis) it's time to dig into...

The Lifetime Customer Value...OR How Much Your Customers Are Really Worth

In order for you to really appreciate the value of any marketing strategy, you must first understand how much revenue and profit your average customer is worth over their purchasing lifetime. This is known as the Lifetime Customer Value (LCV).

By knowing your LCV, you can determine how much you can afford to spend to acquire new customers, as well as reward your existing customers for their loyalty and patronage.

Many business owners don't fully appreciate the value of a customer over his entire purchasing life with the business. Yet without this knowledge, it's almost impossible to make informed and intelligent marketing decisions.

Calculating Your Lifetime Customer Value

Take a quick moment to calculate the Lifetime Customer Value for your business. Enter your details below:

A.	Your customer's average transaction amount	
B.	Multiplied by the average number of purchases your customers will make each year	
C.	Multiplied by the average number of years your customers will continue to purchase from you	
D.	**Total Lifetime Customer Value**	

This is rarely applied yet very simple math. It opens up a new world of marketing and business growth opportunities for you...

For example let's say you own a restaurant (although the same principles apply if you own any business that generates repeat customer purchases; i.e. you sell jewelry, sporting equipment, home goods, or you own a salon, winery, bowling center, etc.).

The Smith family comes to your restaurant spending $50 on dinner during their first visit. Based on your experience you know they'll return on average 20 times a year for the next 5 years before they move away.

So the Smith family will give you 5 years x 20 visits per year, or 100 visits at $50 sales each. That is a total sale amount of $5,000. If your food and overhead expenses are $2,000 that means you have a gross profit of $3,000 for the Smith family.

Your numbers will vary and every business is different. That's why you must run the numbers for your business to use this formula accurately. Some businesses have a lifetime customer value of a few hundred to over a million dollars. It may surprise you to realize that a good, sit-down restaurant, with a liquor license, can easily have a lifetime value of $50,000 or more for a new customer.

Improving Your Lifetime Customer Value (LCV)

- Do you treat your new customers as if they're worth $50,000 over their lifetime?

- Are you tracking your customer's spending and frequency?

- Do you know which customers haven't purchased from you in 30, 60, 90+ days? Do you run targeted promos just for them?

- Are you segmenting your customers and communicating with your VIPs differently than your least profitable customers?

- Can you imagine how your business would change for the better you'd be if you did?

Visit **AaronDavis.com/LCV** if you'd like more tips and ideas on improving your Lifetime Customer Value!

The Cost of Losing a Customer

Along with understanding your customer's lifetime value, it's important to have a clear understanding of the real effects losing a customer has on your business.

In addition to their own LCV, one lost and unhappy customer can have a far reaching impact on your business because negative word-of-mouth travels faster and further than positive word-of-mouth. Realize that when you lose a customer you're not only losing their business, you're losing all of their referrals as well.

If an unhappy customer were to tell 10 friends about their unpleasant experience (or not refer those 10 friends to your business), and each of those 10 friends told 5 others, the total number of people affected by one bad experience would be 61.

If only 25% of those people chose not to do business with you because of negative word-of-mouth, that equals 15.25 people. If each of those 15.25 customers had buying habits similar to the Smith family discussed earlier, the lifetime revenues lost can be astonishing.

When you plug in these figures and expand on our previous LCV example, you get the following:

A.	The original unhappy "lost" customer	1
B.	Tells 10 others of their bad experience	10
C.	Who each tell 5 others	50
D.	Total people knowing bad experience	61
E.	25% don't buy because of negative word-of-mouth	15.25
F.	Lifetime Profit Value of a Customer	$3,000
G.	**Total Lost Profits from one bad experience**	**$45,750**

That's $45,750 from one bad experience -- that's an awful lot of money for letting one customer leave your business unhappy!

Regardless of what type of business you're in, it's vitally important to put systems in place that are designed to keep your customers coming back more frequently and spending more money each time they visit. By implementing a properly designed Cause Marketing and customer loyalty solution you show your customers how much you value and appreciate their patronage by rewarding them and supporting the community.

The 10 Major Profit-Producing Benefits of Cause Marketing to Your Business

Any company would be crazy not to utilize "Cause Marketing" to their advantage, as well as to the advantage of their community. Done properly, Cause Marketing can easily be the most profitable marketing strategy you utilize in your business.

The great majority of customers will gladly visit a new business for a heartfelt cause they believe in. Research shows that 80%-90% of customers will spend more, put up with inferior products or services, as well as switch brands if they feel that their purchase can help make a difference to a cause they care about, or to their community. While this is helpful to any business that implements a Cause Marketing program, it can be especially helpful to smaller businesses that are struggling to compete with larger chains. Just as smaller businesses are looking to attract customers, customers are seeking ways to have their shopping rewarded; they're comforted by the idea that their purchases will help to make a difference in their community.

I've identified the ten of the biggest benefits of using Cause Marketing in your business.

10 Big Business Benefits of Cause Marketing
1. Reduce or Eliminate Discounting
2. Rewards Trigger Increased Frequency
3. New Customer Acquisition
4. Less Defection & More Loyalty
5. Better Customer Service
6. Convenience
7. Saving Money and Increasing Revenue
8. Sponsorships and Cross Promotion
9. Automated Paperless Database Creation
10. Positive PR, W.O.M, and Goodwill

I only have space to fully explain two of the ten benefits in this chapter, but will gladly send a free report which details all ten benefits to anyone who asks for one. Email me at Aaron@AaronDavis.com.

Now, let me explain the first two major benefits of Cause Marketing here: Reduce or Eliminate Discounting, and Rewards Trigger Increased Frequency.

Big Business Benefit #1: Reduce or Eliminate Discounting as an Advertising Strategy

The first benefit of Cause Marketing is that it protects profit margins while making your customers feel better about paying full price. The value of rewards and fundraising combined helps you reduce your reliance on discounting and slashing prices. With the right rewards and Cause Marketing strategy, you can confidently charge full price on every transaction, even raise prices, and your customers won't even blink.

It works by replacing the value of the discount with donations and cash-back rewards which only accrue after your customer actually spends money. The economics make sense because partnering with several non-profit organizations to donate after their members patronize your business costs less than traditional advertising yet produces faster and more powerful word-of-mouth publicity. Non-profits love the ongoing donations which accrue for their cause without any change in behavior, no volunteers needed, no selling, and often no expense.

The High Cost of Discounting

Independent research from Bain and Company, Forrester's, and many other well respected independent research firms have indicated over 90% of traditional advertising expense simply reminds your existing customers to return and pay a lower price when they do.

Despite this research, most business owners regularly discount their products and services with coupon books, mailers, weekly ads, or other similar types of ad media where a large expense is paid up front and a long term commitment is required to keep the strategy going for months on end. Not only is there an expense to distribute the offer but the offer being promoted is another 20% to 50% off (or more).

When utilizing this type of advertising you're hit with two expenses:

1. The distribution of the offer *plus*
2. The cost of discounting your products and services.

Can you see how this vicious cycle of discounting repeats itself over and over again, training your customers to visit your business only when a coupon is available? This results in cheapening your brand within the local community, a recipe for future bankruptcy.

Although excessive discounting is a huge problem for many business owners, it's also the only advertising strategy most merchants understand which is why the costly practice continues. Daily deal websites have pounced on this mindset featuring an online version where you offer a huge discount to customers in the hope of driving them to your business with the savings as bait.

Most of the time, when you utilize this strategy you're only attracting 'groupies' who are loyal to the discount (and not your business). Without a proper loyalty program in place this 'groupie visit' comes at a huge price and has cost many business owners thousands of dollars in expenses and crippled their cash flow to the point that they'll never do a daily deal again.

I often see substantial discounts advertised in the hope of attracting new customers, such as "50% off" or "Buy One Get One Free" (BOGO). Now a more conservative amount in the daily deals era is 20% off the entire bill. Many business owners don't know how to escape this trap and have no idea how to protect price points, increase value, and use a cash-back rewards program to increase revenue while giving the perception of a discount.

Daily Deal and Discounting Bottom Line: Offering your customers a discount or special can work but the proper loyalty strategy must be in place to capture your customer's data and create a *trigger* to bring your customer back more frequently without the additional expense to get them in the door again.

Can Over-Reliance On Coupons or Discounting Actually Hurt Your Business?

There are countless variables and factors involved in why a business fails. I actually like the concept of a coupon because it represents saving money or delivering value to your customer based on an offer. However, I disagree with traditional advertising media on how and when the coupon should be implemented.

As a loyalty expert, I believe in rewarding customers after the sale rather than before the sale. I also like my clients to charge a fair and FULL price for their product or service and avoid the pitfalls of cheapening (discounting) their brand in the community. By using cash-back rewards (and a good Cause Marketing strategy) you can deliver higher value at full price with a happier customer than one receiving a discount. Your customers still receive savings, however higher value can now accompany those savings in a different form than taking money out of the register when a discount is applied.

How To Completely Eliminate Discounting

When you fully embrace loyalty and Cause Marketing, the benefits and value of this strategy completely REPLACES discounting as a core advertising strategy:

- Putting full price in your register today

- Automatically building your customer database

- Satisfying the customer's own need for a getting a good deal

- Creating a trigger which helps generate return visits without additional advertising expenses

- All while supporting your community in the process

A well-executed Cause Marketing and customer loyalty program can help you to reduce, or even eliminate the need to discount by implementing a turn-key solution which not only brings existing customers back more frequently, but attracts hundreds of new customers through the Cause Marketing (or fundraising) function.

What a difference when you compare this strategy to traditional advertising where most of the expense is wasted. Remember, 90% of advertising dollars spent simply remind existing customers to return… and pay less money when they do.

The two most powerful emotions in retailing are recognition of the customer and support of that customer's heart-felt need or local community. When you meet both of these emotional needs at the same time, price becomes less of an issue and value replaces discounting.

Big Business Benefit #2: Rewards are a Trigger to Effortlessly Increase Customer Frequency and Spending

The second benefit you'll gain by utilizing a Cause Marketing solution in your business is that the rewards are a trigger to keep your customers coming back more often. Rewards programs are pretty common but the misconception by a lot of businesses is that rewards are an expense and are associated with discounting, when in reality they're totally different. Many merchants are so used to discounting they often feel higher rewards mean higher costs, but this fails to take into account the reduced costs in discounting, marketing, and advertising.

Although there's a redemption of a reward (and most rewards programs are points based, while research shows consumers prefer cash-back for simplicity and flexibility), unlike traditional forms of advertising, issuing rewards is not an expense, but a trigger to increase customer spending.

Rewards which increase customer spending and purchase frequency, without any additional advertising costs to deliver the value, should be issued generously.

The higher the rewards, the better the ROI (to a certain extent of course) but 20% cash-back rewards will usually produce higher ROI than issuing 5% or 10%! With rewards, numbers are often backwards. For example, 20% looks like a bigger number and therefor a bigger expense than 5% or 10%. But 20% Cash Back Rewards will often be far more profitable than 10%.

Example: Understanding the Value of Rewards

If you had a $0.10 reward to Home Depot, would this make you want to return to Home Depot instead of Lowe's for your next purchase? Probably not. But if the reward were $5.00 or $10.00 you'd start thinking twice. Even if you're dealing with large ticket items a fairly small, yet decent size reward starts you thinking about returning and possibly spending more when you do. This has long been a gift card marketing strategy known as "ticket-lift".

If Home Depot were to make the mistake of thinking rewards were an expense rather than a trigger, they might have lost a visit and a large purchase because of it. The same is true of other businesses, and in today's tough economy even a $1.00 to $2.00 reward might cause customers to visit your business rather than a competitor that doesn't offer a rewards program at all.

If the reward were just $0.25, it probably wouldn't register in your customer's mind. You need to have a decent sized reward in place to earn return visits, leading to higher spending and increased LCV.

In addition, the rewards balance starts your customer thinking about the new rewards they'll earn when making an additional purchase. If the reward your customer receives is too small then they may not return to redeem the balance on larger future purchases since the incentive is not strong enough to drive their decision to purchase from you.

Rewards Are Not an Expense...Here's Why:

It must also be noted that ANY rewards you issue (no matter how high) are NOT an expense at all, it's only redemption of the rewards which triggers the 'expense' and even then you'd still be hard pressed to call it an expense.

Since redemption must happen with a future visit, do you really have an expense at redemption, or a profit margin with the return visit? If you think, however, that the customer would have returned anyway and therefore call redemption an unnecessary expense, you'd be forgetting about increased customer frequency. (I don't have the space to cover frequency in detail in this chapter, but if you contact me I'll send you a copy of my "How Cause Marketing Explodes Customer Spending and Frequency" report. E-mail me Aaron@AaronDavis.com.)

Even better, the redemption expense only applies to your products or services. The average business owner is so used to 'traditional' expenses, such as coupons or discounts which come off the top, that they have a hard time understanding rewards that act much differently.

Think of rewards as an electronic coupon with a far greater profit potential due to how the redemption expense works, without the high costs of delivery to the end user. When you can reduce the costs of discounting, delivery, marketing, and advertising, you'll look at rewards in a totally different way.

The Redemption Ratio, Float & Breakage

In any given month, your store or restaurant will not redeem more than 20% of your outstanding rewards balances issued. Customers save rewards or wait until they really need them, such as in a pinch before payday. Having tracked redemptions for years, I know it's rare to see a 20% redemption ratio in any given month. People like to save rewards until they can take their family or loved ones out for a free dinner.

I have clients who've loaded thousands of dollars onto gift cards their customers purchased five to ten years ago that still haven't been redeemed. This is often referred to as the *float*. They were paid up front, with several years between gift card issuance and redemption. The customers essentially gave the business a long term loan which helps tremendously with cash flow. This same concept applies to rewards.

With rewards it's not uncommon for customers to save over $100 on their cards with no thought of redeeming those rewards; it's like raiding the savings account. These customers might have spent $500 to $1,000 or more in order to earn their $100 reward, but you've yet to feel any redemption expense. Furthermore, there will always be a percentage of rewards and gift value which are *never* redeemed. This is known as *breakage* and studies show breakage can be as high as 28% of total issuance in certain cases. All these factors contribute to improved operating cash flow in your business.

Cash Back Rewards (and Donations) Tax Advantages

Another often overlooked aspect of a Cause Marketing program and rewards redemption is the valuable tax advantages you receive.

When your customer does redeem their reward it's an advertising expense, it can be written off as such, where discounting on the front end of the transaction cannot. At the end of the year, simply pull up a detailed report with all of the rewards you've redeemed as well the donations you've made to your non-profit partners, and hand over to your CPA for accounting purposes. (I'm not a Certified Public Accountant and laws vary by state. Consult with your tax professional regarding any specific tax or accounting strategies questions.)

Applying Redemption Expense Against Product Cost

When your customers do redeem their rewards, guess what? The expense is only on the cost of your products or services and at full price to boot! If we continue with the restaurant example, let's say you issue $1,000 in rewards during any given month but only redeem $200 of rewards in the same month. That $200 in redemption has only cost you ($200 x 30% Cost of Food = $60.) This means you took in $1,000 in sales, issued 20% cash back rewards and it cost $60 in real money to pay for food plus the cost of the program fees during that month.

This cycle repeats month after month. Let's look at the table below for a closer look, assuming your restaurant starts the program doing $1,000 in sales but steadily increases sales by $1,000 over a five month period. Under this example, you issue 20% instant cash back rewards and redeem 20% of monthly sales month to month until bleed off.

The following table shows just how valuable issuing rewards can be with very little expense realized due to breakage. The totals show $15,000 in rewards card sales coming in with just $420 of actual expense. **This is equal to a $35.71 return for every $1 invested in marketing your business!**

Month	Sales	Rwds @ 20%	Redemptions (20% Bleed Off Month to Month)	Total Redeems		Cost of Food		Actual Expense
Jan	$1,000	$200	$40.00	$40	x	30%	=	$12
Feb	$2,000	$400	$80 + $40	$120	x	30%	=	$36
March	$3,000	$600	$120 + $80 + $40	$240	x	30%	=	$72
April	$4,000	$800	$160 + $120 + $80 + $40	$400	x	30%	=	$120
May	$5,000	$1000	$200 + $160 + $120 + $80 + $40	$600	x	30%	=	$180
Totals	$15,000			$1,400.00	x	30%	=	$420.00

Can you think of any other advertising strategy which has such a high ROI, is 100% trackable, guaranteed to have zero advertising waste, and the expense only occurs after a customer has already purchased from you and paid FULL PRICE? It's like going to Las Vegas and playing the $1 slot machines and every time you pull that handle you win a $35 jackpot. How many times are you willing to play that game?

Again, we're still are *not* taking into account the savings on marketing or advertising, as well as increased spending and frequency. Either way, you can clearly see the actual expenses are very small in relation to the numerous benefits.

Now that you understand how Cause Marketing eliminates discounting and creates a trigger for your customers to purchase more frequently, keep those two high-profit benefits in mind, while you consider the following strategies to create more awareness about your Cause Marketing program.

9 Simple Strategies to Make the Most of Your Cause Marketing Program

Cause Marketing is one of the best (if not the best) ways to build your business and here are some ideas you can use to take your Cause Marketing program to the next level. Implementing even a few of these strategies will increase customer awareness and engagement more quickly and deliver a much higher return over the long haul.

1. Become (Or Hire) a Chief Customer Officer

The Chief Customer Officer (CCO) is one of the most important positions in your company. Among other duties, CCOs visit schools, churches, little leagues, rotary clubs etc., to explain the program and help non-profits engage in best practices so they understand their responsibilities in creating donations and driving visitation to your business. In addition, CCO's mingle with customers inside your doors providing exceptional customer service, explaining the loyalty program, signing up additional non-profits, and increasing revenue in a variety of ways. Many businesses have never considered the position of a CCO, but with a world class Cause Marketing and customer loyalty solution in place, it makes sense, as there are numerous ways to increase pre-paid sales, gift card loads, frequency, spending, and much more. A CCO removes the pressure from employees to understand these strategies, helping and training them to be better customer service personnel.

2. Create Marketing Material, Displays and Collateral

There are a number of ways business owners can increase exposure and get employees on board. Any type of marketing materials online (such as your website, Facebook, etc.) and inside your location will be a big help in driving awareness and involvement. You might implement card sleeves, table tents, posters, flyers, banners, or other similar types of presentation materials which explain the program. Education is critical and you should take every opportunity to educate your customers. Materials should be displayed with an emphasis on helping organizations raise money on a continuous basis.

3. Set a Meaningful Donation for Non-Profits

Fundraising donations should be something that really engages both your consumers and non-profit leaders. It's tough to engage people when the donation is only 2% or 3% of the sale. Unless the average ticket is substantial, the minimum donation should be 5%. Even then, 5% is a good starting amount and there are many ways to increase this donation based on frequency, spending, or promotion within the non-profit organization. Again, the donations and reward percentages are only realized after a FULL PRICE sale without any advertising or distribution costs. Discount strategies, such as 20% off promotions or 2-for-1 sale offers, are far more expensive than increasing donations and rewards tied to actual full price sales transactions.

Donations and rewards are not really an expense at all. Both of these balances not only show consumers you value their business, but they encourage future spending and visitation to your business. They also inspire W.O.M. champions as reported in numerous studies.

When you implement this strategy you'll create tremendous goodwill and generate many more return visits with a higher average ticket. This doesn't even count the many new customers who'll choose your business as a result of donations to their non-profit organization. As mentioned above, a minimum donation should be 5%, but 10% or 15% is even better. Not only for the non-profit, but for your bottom line profits as well! Customers will be more likely to visit your business more often than if the donation ratio was only 2 or 3%.

> ### The Power of Word-of-Mouth Advertising
>
> Just about every business will agree that the best form of advertising is word-of-mouth. Cause Marketing provides you with a strategy to take WOM to a much higher level. But to get to that higher level, you can't be skimpy on rewards and donations.

4. Set a Meaningful Cash Back Reward for Customers

One of the worst mistakes you can make is reducing rewards. Again, this mindset comes from misguided understanding of customer frequency, spending, and visitation. Don't forget about traditional discounting and advertising costs -- instead of a 20% discount (which almost 100% of merchants are willing to give) the same amount might be split with 10% fundraising and 10% rewards. The 'expense' of these two combined is much lower than a 20% discount. For a complete detailed explanation of Cause Marketing and pricing review my whitepaper "Understanding the Math and Value of Rewards. (Email me at Aaron@AaronDavis.com for your copy.)

In the case of rewards, the issuance alone costs you absolutely nothing and generates incredible consumer goodwill practically guaranteeing a return visit. Often times the customer won't even redeem the reward but still increases frequency due to the accumulation of rewards and the feeling of goodwill.

The reward is extremely important for making your customer feel appreciated while simultaneously supporting the emotional need to support their charitable organization. Verify both the Reward Ratio and the Donation Ratio are at least 10% each (not combined) for best practice program design. You cannot go wrong with an aggressive reward and donation structure, especially when your customers are paying full price (no discounting).

5. Contact the Local Press

The idea of a fully accountable and transparent fundraising program can be a huge benefit to schools, local business, and customers alike, so alert the local media when you support the community. Big corporations use the media all the time to publicize their own charitable interests, so why not you? One idea is to host a press conference at your business and invite non-profit leaders and volunteers from all over town to come in and kick off their fundraising program.

With school leaders and key non-profit decision makers present, the news will pick up the story and help spread the word. The key idea is find a way to let the entire community know you have the capability to reward them and fund their charitable organization with no change in behavior and complete accountability. The Cause Marketing capabilities of your program should give you exposure in a variety of ways -- contact newspapers, radio, and any type of media you can think of for free publicity. When the program is explained, you may very well qualify for added coverage without any cost.

Once people know you're supporting the local community, the entire program will grow rapidly. After all, who doesn't want fundraising donations without having to sell anything, ask for volunteers, or change any behavior other than buying goods and services they already purchase? A stored value program that delivers 100% accountability and transparency through a trusted 3rd party source is one the most powerful innovations in the history of fundraising and all that's required is to let the press know, let people know, and let the community know. Anything that gets the word out will increase the expansion and engagement of your program and be a triple-win for everyone involved.

6. Recruit Sponsors to Finance Program Expenses

Printing and designing marketing materials has a hard expense associated with it, so why not find sponsors to take care of 100% of the costs in either cash or trade? Make sure you're familiar with all the ways a cause marketing program is vastly superior in advertising value than any other venue these sponsors currently employ. You can write letters and presentations targeting corporate sponsors with whom you already do business. Pepsi or Coke, Sysco or U.S. Foods, car dealerships, real estate agents, financial planners, you name it, there are scores of business contacts that can benefit tremendously from being tied to a local community fundraising program. Not only can a sponsorship fund all the program costs, you can generate additional revenue in the process as well. Send me an email if you'd like more specific strategies and ideas for sponsorship: Aaron@AaronDavis.com.

7. Train, Engage, and Motivate Employees

Make sure your employees are engaged and expertly familiar with the fundraising and rewards program so they can properly explain it to customers upon request. Some of my most successful clients create a bonus structure for their employees who introduce the most non-profit groups to the business. One restaurant is giving 2% residual income to their service staff for all non-profit group sales activity when they sign on to the program. This particular business owner now has all the employees asking customers if they are tied to any church, soccer club, school, etc. The staff will then forward the lead or key administrator contact to the business owner for follow-up and enjoy a nice bonus as a result. There are many simple ideas that can be implemented to engage employees. A successful program leads to happy customers and when the customer is happy, employees benefit.

8. Send Mobile Text and Email Campaigns to Fundraiser Participants

Your customer database can be queried based on individual fundraiser participation and that means you can send individual mobile text and email campaigns to each specific fundraiser database. This helps you communicate the program's virtues with the best message, who to target, what to say and many other strategic decisions. This allows you to send the proper campaigns to get your customers more engaged and regularly communicate the value, advertise new specials, highlight ongoing money raised on a monthly basis, and even rank the top donation generators inside the non-profit organization to stir friendly competition and drive more sales back to your business.

9. Meet Regularly with Non-Profit Leaders

Aside from all the great marketing work you can do as illustrated above, let's not forget what the non-profit leadership can and should be doing to help promote the program.

Non-profit leaders should be constantly promoting the benefits of the program to their members i.e. including updates in their newsletters and emails, making personal phone calls to members, hanging posters inside facilities, sending special snail mailings, and everything else possible to keep awareness at a peak.

Something else that works well for my clients is hosting periodic complimentary lunches with the non-profits. They get to sit down, one-on-one, and review the program's activity and marketing strategy. I've found that most non-profits need accountability and reminders even though they're the beneficiary. Many non-profits are so used to old-school fundraising techniques they often forget about their responsibility in this type of program and how their engagement can be a key to its success.

How to Select a Cause Marketing Provider?

If you've made it this far I'll assume you agree your business can benefit from a Cause Marketing and customer loyalty solution. But how do you select a provider, where do you start when looking for solutions, and does it really matter who you choose?

First of all I don't think you really need another solution with a bunch of features. I know you're already too busy running your business and keeping up as it is. You're probably overwhelmed with all these new technologies and solutions and don't have time to really track and understand new customer needs, which are changing every day. And maybe you don't have the time or expertise to develop the proper promotions, and marketing strategies, which protect your price points and eliminate discounting.

So here's how you find the right Cause Marketing and customer loyalty provider. It's very simple. Just ask them three questions when you call. Don't ask them about email, or rewards, or points, or features or anything like that. Ask about how they would solve your problems. How do they deliver on the specific needs of your business? Ask marketing questions like this:

- "What plan would you develop for me to protect price points so my customers are happier paying full price rather than a lower price?"

- "What type of Cause Marketing solutions do you have in place? And how important do you feel they are at developing relationships and increasing new customer acquisition?"

- "Will you help me bring in sponsorship money so I don't have to pay for the program?"

Now those are some interesting questions! And don't elaborate on them, they don't need a whole lot of explanation. Just let the company you're investigating answer the questions. Whoever you're talking to should be jumping for joy as soon as you ask them, knowing that you're exactly the right client for them! However, more than likely they'll say something like "Um... what do you mean?" As soon as you hear those words, hang up the phone and try somebody else! You want someone who understands these questions more than you!

If you can find two or more companies who know how to answer these questions, it's easy to compare and choose the right one. But don't just choose based on their features. With technology they can make it look so confusing you wouldn't know what to choose--but they can't mess up the right answers to those marketing questions.

When it comes to Cause Marketing or customer loyalty you don't need another solution, you don't want to just buy a box of software and be wished "good luck". You need to know how they're going to help you develop the proper promotions and communication; how they're going to help you succeed and become more profitable, you need someone who takes the time to develop custom ideas and strategies which are proven to work.

That concludes the chapter on how to use Cause Marketing to grow your business. Hopefully you have discovered some new concepts and strategies in implementing Cause Marketing as a customer loyalty machine as a way to dramatically improve market reach and profitability.

About the Author

As a leading Cause Marketing, customer loyalty, and credit card processing strategist, Aaron helps forward-thinking business owners restructure (or sometimes just fine tune) their business systems, merchant services, and marketing efforts to boost bottom-line profits.

Since October of 2006, Aaron has worked with over 400 clients in more than 31 different industries, helping small and medium sized businesses at the local level, as well as regional and national franchise operators all across the US, to grow their business.

Through his consulting programs, workshops, and training Aaron helps his clients make more money, reduce expenses, and implement smart business systems to increase marketing ROI, Customer Lifetime Value, and positive Word of Mouth.

To learn more about how Aaron Davis can help maximize your business growth, or to inquire about Aaron's availability as a speaker or coach, visit www.AaronDavis.com.

Request Your FREE 30 Minute Cause Marketing Strategy Session Today!

Since you just finished reading Cause Marketing: How to Produce a $35.71 Return for Every $1 Invested in Marketing Your Business, you may decide that you want to take action and create your own Cause Marketing machine to cut costs, build customer loyalty, and improve your bottom-line profits, all while giving back to the local community. If so, you might not have to do it alone!

You may qualify to work with me to create and implement the systems, strategies, and tactics contained in this chapter, and I'll give you a simple risk-free way to find out.

You can request a FREE 30 minute coaching session to evaluate your business systems and get simple strategies you can use to put more money into your bank account.

It's just you and me, on the phone -- there's no risk, no catch, and no obligation to buy afterwards. We'll just talk and if you like what I can do for you, then I hope we'll get the chance to work together. If not, we'll depart as friends. Either way, you'll get a free coaching session and plenty of killer tips for your time, whatever you decide.

To get started simply visit: http://AaronDavis.com/30 on your mobile phone or internet browser and fill out the form on the page. Once that's completed you'll receive an email confirmation and I'll contact you with scheduling options.

Visit http://AaronDavis.com/30 to get started today!

Chapter 12

The Secret to More Customers and Clients with Less Effort

Alex Navas

"Efficiency is doing things right; effectiveness is doing the right things."

Peter Drucker

I'm a huge proponent of effectiveness. In fact, as I looked up the very definition of effectiveness, I understood why I love it so much.

Dictionary.com describes effectiveness as **adequate to accomplish a purpose; producing the intended or expected result.**

If only more entrepreneurs and businesses grasped the power of effectiveness, especially as it relates to their marketing and customer acquisition, we wouldn't see such an enormous failure rate amongst businesses. Instead, we would witness a tremendous economic turnaround caused by thriving businesses that are effectively positioning themselves in their marketplace.

Some time ago, I was watching a show called The Hero, which featured a number of regular people who would go through physical, mental and psychological challenges to find out what they were really made of. In the end, the winner would be chosen based on their performance and selfless choices made throughout the show which benefitted the entire team, not just themselves individually.

For one of the challenges, a firefighter had to carry extremely heavy bags down the bleachers at a football field, drop off the bag at the center of the field and run back to pick up the next one, all within a specific time period. Not completing the task meant that he would lose out on money for a charity and he would be forced to leave the show.

As he began, he went up and down the bleachers carrying the bags one by one and became quickly exhausted. I was exhausted just from watching him doing the challenge. However, for the last few bags he decided to do something differently.

Rather than running all the way up the stairs, grabbing the bag and running down the stairs with the bag in hand, he grabbed the bag, ran to the edge of the stands and threw the bags down to field level. He was then able to pick up speed since he would now be able to run down without the extra weight of the bag. He then picked up the bag from the floor and quickly brought it to the center just before time ran out.

The objective of the challenge was to get the bags to the center of the field and the choice was his on how he'd accomplish the task. At first, he decided to do things the hard way. After a while, he figured out a much better way to do it that took far less effort.

While we may not be facing the same physical challenge as the fireman on the show, we have similar decisions to make on how we move our businesses forward. We may know the end result that we desire to achieve, yet we often don't think about it in terms of choosing the most efficient path to get that result.

Identifying this is the key to maximizing your time and money and is where dramatic improvements lie.

The Biggest Enemy to Your Business Success

Many businesses get started with very limited real world training and experience on how to market their products and services. As a result, they struggle through their first few years not knowing exactly how to go about getting new clients and customers to purchase their offerings.

Admittedly, some have been in business for much longer and continue struggling with this very thing. They've managed to get customers by chance, and as we know, chance is not a bankable business strategy.

When I first entered the business world in 2000 at the age of 21, I was given an opportunity to become a self-employed mortgage loan officer with the promise that I'd be able to pave my own way, work when I wanted to work, and earn more income than I had previously earned working for other people. With all that was offered, why wouldn't I jump into business?

This is where my marketing training began. I remember the owner of the company handing me a phone book and telling me all I had to do was call people one by one until someone was interested enough about mortgages to engage in a real conversation with me. It sounded easy enough... until I got on the phone. I spent hours every day working up the courage to call hundreds of people, leave countless voicemails, get hung up on repeatedly and cursed at on the phone. I realized quickly that this was not the path I wanted to take to build a successful business.

Aside from cold calling, I was also instructed to print out thousands of flyers and to pass them out wherever I went. This included putting them on car windshields, in laundromats, grocery stores, and handing them out to random people all in the hopes of being lucky enough to get a client. For the first year in business, I did as instructed and it was the worst year of my life.

If you're anything like me, you're probably thinking, "there's got to be a better way."

Frankly, getting busy with activities such as these may feel productive, but they're not effective. You certainly are doing things, but they aren't quite the right things.

Techniques such as cold calling and handing out flyers may help spread the word about your business, but it will not effectively address the wants and needs of your potential clients. It's not about you and your product or service; it's about what your client wants. Offering them an unanticipated opportunity will most likely fail to capture their attention. The key is to identify with your potential client.

Cold-calling and mass-posting techniques will not produce the intended result in the minimal time, and it's why you may find yourself not serving as many people in your business as you have the opportunity to serve. I know how frustrating that can be.

"It's easier to do a job right than to explain why you didn't."

Martin VanBuren
8th President of the United States

Time and effort spent on the wrong things will remove your ability to generate the right results you are after.

You need to develop the right marketing mindset and methods to cut out all the low impact activities from your day while producing a considerable increase on your investment of time, money, and effort.

Big Company Strategy for The Small Business

Every year, large companies like Apple and Samsung spend tens of millions of dollars preparing for their next product launch. They coordinate teams of experts to manage and execute proper media coverage, event planning, social media engagement and effective communication with distribution partners. They're able to attract large crowds of hungry and eager buyers interested in virtually every product they produce.

This may be inspiring for a small business owner, but may also seem impossible to model. How can the limitations of small businesses compete or duplicate what large corporations do on a consistent basis?

Is our only available strategy to reach people one on one? Do we have to settle for growing our business slowly by reaching one person at a time rather than reaching the masses?

I assure you that we have tons of opportunities to mimic what they do without the resources they have readily available to them. Even sole proprietors have the ability to reach the masses with their products and services, but it all starts with the right mindset.

To illustrate this, let's think about a fisherman. A fisherman's business is to catch fish. You have to understand that a fisherman has different tools to get the job done. They have the option of trying to catch fish with their bare hands. While I imagine it would be difficult, if they've done it long enough they may be pretty good at it.

Other fishermen may use a spear, which seems like a better tool to use than bare hands. Still others may prefer to fish with a fishing pole. After all, the fishing pole increases their range and is designed to actually get the fish to the bait at the end of the fishing line. Once the fish eat the bait, they are trapped, and the fisherman is ready to reel them in.

Marketing is quite the same. We are fishing for our customers and clients. Some business owners and professionals use primitive tools like the phone book or flyers, just like I used when I first got into business. We can't blame them; perhaps it's all they know.

Then there are those who are slightly more advanced, using networking groups and direct mail letters sent to a purchased mailing list. They may have several referral strategies that they depend on and occasionally use emails and postcards in the hopes of obtaining a new prospect. These are all "fishing" tools for getting new business.

The question is, when have you seen these large companies use one-on-one techniques to get people to buy their products and services?

The reality is that they don't do it. You may see a variation of the examples I gave you, but they do business very differently than traditional small businesses. They don't invest resources into getting one customer at a time. They invest in marketing and promotions that would capture many people at once so they can get the biggest return on their investment.

Let's get back to our fisherman example. Which fishing tool would you recommend to effectively catch more fish? Should he use his hands, a sphere, or the trusty fishing pole?

In my opinion, the answer is much easier than you think, although it may be somewhat unexpected. Which would I choose?

NONE OF THEM!

You see, they all limit the number of fish he can catch at once. If I were that fisherman, I would quickly abandon those tools and exchange them for the greatest tool of all; the fishing net.

How about you? Would you rather fish for customers and clients with a fishing pole or a net?

This concept is the exact strategy that big businesses use to sell out of products, create raving fans and reach the masses.

Rather than client attraction, this is what I call Audience Attraction. This is where you focus on reaching many people at once rather than one at a time. It's the most leveraged way small businesses can effectively grow their business with less effort.

The Audience Attraction Advantage

Imagine every time you were in need of more business you were able to tap into an audience, a large group of prospects that are highly qualified and have already expressed interest in what you offer? Would that help you grow your business?

If you can see what an incredible asset this would be for your business then read closely because I want to share with you how to integrate Audience Attraction in your marketing to take back control of your customer flow. After all, having no customers means having no paycheck, right?

So what's the big deal about marketing your business the Audience Attraction way? There are actually several benefits that don't only affect you but also your bottom line.

Investing time and effort to build your audience up front can lead to an ever-increasing quantity of leads and prospects that keep you and your sales staff busy with the right kind of people. Rather than building awareness for your business one person at a time, you'll be able to exponentially increase your visibility since you are only marketing where large groups of your target market already hang out or congregate.

Because Audience Attraction positions your business in front of large groups of prospects, it reduces the amount of time it takes to reach a certain number of people and decreases marketing expenses since you'll be more effective with every new marketing strategy you put out. When you reach more people at once, you can do less marketing and still have a bigger impact.

> "I am a real ham. I love an audience. I work better with an audience. I am dead, in fact, without one."
>
> **Lucille Ball**

The Foundation for Audience Building

Now that you see the importance of marketing to audiences rather than individuals, it's time to lay the proper foundation to successfully integrate leveraged marketing in your business.

The first step in audience attraction is to **know the audience**. If you don't know who your audience is, there's absolutely no way you'll find them in large quantities. In essence, you have to know who they are before working on getting them to you.

Imagine you were an event promoter and you were tasked with selling opera tickets. In fact, it was your job to sell all the tickets to this important event. Where would you begin? How would you get started to successfully sell tickets to the opera?

I'll tell you where you wouldn't begin. You most likely wouldn't begin by purchasing an ad in Sports Illustrated for Kids. You'd probably avoid posting Opera promotions at a professional wrestling or monster truck event.

If you decided to start with these venues, you'll very quickly notice a disconnect between your product (opera tickets) and the audience you are directly marketing to (children interested in sports, wrestling fans, or monster truck enthusiasts).

Of course, there may be a few people you reach purely by luck, but luck is not a repeatable marketing strategy. Audience Attraction begins with knowing who your ideal customer is and it's the one step most businesses miss. What a huge mistake.

Let's go back to our fishing example from earlier. If you were fishing for whales, you'd need to equip yourself with harpoons and go deeper into the ocean where whales are found. However, the same harpoons wouldn't be helpful if you wanted to catch goldfish. In fact, you'd also need to sail to the exact location where goldfish swim rather than go where whales are located.

Your audience is very similar. Time after time I hear business owners and professionals say, "But Alex, my services work for everyone." While that may be true, how in the world can you market and position yourself in front of everyone. That would be very time consuming and expensive.

It's much easier to target a specific group of people, an audience, because you'll be able to utilize marketing that speaks directly to their dreams, desires, wants and needs. Your audience-specific marketing will capture their attention and make them interested in what you offer; because it speaks directly to them.

If you're still not convinced that it makes sense to narrow your marketing focus and choose a specific audience, then I have something for you to consider. It's my personal list of the top 10 reasons to choose an ideal audience. I use it in one of my courses called Expert Branding Formula, but I think it'll help you see why it makes total sense to put this practice in place to get much better results with your marketing. Are you ready? Here we go.

Top 10 Reasons to Choose an Ideal Audience

1. Make more money with less marketing effort
2. Create benefits that speak directly to your core audience rather than a generic message to the masses
3. Build your visibility and credibility faster
4. Reduce or eliminate your competition
5. Create a distinctive brand for your business
6. Become an expert more quickly and with less hassle
7. Command higher fees/prices since you're a specialist to your ideal clients
8. Gain respect from your colleagues
9. Reach influencers faster
10. Have your competition become a referral machine for you since you specialize and they don't

Do you see the power of choosing an audience yet?

Before we move onto step two of my Audience Attraction strategies, here is a quick way to narrow down your audience. Spending 30-60 minutes going through this either alone or with your core team can prove to be invaluable when it comes to getting the most out of your marketing.

3 Ways to Choose Your Ideal Audience

Geographic Based – narrow down customers by the area or location where they live or work. This includes their town, subdivision or the nearest metropolitan area. If you narrow down your audience geographically, you may opt to be the dentist of choice in Albuquerque, New Mexico.

Demographic Based - choosing customers based on their characteristics such as marital status, gender, age, education, religion, or other personal traits. For example, you may choose to be a marriage counselor rather than a general relationship counselor and target married couples specifically with your marketing.

Psychographic Based – yet another form of selecting your audience is by identifying their behaviors, values, and interests among other things. You can focus your real estate business to serve those people who are members of exclusive country clubs.

With your ideal customer identified, you're now ready to move to step two. You see, without knowing your ideal customer, all other steps will fall short because you simply don't have this specific group of people in mind which means you can't envision how to properly communicate to them in a way that will influence them to take the next step towards yes to you and what you offer.

Audience Persuasion Strategies at Work

Now that you've identified your core audience filled with your ideal customers, you need to craft a marketing message that compels them to come to you. We know who they are so it makes marketing your offerings much easier since we now know what makes them tick.

It's important to know that your marketing isn't really about you and what you offer. Your marketing is centered on their wants, needs and desires and how you can deliver on those exact things. The sooner you understand this, the faster it will take you to craft compelling messages that make what your offer seem like the best fit for them.

Let me start by giving you an example.

When my son was younger, we were looking for a dentist to make sure his teeth were nice and healthy. We called around many places looking for a good dentist that would be welcoming to a child. Upon investigating, we came across a dentist office that did things a little differently. When we first got there, their waiting room had all types of children's books, a doodle board, and walls that were chalkboards where children can write on the walls. It was a fun environment.

The common person may have thought, "What does this have to do with a dentist office?" However, as a student of marketing, I quickly realized what was happening here.

You see, this dentist office knew their ideal customers were children who didn't like going to the dentist. Rather than settling for what would be considered the norm for an office like theirs, they marketed themselves not as a dentist office, but as a unique experience for children to get great dental care while enjoying the process. In fact, when my son went in for his checkup, the seat was laid back and above him was a TV monitor so he can focus on the cartoon that he chose rather than the treatment itself.

The dentist and staff knew that parents were often frustrated and embarrassed by their crying or whining children while waiting impatiently for a procedure that was uncomfortable for them. So what did they do? They identified the problems and marketed the solution very effectively to their core audience.

This is the true value of crafting a specific marketing message catered to the audience you serve. When you can pinpoint how your products and/or services solve their biggest challenges, you win, and winning means the difference between a struggling business and one that thrives in any economy.

"People don't care how much you know until they know how much you care."

Theodore Roosevelt

As harsh as it may sound, our customers don't really care about you and I, our businesses, or even our products and services. **All they want to know is how we can help them and make their lives better!**

Defining a powerful marketing message helps you stand out with less effort since your competition is simply stating what they do rather than directly addressing the challenges their prospects have.

While your competitors focus on marketing their features (the details of their products and services), you lead with marketing the benefits (what's in it for them) as it directly relates to what they're currently experiencing.

I want to show you what a difference a strong (and specific) marketing message makes when speaking to groups of prospects. The example below is one that I shared with a group of real estate agents in helping them communicate what they do more effectively. Notice the traditional communication from real estate agents on the left compared to the customer-centered marketing message on the right.

Competition - Features	You - Benefits
I help people sell their homes	I listen intently and bring clarity to disenchanted people worried about selling their home
I help people realize their dreams of homeownership	I educate and assist frustrated renters to buy their first home while removing the confusion and anxiety throughout the buying process.

Why did we use descriptive words like "listen intently," "bring clarity," or "educate and assist frustrated renters"? Because those things directly address issues that homebuyers and sellers have when they've worked with a real estate agent. They often don't feel understood, or have felt that the agent was simply trying to get a paycheck rather than helping and educating them about the best options available to them.

This makes for a much stronger marketing message that resonates with the audience you're serving. Without knowing your audience, you don't know what they're struggling with, so you end up with weak marketing messages like "I help people buys homes."

If you truly want to communicate in a more valuable and influential way, you absolutely must get down to what your prospects truly want from you. In other words, what is the end result they're looking forward to once they receive what you offer?

People don't spend money simply to have more stuff; they spend money to have whatever that "stuff" allows them to have. You don't get braces on your teeth because you particularly like metal in your mouth. You do it because you want a beautiful smile that gives you more confidence.

Likewise, your prospects want something that your product and service delivers. This is what transforms marketing from OK to excellent; the communication of the end result your customers are seeking. Having a powerful marketing message allows you to turn audiences into raving fans.

Here's a little exercise. I want you to begin going deeper on the benefits your customers get from working with you. Let's go deeper into what you truly offer than simply the face value of your products and services.

I'll get your brain started by using my business as an example. I'm a marketing consultant who specializes in helping service based businesses increase their revenue and referrals by marketing to audiences rather than individuals. Interestingly enough, while I help businesses with their marketing, they don't hire me for marketing itself.

Let's go deeper into what I actually provide. To do this, I'm going to go 7 questions deep by asking "Why" after every answer.

What's important about marketing to my clients?

1. It helps them get more customers to their business (Why is that important?)
2. Having more customers allows them to generate more revenue (Why is that important?)
3. Having more revenue helps them continually grow and create a valuable business (Why is that important?)
4. Having a valuable business helps the owners create something sellable that can lead to more financial freedom (Why is that important?)
5. Having more financial freedom means they can have a profitable business that allows them to spend more time with their families and doing what they love (Why is that important?)
6. Having more time and money with their family allows them to cultivate great relationships with their children that will last a lifetime (Why is that important?)

7. If they have rewarding relationships with their children, they will feel that their life matters and they've made a great contribution to society.

If you notice, answers 1-4 are fairly superficial. If you stop there, you'll miss out on the most important reasons people buy from you. After reviewing these answers, you'll realize that businesses hire me to help with their marketing so they can have more freedom to invest in their families and create a life of contribution. In fact, without the right help that I provide, they'll be settling for less freedom than they could have access to which is not what they want.

Do you see how important it is to go deeper into what your prospects actually get from working with you? You can stick to the superficial reasons and continue having less-than-optimal results with your marketing or you can choose to go deeper and really pull at the heartstrings of your prospects. They'll know you care because you know what's most important to them unlike most of your competitors.

Give it a try. Go 7 levels deep to really find out what you provide.

What benefits do your clients get from working with you?

(Don't forget to ask, "Why is that important" after every answer)

1. _____

2. _____

3. _____

4. _____

5. _____

6. _____

7. _____

Are you starting to see the value of Audience Attraction marketing? You target more people with less effort and communicate your benefits specifically related to their needs

We're making great progress here but it's time for the last step in the process. Remember, you have a choice of how you market your business and the type of marketing you use. You can do marketing the traditional way that gets minimal results or choose to market to many and fill your business much faster than what you've been used to. Again, wouldn't you rather fish with a net than fish with a pole?

Infiltrate Existing Audiences for Maximum Results

Step number three of Audience Attraction is to strategically approach groups of prospects rather than going to people one at a time. By mastering this skill you'll no longer have to worry about where your next client comes from. You won't just be attracting individuals, you'll be attracting groups of people interested in your offer and marketing message.

When I was in the mortgage industry I held marketing boot camps for professions such as realtors, accountants and financial advisors. Marketing wasn't my profession but I was good at it. I figured if I could help others with marketing, then they would refer some of their clients to me. I had about 15-20 professionals come to me through my boot camps and workshops. I knew that each of them helped hundreds of people and could refer some of those customers to me.

Most others in the mortgage industry at the time were looking for individual customers they can help provide a mortgage to, but I chose a different route. If I was able to help key influencers, people who had access to many ideal prospects, then I wouldn't have to spend time looking for one client at a time. I would just help someone who would be able to send me dozens or hundreds of prospects over time without my effort. That was a win-win scenario for me. That's how I realized the power of Audience Attraction.

I wasn't necessarily making any money through educating others on marketing, but I was making an investment by educating them on how to market *their* business. Not only did they refer me to their audience as I had hoped, but I became to "go-to" expert for them and their clients. I can tell you with certainty that no matter what business you are in, you have the same opportunities to get in front of audiences that are just one relationship away.

If you follow this path you will begin to see your competition as collaborators, which is a great position to be in. You open up new opportunities that perhaps didn't exist before with the old style of marketing your business. People began to collaborate with me and I collaborated with them. As a result, the gaps between us were filled. It also created an audience that I could tap into.

On one occasion I connected with a business coach who had an audience of about 20,000 real estate agents. We connected through social media. At first we only had a few similarities and a couple of mutual Facebook friends. But in a matter of weeks we developed a friendship and decided to collaborate with each other. After thinking through some options we partnered up and decided to launch a program called Expert Branding Bootcamp, which was geared toward real estate agents. Within 45 days from launching this brand new program we were able to generate $25,000 in sales from scratch.

Our success was possible because he had the audience and I had the ability to make something out of nothing. *By tapping into his audience, I suddenly had access to 25,000 real estate agents that would have taken a lot of time and money to acquire on my own.* This collaboration worked because I brought value to someone else and their audience, so they made their audience available to me.

Connecting and collaborating with other businesses, professionals, leaders and influencers can open many doors for you and your business. Not only can you gain access to a whole new audience, but you can develop friendships and business relationships. If you partner with somebody and the collaboration is successful, they may come back to you later with new ideas and opportunities that wouldn't be available otherwise.

One of the biggest problems that prevent business owners from collaborating and gaining access to existing audiences is the fear of approaching others. Many of us have faced rejection in our lives that could make us wary of those we are unfamiliar with. However, if we are truly dedicated to growing our businesses, we have no choice other than getting over that fear. It's not worth it to hang onto the fear and settle for less than the best in our business as a result.

There is only so much you can do on your own. By collaborating with others who already have audiences, you can serve your market at a much higher level than you ever could by yourself. Just by having the "what can I do for you" attitude, you can form successful partnerships with complete strangers in a very short amount of time.

Knowing how to establish partnerships can help you get your foot in the door and make valuable connections. It is very possible to approach people who already have a name for themselves in the industries you serve and not get turned away.

The key is to have the right attitude and to understand that people are just people. Ask them how you can help them, what gaps can you fill for them, and how you can help them find solutions to their current challenges. Aim to create a win-win situation where you can serve their audience and still gain valuable experience, skills, and potential customers.

Who can you think of that already has access to the people you serve? Are there any other business owners who have the same type of clients as you and offer a complimentary product or service to what you offer? These would be great collaborations to consider.

One of my clients is a local auto mechanic shop. He was looking to get more clients so we connected with a neighborhood carwash nearby. I negotiated a collaboration in which the car wash gave my client free carwash certificates to give to his clients, which would be an added value to people who went to get their car repaired.

On the other hand, the carwash gets their business in front of all of the mechanic's clients since the mechanic is marketing his carwash through the free car wash vouchers. Basically, everyone wins in this scenario. The carwash was able to tap into the mechanic's audience without any promotional costs other than a free carwash to people who came over from the mechanic's shop. My client, the mechanic shop owner, was able to give new customers a free carwash. This was different from what other mechanics offered and it helped him get new people in the door.

While I'm sharing various examples here that you can directly or indirectly model, the most important part is the strategy itself. You must ask yourself, "Who has access to an audience of my ideal customers and what value can I offer to get in front of them?" Answering these very questions will change your marketing forever.

Integrating Audience Attraction in Your Business

If you ever wondered how to get more from your marketing, Audience Attraction is the most effective way to go. Not only will it save you time and effort, it will also allow you to focus your marketing budget on reaching the maximum people with less of the wrong types of marketing.

How do huge billion dollar corporations grow rapidly and sell out quickly? They focus their marketing efforts on getting in front of large groups of people interested and ready to buy what they offer. Now you have the knowledge to do it yourself.

It no longer matters how big or small your business is; you have the ability to target the masses in ways that didn't exist just a decade ago.

Remember, the first step of the process is to choose WHO your audience is. Without knowing your audience you'll continue shooting blindly, hoping something will stick. But knowing your audience will transform the way you connect and communicate with them, helping you stand out in a crowded marketplace.

Once you know your audience you can craft a marketing message that speaks directly to their core wants, needs and desires. When you demonstrate that you know them and can relate to their challenges, your solution becomes the obvious choice compared to all other options. Buying becomes a lot easier when your customers feel they're understood. Unlike most businesses that keep their marketing superficial, you're equipped to go deep and know the end result they're after.

Lastly, with your new understanding of your ideal clients and the ability to communicate influentially, it's now time to tap into others who have access to your prospects. There's no reason you should try to create a group of your own when there's others who've already put the time and effort to gather them for you. All you have to do is lead with value and find the win-win scenario that would make collaboration worthwhile for everyone involved.

It's now time for you to shift your marketing from fishing with a pole to finishing with a net. Go out there, implement these short exercises, and put yourself in front of the people who need you most. There are groups of people waiting to be found by you so they can attain the results only you can provide.

About the Author

Alex Navas is an internationally recognized strategic business coach, speaker and marketing strategist who helps entrepreneurs and business leaders attract audiences of prospects into their businesses, become recognized experts, develop high value offers and create profitable partnerships. He started his first business at the age of 15 and has mastered his marketing and relationship building skills since then.

He later launched, grew and sold two successful mortgage companies before dedicating his life to equipping business leaders on creating profitable and purposeful businesses through effective marketing strategies that generate consistent and systematic growth. As the creator of the Expert Branding Bootcamp and Audience Attraction Strategies programs, Alex is passionate about sharing his knowledge and expertise with others through webinars, teleseminars, workshops, and conferences and can be found at www.AlexNavas.com.

Claim his top 3 proven audience attraction strategies to boost your business within the next 30 days at www.AudienceAttraction.com absolutely free.

Free Resources from Alex Navas

Through this chapter, you've discovered the true power of the Audience Attraction strategy for marketing your business. As a thank you for reading this chapter, I'd love to offer you something of incredible value to add help you not only learn more about these strategies, but also help you implement the in your business.

I've created a video series that will walk you through exactly how to begin using these Audience Attraction strategies to dramatically increase the people you service and directly impact your revenue.

To get your free Audience Attraction strategies video series, go to http://www.AudienceAttraction.com.

You can also find additional marketing and sales training and resources at http://www.AlexNavas.com.

Chapter 13

How to Generate More and Better Leads Quickly and Inexpensively

Archer Atlas

You might not know this, but right now there's an incredible opportunity just waiting to be seized upon by you and your business. This opportunity is pretty much unparalleled and incomparable to any other, probably in the history of business and marketing. What's intriguing about this opportunity is that the technology behind it is over 130 years old, and has been used over that time to produce trillions of dollars in revenue.

The opportunity I'm talking about is in using the telephone to increase your business' sales and bottom line. In this chapter, you'll discover that not only is the telephone a super-underutilized tool for:

- Growing your business
- Producing more qualified and better leads
- Increasing conversion of those leads into clients
- Getting those clients to buy more and buy more often

But you'll learn the right way to go about doing this... producing the best results for your business and its bottom line in the most efficient manner.

If you're serious about growing your business and producing the best results possible, then you'd have to be out of your mind to neglect the opportunity telephone sales brings to the table for you. Since I'm sure you're not insane (after all you wouldn't be reading this if you were), let's get down to business and I'll show you how.

Why Right Now is the Greatest Time in History

Before we can really dig in, I want you to take part in a small mental exercise. Think about this...

- How many pieces of "spam" mail have you received?

- How many spam emails do you get in an average month?

- How many of them are offers from companies trying to sell you SEO (search engine optimization) services or some other product or service?

See what I'm getting at? If you're like most business people, you probably get a ton of emails asking you to do and buy all sorts of things.

Now compare that to how many sales calls you get. Then compare it to how many sales calls you've gotten in the past. Notice a trend?

People and businesses are moving away from using the phone to sell.

For me personally, I'm amazed by how much the volume of sales calls I've received has fallen over the years. Right now, I'm getting next to none. In the past, sometimes I'd get up to a dozen calls a day. In fact, I used to have my phone hooked up to recording software constantly so I could record all the pitches I'd get. I would get *that* many.

Along the line, something changed. The telephone lost its luster. It was seen as being too difficult to use to get results. There were easier methods available.

The Path of Least Resistance

People will usually choose the path of least resistance. And there are other, seemingly less resistant paths to take. There's email, snail mail, Facebook, LinkedIn, PPC, search, etc.

Most business people hear about telemarketing or cold calling and they head for the hills. The phone is last on almost everyone's list. People have gotten fearful of using the telephone to grow their business, and therein lies an opportunity.

Right now, there is less competition than any other time in this generation. Less people and businesses are using the telephone to increase their sales, making your telephone calls all the more noticeable, impactful, and effective. This is a golden opportunity.

It's like the famous warren Buffett quote, "Be fearful when others are greedy and greedy when others are fearful." The other businesses out there—along with your competition—are all being fearful of the telephone and greedy with the other, seemingly less-resistant types of media. Now is your time to be greedy with the telephone and a little bit fearful, or at least cautious, of those other avenues.

I'll say one last thing about the opportunity found in this lack of competition. Imagine a scenario where you're a single man and there are two beautiful single women you'd like to ask out on a date. Now, let's say one of these women is in a room filled with men that are constantly hitting on her, and one woman is in a room with just her and you. If you're the man, who do you think you'd have a better shot at getting a date with? The one woman in the room full of men hitting on her, with you being the 25th guy to ask her out? Or the other woman, whom you're alone with, who hasn't had to hold her defenses up all night from repeated "attackers?"

Now let's take it a step further by imagining a scenario where you not only have the opportunity and advantage of being noticed and commanding maximum attention, but you also have the "tools" necessary and have been trained in the best possible and most effective ways to ask for that date and get it.

See what I'm getting at? All things being equal, you're going to want to be the guy asking the second woman—with whom you have no competitors for her attention—out on a date. And you're most certainly going to want to be trained in the best possible methods for asking for and getting that date.

That's what this chapter is all about. Like I said, you have a golden opportunity in front of you. The question is will you have the fortitude to go against the grain of what everyone else is doing and make yourself and your company stand out, command attention, and obtain extraordinary results? After all, when you go against the grain, you get against the grain results. By doing only what the average person or company is doing, you're guaranteed to get average results. Which one will it be?

What Exactly is a Cold Call?

I'm probably going to burst some bubbles right now. For one, all we've talked about so far is this great opportunity you now have right in front of you. It's been all sunshine and puppy dogs. It's been all theory and no practice, so far. Well, here's where the rubber hits the road.

I've been driving home the point of opportunity and not getting into specifics so far for a few reasons. For one, opportunity—this opportunity—is the most important thing to take note of. It's in your benefit to know and understand that this opportunity exists and is real and that you can benefit directly from it. I have to drive that point home because the fact of the matter is, what we're about to discuss isn't glamorous, sexy, or even very attractive (although the results it produces certainly are). It involves actual work and training.

This training has a huge ROI and is worth every second because of the results it produces, but there's a real reason most people hear the words telemarketing, telephone selling, or cold calling and go running for the hills. But just as with everything in life, anything that's worthwhile requires effort, persistence, and stick-to-itiveness. After all, if it were so easy, everyone would be doing it and there wouldn't be this golden opportunity at all.

That said, allow me to peel back the curtain for you and show you exactly how you can benefit from this un-sexy, un-glamorous, and un-attractive wart addled medium that produces such lovely, beautiful, and wonderful results.

First, let's define exactly what we're talking about. But before we do that, let's give it a name: cold calling. Cold calling is the act of calling someone on the phone, unsolicited, and engaging them into your sales cycle. That's basically it. Not so horrible sounding, huh?

That's because it's not at all. It's not horrible sounding and it's not horrible in practice. Don't get me wrong; it's not exactly easy either. Like I said before, there's a reason this opportunity exists and is so great. It's because others are unwilling to do it, instead choosing what they feel are "easier" methods.

OK. So that's cold calling and that's what this opportunity is all about. It's ultimately about contacting the right prospects, generating interest in them, qualifying that they are indeed the right prospects that can benefit from your goods or services, that they will benefit you and your company if a relationship happens, and that the both of you will be better off as a result of this contact and relationship.

That's the big picture and the end game of it. Let's zoom in a little and take a look at the nitty-gritty and the purpose of a cold call.

The Three Purposes of a Cold Call

There are only three purposes on a cold call, ever. Just three. Listed, they are:

- Generating qualified leads
- Setting a sales appointment
- And closing a sale

That's it. Anything else is simply a waste of both your and the call receiver's time and is ineffective, inefficient, and just overall bad business practice.

In fact, I'm going to limit this chapter's scope to only the most effective purpose of a cold call there is: *Generating qualified lead*s.

While setting appointments and closing sales over the phone on a cold call can and does happen—and often—it's not the most effective use of the telephone or your telephone time.

I know this all too well, as I got my start in sales as a stockbroker, working for a small boutique firm on Wall Street. And I made my living from closing sales over the telephone on a cold call. In fact, at that time that was my preferred method of acquiring clients. I'd spend thousands of dollars on new "good" leads, pick up the phone, and call a prospect once, cold. If he bought then and there, he'd be my client. If not, I'd tear the lead card up, throw it in the air, and let it rain down on me and the floor, never to speak to that prospect again.

Oh how stupid and wasteful!

For one, I just spent good money on obtaining that name and number. Why would I waste it by throwing it out just because the guy on the other end didn't want to buy what I had on the spot? For two, do you have any idea of the odds against getting the person on the other end to actually buy then and there? They're some long odds, and you'd have to have a bunch of things lined up in your favor in order for this person to buy, right then and there. Let me list them:

1. He'd have to be in the market for what you had to offer and have a current need or desire for it.
2. He'd have to believe you and trust that you are who you said you are, and that you're from the company you said you're from.
3. He'd have to understand, comprehend, internalize, and see the benefit in what you had to say.
4. He'd have to feel he had received enough information to make an informed buying decision.
5. He'd have to like you enough to pull out his wallet and pull the trigger on a sale.
6. On top of it all, he'd have to be in at least a decent—if not good or great—mood and feel good about buying.

If the prospect just opened an overdue bill he got in the mail before picking up the phone, or he got into a fight with his wife last night or before leaving for the office this morning, you can most likely kiss your chances of getting him to buy then and there goodbye. And if you "tear up the card" or burn your bridges that lead to him, like I used to do, you can kiss him, his business, and what a relationship with him can bring you, goodbye forever too.

As you can see, the odds of being effective with this type of cold calling and selling are really against you. In fact, just reason number one on the list above—having the prospect be in the market for what you have to offer and have a current need or desire for it—automatically eliminates 97% of all prospects.

At any given time, there are only 3% of the total amount of prospects actively looking for any given product or service, with a current need or desire for that good or service. That's it: just 3%.

You wouldn't think it's a smart business model to only target that 3% of current buyers that are actively looking for what you have to offer and have a current need or desire for your goods or services. You have to be insane to conduct your business like that. But that's exactly what many businesses have done, will do, and are currently doing. Incidentally, that's why so many companies have abandoned cold calling and using the telephone in their businesses to increase their sales and bottom line.

So the third option above—trying to close a sale over the telephone, with a cold call—is out and out ineffective and inefficient. Let's move on to purpose number two: setting appointments over the phone.

Why Setting Appointments Over the Phone Isn't the Answer

I'll admit this method of cold calling—cold calling for the purpose of setting sales appointments—is far more effective than simply trying to close a sale over the phone, right then and there. That said, it is still not all that effective and efficient. Here's why…

Let's say you call up someone cold and out of the blue and ask for an appointment. First off, to get an appointment with this prospect, you'd have to meet certain criteria. Now this criterion is nowhere near as stringent or eliminating as the list above, where a sale on the first phone call is the goal. But it still eliminates a huge portion of the total amount of prospects.

For someone to answer "yes" to your request to set an appointment they wouldn't necessarily need to be in the market for your good or service, or have a current need or desire for them (but it sure would help). However, they would need to obviously be "open" to the idea of meeting, "open" to the prospect that what you have to offer may be of benefit to them, and "open" to the prospect that the time they exchange in order to see you will be worthwhile.

Bottom line, they must be open to all these things: they'd have to be thinking about what it is you're offering when you just so happen to be calling, they'd have to be in the market for your offerings, or they'd have to have a current need or desire for your products.

Does that give you better odds than you'd have in just trying to close a sale on the spot? Definitely! But there's still a bunch of stipulations and conditions that'll have to be met for you to get the appointment. The odds are still against you.

The Target Triangle

If you look below at the illustration, you'll see what I refer to as the "Target Triangle." I've seen others refer to it as a sales pyramid or a sales funnel, but I like alliteration so I call it the Target Triangle. More important than the naming of this is the principle behind it.

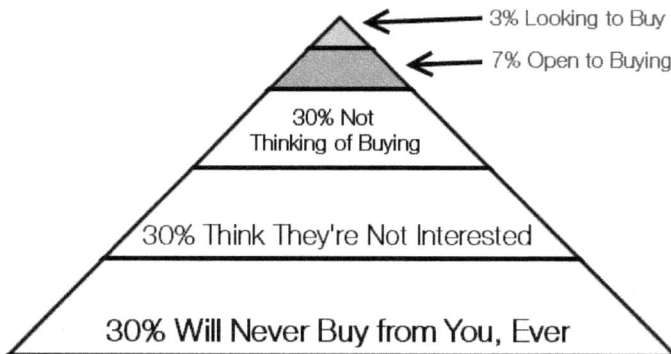

You'll see the triangle has 5 sections. The top section represents the 3% that are buying now. The second section represents the 7% of those that are open to buying. The bottom three sections are all 30% each and represent those that aren't thinking about buying, those that think they aren't interested in buying, and those that will never buy for any reason, from top to bottom respectively.

I have to give credit where it's due. I learned this principle from the late great Chet Holmes and it literally changed the way I do business, the way I think about business and generating leads and acquiring clients— and to be quite honest—it has changed my life.

As we talked about before, when you set closing a sale as your purpose for cold calling, you limit yourself to only that top 3% of the triangle. You're excluding the other 97% of the total prospects out there for your goods or services.

When you make the purpose of your call setting a sales appointment, you're limiting yourself to those top two sections of the pyramid—only 10% of the total prospects. You've excluded yourself from doing business with 90% of the total market. Is it better than only trying to close a sale on a cold call? Without a doubt. It's 233% better, on average. But there's still tons of room for improvement. By the way, this is the level that most business operate at. Conservatively, I'd say 90%+ of business out there only target and focus on the top two section of the pyramid—10% of the total market.

Right now, I'm going to show you how you can be seven times as effective as you'd be if your purpose for calling was to set an appointment, and twenty-three times more effective than you'd be if your purpose was just closing a sale on a cold call.

Anyone that doesn't want to be seven to twenty-three times more effective should simply close this book right now, because these kinds of increases can turn the most meager results into significant revenue and profits for your business.

The Four Ways to Grow a Business

But first, let's quickly go over some basic numbers so we can quantify how much this strategy can be worth to you and how much it can help you grow your business.

There's four ways you can grow a business. You can increase the number of prospects, you can increase conversion from prospects to clients, you can increase the average order value, and you can increase the average order frequency.

Now what we're dealing with here is strictly focusing on the first way to grow your business: increasing the amount of prospects. Let's run through an example quickly.

Let's take a hypothetical company in a hypothetical industry that has 10,000 total buyers. Now let's say this company does $1,000,000 a year in revenue, and they do this by marketing and selling to customers in a manner similar to what most companies do—meaning they spend their time, money, and effort focusing on only the top two sections of the triangle, which accounts for 10% of the total buyers.

So follow me on the numbers: this company markets to and appeals to only 10% of their industry's 10,000 total buyers, giving them 1,000 prospects. Now to get to that million dollar revenue, they'd have to convert some of these prospects into clients and have these clients buy some goods and services. For simplicity, let's say this company converts 10% of these prospects to clients, so they now have 100 clients accounting for $1 million in revenue.

Each client is worth an average of $10,000 a year in revenue. For our purposes, it's not important whether they come to that number by averaging $10,000 per transaction one time per year or whether they get to that figure by averaging $1,000 per transaction ten times per year, but we'll go with the latter numbers.

So here we have it:

This company attracts 10% of the total number of prospects for 1,000 prospects they market and sell to. They convert 10% of these prospects to clients who purchase an average of $1,000 worth of goods or services an average of ten times per year, totaling $1,000,000 a year in revenue. With me so far?

- 10,000 Total Buyers x 10% Target Rate = 1,000 Prospects
- 1,000 Prospects x 10% Conversion Rate = 100 Customers
- 100 Customers x $100 Average Order x 10 Orders Per Year = $1,000,000 in Revenue

Now, let's say we were able to increase the amount of prospects. If you really think about it, it's not very hard to imagine an increase in this number. After all, we're only targeting, appealing to, and marketing to

10% of the total amount of prospects. An increase to this number is not unimaginable, but highly likely.

Let's say we live in an ideal world where we're able to target the top four sections of the triangle, instead of just the top two. That right there would increase the amount of your prospects *seven times* over. You'd go from targeting 10% of the total number of prospects to targeting 70% (remember, that last 30% will *never buy*).

Targeting 10% of Total Buyers:

10,000 Total Buyers x *10% Target Rate* = 1,000 Prospects

1,000 Prospects x 10% Conversion Rate = *100 Customers*

Targeting 70% of Total Buyers:

10,000 Total Buyers x *70% Target Rate* = 7,000 Prospects

1,000 Prospects x 10% Conversion Rate = *700 Customers*

If we apply these ideal numbers to this hypothetical example, we get staggering results. We'd go from having 1000 prospects out of the 10,000 total buyers being attracted and taking notice to have 7,000 of these prospects becoming this company's prospects. That's a 600% increase. And with all other things being equal, this company is looking at a 600% increase to their revenue, increasing it seven times over. Pretty fantastic, don't you agree?

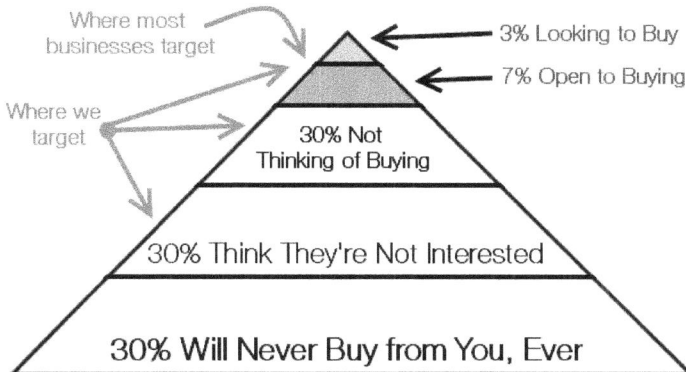

But let's pause for a second for a dose of reality. This isn't an ideal world and you're not going to go from having 10% of the total market take notice to having 70% take notice. It just isn't going to happen. If you're lucky, or good at employing the strategies we'll be talking about later, you're going to get only the top three sections of the triangle to take notice. But that's still a marked improvement of going from 10% to take notice to getting 40% to take notice.

If you do the math, you're looking at a fourfold increase to sales, which is nothing to sneeze at. That said it's time for another reality check. This fourfold increase in prospects taking notice doesn't happen overnight and it doesn't happen by doing nothing more than what you're currently doing. It's going to take work and strategic thinking. But it can and does happen often.

Nearly every time you see a company make dramatic strides in sales improvements and make breakthroughs in bringing their company to the next level, you'll see this kind of strategic thinking behind it. I've personally seen companies double their revenues in a year—and then turn around and double them again the next year—employing this same type of strategic thinking and implementation.

What Does This Have to do with Cold Calling?

At this point you may be asking yourself, "What does this have to do with cold calling?" The answer is simple: EVERYTHING.

If increasing the amount of prospects is the name of the game, there is simply no better tool for accomplishing this goal in the fastest and least expensive manner, period.

I began this chapter talking about opportunity, specifically the amazing and fruitful opportunity that's presented to us by telephone selling and the lack of competition users of this methodology have. But lack of competition isn't the only benefit and opportunity that cold calling presents. As I stated before, cold calling is the fastest, least expensive way to generate leads and grow the amount of prospects that take notice of you and become your prospects (taking them one step closer to becoming your clients).

Right now, technological advances have made it so that your business can make unlimited calls to a virtually unlimited amount of prospects worldwide for pennies. Not only that, but you can call a prospect today, qualify them, and get engagement, illicit interest, and then have them become a paying client virtually overnight. Try doing that with other mediums of marketing and contact. With cold calling, you've eliminated the lag time and "dead air" between a prospect being a prospect, to becoming a qualified lead, to becoming a paying client.

Not only that, but cold calling is the form of marketing that gets the absolute, bar-none most engagement with prospects. Plus, it's the most interactive medium of connecting with prospects, allowing you to better control the direction of the conversation (both verbal and in the prospect's mind).

Even more importantly, it allows you to answer any questions the prospect may have, right there on the spot. On top of which—and probably most importantly—it allows you to ask for, and receive, answers to the questions that are most important to you and your business. This allows you to more quickly qualify prospects and save even more time, effort, and money that might have otherwise been wasted marketing to an unqualified prospect.

Moreover, there has never been a better time to cold call than right now. As I said before, people will often take the path of least resistance. And most will do whatever they can to avoid doing things they fear or that might appear to be difficult. This presents the golden opportunity we've talked about with cold calling.

While everyone else is taking what they believe to be the path of least resistance: using email, search engine optimization, and pay per click (and etc.)—all fighting and competing with each other—you're standing nearly alone, standing out, commanding attention, and generating the leads that become clients that bring in the revenue and bottom line profits your business needs and deserves.

Lastly, if you're a smart business person, you'll know it's never a good idea to have all—or even most—of your eggs in one basket. By adding cold calling to your repertoire, or increasing your emphasis on the cold calling you're already using to generate leads, you're simply adding another arrow in your quiver, making your business stronger and more impervious to damaging changes and threats that pop up from time to time.

More importantly, this is a golden, indestructible, accurate, and effective arrow that has proven itself to be an amazing asset when it comes to hitting the target of increasing leads and prospects and thereby helping you grow your business.

Cold calling really is that good and powerful of a tool to help you grow your business. And without further adieu, let's get into specifically how to effectively utilize cold calling in your business.

The 3 Major Components of Successful Cold Calls

A successfully lead generating cold calling strategy has three major components:

- Leads
- A Lead Magnet
- A Pitch Script

These are the three pre-requisites you must have in order to be effective in cold calling to generate leads, and each is important in its own way.

Most people focus solely on their script and become surprised when they don't achieve the results they want. Some others pay no attention to providing a valuable lead magnet and find themselves with lack-luster results.

In order to really give yourself and your business the best chance of succeeding, you must have all three components working together as a well-oiled, lead-generating machine.

Using the Right Leads

One of the things businesses and salespeople overlook the most is sales lead selection. This cannot be overstated as a catastrophic mistake; one that is made entirely too often and is probably most responsible for sales failures, especially when it comes to cold calling.

So many companies today rely on cheap, outdated, and completely "beat up" sales leads. Not only is this not effective or efficient, but it costs these companies greatly—both in time and opportunity.

With all other things being equal, the average company can see tremendous increases in their sales numbers simply by either obtaining new sales leads or getting their sales leads from a better source. This is the number one, easiest way to reach sales goals and improve sales numbers in almost any business. Having the right sales leads is that important and powerful.

Back when I was starting out on Wall Street and I "graduated" from being a "cold-caller," whose only job was to qualify leads, to an "account opener," who was responsible for opening accounts over the telephone, I learn a valuable lesson about sales leads.

As a cold-caller for my firm, I enjoyed pretty much instant and appreciable success at generating qualified leads. However, when I graduated to the position of account opener, I had major struggles. For one, the purpose and goal of the account opening call were completely different from a qualifying and lead generating call (and required more skill).

But that wasn't the only issue. Over the course of my three or so months as a cold caller, my firm had gone from calling "brand-spanking-new" leads to now calling the "left-overs." These leads consisted of people who either didn't pick up their telephone when called previously (they were all called previously) or the lead itself contained inaccurate information.

As you can imagine, calling these leads didn't generate very good results at all.

After a three week period of dialing my fingers off, trying my best to get my first account opened (and undergoing the tradition of getting my tie cut off and placed on the bulletin board), and failing to do so, I had a heart to heart with the president of my firm. I asked for his advice on account opening and whether he had any tips on how I can get this first account opened, and how I could become successful at opening accounts in general.

The very first thing he asked me was about the quality of my lead supply. He asked whether my leads had the correct contact information, the source of the leads, and how old they were. When I told him about my leads, he answered, *"of course you're not going to do well with such outdated and poor quality leads. Go get yourself some new leads and you'll see the difference."*

That was some sage advice, for sure. That night, having no money to buy new leads (cold callers and account openers aren't generally paid well), I went to the library at my alma mater, Fordham University, and started photocopying their Dunn & Bradstreet books from the reference section. The next day, I open my first account (and got my tie cut and hanged on the board). The day after that, I opened another account and was well on my way to becoming "on my own" as a stock-broker, working for myself.

I cannot stress this enough: quality leads can be the difference between success and failure, or—even better—they can be the difference between success and even more and higher levels of success.

One last quick story on the power of having good, new leads from my stock broker days…

A few months down the road, after I became a stock broker that worked for myself, I learned an even more powerful lesson on using the best possible leads. For my first few months as a broker, I used the "free" leads I was able to either photocopy from D&B books in the reference section of the library, or other leads I was able to download from the library computers that had subscriptions to other business sales leads services. When I started making a little more money, I started buying newer leads from D&B and InfoUSA, for a few pennies each.

Then something happened that opened my eyes in a whole new way: a new, ultra-successful broker joined my firm. And when he was making cold calls, he used leads I'd never seen before—and achieved cold-calling success like I'd never seen before, too. It was then that I was introduced to "premium" leads.

Instead of the generic business leads that I bought from other companies, that were simply leads for presidents, CEOs, and owners of businesses, these new "premium" leads were more qualified for my purposes. They were leads for people who were investors, and who had shown an interest in wanting to invest more money, by requesting information on investing. They were also premium in that they cost anywhere from 50 cents to two dollars each. But in the end, they were well worth it and paid for themselves.

As soon as I started buying and using these leads, I instantly started having more, better, and longer conversations with a higher level of engagement with the prospects I was calling. Not only that, but I started opening more, higher valued accounts that brought in more commission for my firm and me. Bottom line, my production increased dramatically and I made a ton more money.

The moral of these two stories is that you're going to always want the newest, best-quality, most pre-qualified leads you can get your hands on, regardless of price. In most instances, the more you pay for leads, the more efficient, effective, and successful your calling will be.

Having stale, outdated, and poor quality leads is only going to hurt you. And even when you're armed with the best products or services, with the best marketing, and the best of everything else, it won't do you any good if you're targeting the wrong people. You have to be sure that your message and your market match, and having the correct targets and sales leads is the very first part of that equation.

The last thing I want to say about leads is this: You want to test different lead sources out before you spend significantly on leads. Most companies give free samples or trials. Be sure to use them and judge for yourself. Having the right, good quality leads is so very important and you want to make sure you get this right.

One company I use that has been a very good, accurate, and inexpensive source of business sales leads has been infofree.com. I don't get paid anything for endorsing them, but I wanted to mention them, as I think they are a very good source for business leads that can help you.

Using the Right Lead Magnet

The second thing you absolutely need to have in order to effectively generate leads via cold calling is a good quality lead magnet.

Let me take a step back and explain exactly what I mean by a quality lead magnet. First off, let's take a big picture look at exactly what we're trying to accomplish through lead generating cold calls.

Our goal is to generate qualified leads. How we'll be doing that is by offering value to our prospects in exchange for them "raising their hands" expressing interest in what we're offering, and qualifying themselves. This makes for an even exchange of value for value with the prospect, and without this, you're giving the prospect no reason to move forward with you, thereby limiting your potential results.

That said, a lead magnet is simply something of value to your prospects that you offer in exchange for a prospect to qualify themselves. This lead magnet can be anything that has perceived (and if you're smart, actual) value to your prospects.

I want to be clear that I'm talking about a lead magnet that has value to your prospect. The keywords there are *your prospect*. This lead magnet should be valuable to the prospect and not just you. It shouldn't be a brochure or other piece of company or product information. It should demonstrate value outside of your company or products and it should have value to your prospects regardless of whether or not they choose to do business with you now, down the road, or ever.

The mark of a good lead magnet is that it's kept by the prospect long after they've made a decision as to whether to buy from you or not. It should provide genuine educational value to your prospects and help them in some way—whether that's in solving a problem they may have, educating them about a particular issue they may face, or any number of different ways that provide genuine value to your prospect.

An entire book can be written on this concept alone, and you'd probably be very well served in reading it. I'll leave off by simply listing just a few different forms a good lead magnet, that can help you generate more qualified leads, can take:

- White papers
- Case studies
- Newsletters
- Articles
- Presentations
- Audio recordings
- Videos
- Webinars
- Speeches/ transcripts

Any of the above could make for good lead magnets to use in your lead generating cold calling plan. The key is that you use a lead magnet that provides genuine value to your prospects and that gives them a reason to "raise their hand" and qualify themselves to you.

Forming the Best Possible Pitch Script

The last major component to a successful lead generating cold calling strategy is the pitch script itself.

Frankly, I think that this is the most over emphasized part of cold calling. I've seen people work for hours and even days on end, tweaking and adjusting their pitches on paper or in a word processor, all the while never getting on the phone.

What good would the greatest script in the world do you if you don't actually use it? On the other hand, there's a good chance you can see some pretty decent results with a terrible pitch, so long as you do it enough times and have enough people hear it.

What we're going to talk about is neither of these scenarios. We're going to construct an effective pitch that gets results for you, without you having to "pound the phone" over and over. I'm not saying it's not going to require some work or that it'll be easy. But I am saying that if you deliver a good, strong pitch that demonstrates your value effectively to your prospects, you will be able to see good lead generation results, without having to make hundreds of calls a day.

We'll go deeper into this concept later on in discussing how to set realistic telephone goals and how to hit your numbers, but for right now I'll say this: by following a script and system similar to the one in this book, you should be able to generate two to four leads per caller, per hour on the telephone.

But let's take a step back for a second and go over the basics of a successful script. Now, we've already discussed sales leads and the concept that you should get yourself the highest quality, newest, most accurate leads you can find. That's not only going to make your life and your job easier, but it's going to affect your script, too.

The idea is to acquire the best leads possible that are most likely to be candidates to do business with you, and then to set up your script so that you cast the widest net possible when contacting these leads, and so that you appeal to the highest amount of prospects you possibly can.

If you're using old, outdated leads or leads that don't apply to your business, you might be wasting your time, especially if your goal is to initially appeal to the maximum number of people you call.

Key Concepts of a Successful Pitch Script

OK. So you've done what's smartest and acquired good leads with the goal of having a script that casts a wide net and appeals to the maximum amount of prospects you call. Now is the time to write your script.

As I've said before, I believe strongly in getting the best possible leads and constructing a script that casts a wide net and appeals to the maximum amount of prospects. If it looks like I'm repeating myself, it's for good reason; this concept cannot be overstated. It's that important. That said, I've found that short, to-the-point, and simple scripts produce the best results.

Not only that, but probably the biggest keys to success in cold calling have almost nothing to do with the actual content of the script itself, but rather of your mastery of the material and your consistency in delivering the pitch.

I'll repeat that. Even more important than the content of the script itself is your mastery—and consistent delivery—of the script. That means that in order for you to achieve real, lasting success with lead generating cold calling, you need to know your script like the back of your hand, that you must practice it to where it becomes second nature, and that you should deliver it in a consistent way, across different individual deliveries to different prospects, and across different callers, where everyone delivers the same opening script, exactly the same.

Ideally, your script will be short and to the point, so there's no excuse to not know it like the back of your hand, and with practice, you'll find that consistency of delivery comes naturally. This isn't rocket science.

Now I'm sure you're getting antsy with anticipation waiting to read some scripts, so I'll get to it right now. But first, one last thing...

The most important thing about creating your script is that you make it all about the prospect, not about yourself, and not about your company, your products, or your services. Make the script about your prospect and how they benefit. That is without a doubt the most important concept of your script.

We'll cover that further, later on and give some good examples of this. Just know for now that if you want to achieve any measure of success, you absolutely have to make the pitch about "them" and not "you."

A Quick Word on Tone

Before we can dig deeply into the script, first here's a little you should know about tone. When you're calling prospects (or having your sales team doing the calling), it's important that you have a tone of voice that conveys excitement and confidence. Excitement sells. It causes people to pay attention. Non-excitement is boring and loses people before you can even demonstrate your value to them.

Just be careful not to overdo it. Your excitement needs to be real and not just some hammed-up salesman speak, which really shines through on the phone and raises red flags in your prospect's mind.

The good part about all of this though is that it really shouldn't be all that hard to be genuinely excited. By following this strategy, you're going to be generating qualified leads and those qualified leads will lead to results for you. How could you not be excited about that?

As for having confidence in your tone, that should come very easily too. For one, what you'll be asking for is pretty much a very "easy sale." As you'll see in the sample script, you're offering value and not asking for anything unreasonable in return.

For two, you are offering value to your prospects and not just asking for orders like most unqualified salesmen do. The fact that you're providing something of real benefit should give you even more confidence in your position. You're not just another salesman; you are someone who educates and advises the prospect.

By following this course of action, you're going to be setting yourself up as more of an expert, authority, and advisor than anyone else that calls on your prospects. Remember, you're providing value, not selling. Let this be a source of immense confidence for you.

The last point I want to say about tone is this: you're speaking to a peer, let your tone demonstrate this. It doesn't matter if you're speaking to the CEO of a Fortune 500 company or the owner of a small business in your neighborhood—you want to speak to these people as a peer. You are not one of their subordinates and you will never accomplish what you want by acting like one. You will only command attention and produce positive results by speaking to your prospect as a peer.

What makes this very easy to do—if you follow the advice laid out here—is that you are not like everyone else that calls these people. You're not asking for anything initially. In fact, you're doing the opposite; you're offering value to the prospect. With that, there's no reason to think of yourself as anything other than a peer to your prospects, regardless of their position or the size of their company. You are a peer. And you're offering value to the prospect.

There's much more to be said about tone, which really is an extremely important part of not only cold calling, but of all verbal communication with others, in sales and in life in general. Sadly, the space provided by this book limits me from saying more.

Next, we'll run through a sample script and then break it down and analyze it, so that you can construct one you can use to help you generate more leads in your business.

Sample Pitch

Here is a sample lead generating cold calling pitch. We'll break it down further below, but for now let's just dig right in.

Hello John, Archer Atlas. Reason for the call, I want to send you over our bestselling book on business growth and invite you to an upcoming webinar "The 5 Most Dangerous Trends Facing Manufacturers Today." Fair enough?

That's it. Short, sweet, and simple. Over the years, I've used a script just like this to generate thousands of leads, many of whom have become clients of mine.

The reason it works is because it is simple, short, and sweet. It's also disarming. You're starting off giving something away and asking a logical question where the completely rational answer is yes.

Who doesn't want a best-selling business book for free? Who wouldn't want the option to attend a webinar that is of interest to them and their business?

Let's take a step back and go over this, line by line, so we can see what exactly is going on here, why it works, and how you can construct a similar script for your business.

First off, the very first lines of the opening demonstrate that you're "all business" and not there to waste any time.

Hello John, Archer Atlas…

Notice I didn't say "Archer Atlas, president of Atlas Advisers…" or something similar. I didn't for two very important reasons. For one, my company at this point is irrelevant. I'm not selling my company or its services. I'm merely offering some value. For two, saying the name of my company takes up valuable time in the pitch and doesn't give any selling benefit to me at all.

The final reason I'm not identifying my company is because it might just create some engagement with the prospects. Here's how: By not saying my company name, it might create some intrigue in the prospect's mind. He (or she) might just ask himself a question about me or my company at that point. If he verbalizes this question by asking what company I'm from, he's just further engaged himself in the conversation. This gives me a better chance of turning this prospect into a qualified lead.

Reason for the call…

By transitioning directly from stating my name to getting to the reason for the call, I've further demonstrated that my time is valuable, that I value the prospect's time, and that I am 100% all business.

Most times, the people being called are busy, and with your call, their day has been interrupted. This interruption or intrusion can easily be overcome by demonstrating value to the prospect. However, your further wasting of their time (and yours) is much harder to overcome. That said, you should always get right into your value.

Don't ask about their day, ask how business is going, or state any other platitudinous question. Not only is it condescending to ask these questions of someone you don't know personally, but it is a time waster and shows you do not respect your time or theirs.

Having this as my position now is a 180 degree change from my previous stance on this issue. But I feel very strongly about this (the converted are always the biggest evangelists) and cannot stress it too much. Do not ask nonsensical questions about the other person's day on a cold call. You don't care. The prospect doesn't care. And it's a major turn-off and time waster.

...I want to send you over our bestselling book on business growth...

The key here is to offer something of value that will benefit your prospect.

As well, you just gave a good reason—right there—for the prospect to stay on the phone and keep actively listening. You're offering something of value that can be of benefit to them. More importantly, you're leading off with this offer of value. Many times, that action is enough to get a positive response from others. People want to reciprocate. The power of reciprocity is a very strong thing. If you do something for someone else, many times they're going to feel the need to want to do something for you.

And with that:

...and invite you to an upcoming webinar "The 5 Most Dangerous Trends Facing Manufacturers Today."

You've offered to give the prospect something of value. Now is the time (if ever in the call) to try to "cash in" on that goodwill by asking something of the prospect.

Now this "request" was a little tame and also provided value, but it's still a request of the prospect, nonetheless. The key is to ask something of the prospect at this point. It always helps when it is a reasonable and rational request. You'd be laughed off the phone and hanged up on if your pitch offered a stick of chewing gum in exchange for a million dollars, so be sure to be reasonable in your request.

Fair enough?

Finally, the close. It's a soft close, but what you're making is a pretty soft offer. And that's the point. You want to maximize the amount of people who say yes at this point in the buying cycle. You can go back afterward and further qualify or disqualify prospects, but at this point the important thing is getting the maximum amount of people to say yes to your reasonable request.

It's worth noting that some people who employ this strategy for generating qualified leads ask, "does that sound reasonable?" rather than asking "fair enough?" I'm partial to "fair enough" myself, but both have worked well for my clients, colleagues, and me.

So that's the meat of one type of lead generating cold calling script (there are a few other types). The conversation can go any of three ways from there. For lack of space, we'll only be able to very quickly go over two of these paths that your calls can head down.

The Prospect Responds "Yes"

If and when the prospect responds with a yes, it then becomes time to ask some further qualifying questions, to verify or obtain correct contact information, and to close the call by giving your contact information and setting the prospect's expectations for what comes next.

There are two types of qualifying questions: reference questions and value questions. Reference questions are questions asked for reference, such as a stockbroker asking a prospect to name a stock he or she current holds or what brokerage firms they currently do business with.

These questions are for future reference and can be used to refresh the prospect's memory about the conversation when speaking to him or her in the future. The answers to these questions can also be used for reference in future correspondence with the contact, to demonstrate that you're not sending them a form letter, that you have spoken with them in the past, and probably most importantly, that you've listened when they've spoken.

Value questions ask for information that is of value to you. Their answers can further qualify the prospect, disqualify the prospect, or give you valuable selling information that can aid in a future sale to this prospect.

For example, if you were in the business of selling new workstations, and you found that most of your current clients used your new workstations to replace their five year old or older Windows Vista workstations, some great value questions might be as such:

Are you currently using a Vista workstation? When were they installed?

If the answers to these value questions are ever "yes" and "five or more years ago," you'll know you have a very qualified prospect. These are just a couple of examples of good value questions.

After asking qualifying questions and receiving answers to them, your next step would be to ensure you have all the proper contact information for the prospect.

You're next step would be to give your contact information and wrap up the call. This includes recapping what the prospect will receive from you (your offer of value) and setting the prospect's expectations moving forward (when they'll receive the valuable offer, when you'll get back to them, the next step, etc.).

So that's what happens when a prospect takes the first path, the path of "yes." Moving forward, let's get into what happens when the prospect takes the second path, the one of "no."

The Prospect Responds "No"

No matter how great you or your company are, no matter how valuable what you have to offer is, and no matter how well you deliver your pitch, some people will still say no. It's a fact.

When the prospect responds with a "no," "not interested," or some other non-favorable response, this can be for any number of reasons and really shouldn't be taken personally. After all, *most* people will give you a response of some variation of "no." Such is life.

Many times a prospect may say no simply because they aren't a real prospect in the first place. They may have no need for what you offer, and by saying no, they have done you a favor of freeing up your time to pursue *real* prospects.

Another reason for a prospect saying no is because they don't understand or see the value in what you're offering. If that's the case, then it's your job to properly demonstrate your value to them. Be completely confident when doing this. After all, you might just be doing the prospect the biggest "favor" they've ever received in their lives. Approach all of your "no" saying prospects like this and you're sure to covert a decent amount of them to start "seeing the light."

The most important thing to remember when responding to a prospect that said no is that you aren't really selling anything. You've offered value and asked a reasonable request. Most prospects that say no do so because they didn't clearly see or understand the value offered to them or the nature of the request asked of them. And while it's your job to bring them clarity, you should do so while stressing the fact that you are not trying to sell them anything at all, in this point in time.

You're simply offering value and asking a reasonable request. Further demonstrate your reasonability and reason with the prospect.

There are many more and different ways to effectively handle "no's" and other objections, but for this limited amount of space, the few listed here will go a long way for you.

A Quick Recap

Here's a quick recap of the steps involved in a successful lead generating cold calling pitch script.

- Introduce yourself by name and get right into the reason for the call
- Offer a lead magnet of value to your prospect
- Make a reasonable request of the prospect
- Close with "fair enough?" or "does that sound reasonable?"

If the Prospects Says "Yes":

- Ask qualifying questions (reference questions and/or value questions)

- Verify the prospect's contact information

- Provide your contact information

- Wrap up the call by telling the prospect what they'll receive from you and when

- Set expectations going forward or explain the next step

If the Prospect Says "No":

- Clarify your value and the value you're offering

- Clarify the nature of the request and how you both benefit

- Remind the prospect of the nature and purpose of the call

- Reason with the prospect

This is a very broad view of what can be a more complex process. That said, I honestly believe you have enough information provided to you in this chapter to be able to successful start generating a significant amount of qualified leads for your business via cold calling.

In Conclusion

There are thousands of ways to increase the amount of qualified leads flowing into your business. What we've just covered is one way to do this. It's certainly not the *only* way—and I'll admit it may not even be the *best* way for *your business*. But what I will say is this…

This method works. And it works well.

I've used it throughout my career—both in the distant and recent past, as well as in the present—to successfully generate thousands of qualified leads, of which many have become my clients. This method has been "field-tested" and has proven itself over and over again, by my own clients, my colleagues, and by me.

The best part about this method is that it is working better today than ever. Using these same techniques, I've personally been able to fill up my training webinars with only an hour a day (at most) of calling, generating a minimum of four qualified leads per day for this purpose, personally.

As I've said before, right now there is an amazing opportunity for you to generate qualified leads for your business, both quickly and inexpensively. There's honestly never been a better time than right now to generate more leads for your business through cold calling. This chapter presents you with time tested, working, real-world methods to grow your lead base.

It's a great start, but there's more you can do and more to explain than can ever be demonstrated in just one chapter, or even a book. But what you have right now can and will get you much of the way there, if you're willing to apply it.

Do yourself a favor and start applying this material. I'm telling you, you won't be let down. Thirty days from now, you could be well on your way to growing your business and your lead base—or you could just be thirty days older. The choice is yours.

About the Author

Archer Atlas is a leading business growth expert and highly sought after authority on business development, sales and marketing. Through his consulting programs, books, newsletters, and seminars, Archer helps his clients grow their bottom line by focusing on improvement in five core areas: strategic differentiation, lead generation, conversion, transaction value, and purchasing frequency.

Archer's latest book, "ASK: Unlock the 5 Proven Paths to More Clients, Revenue, & Bottom Line Profits," was written with the aim of helping business leaders more strategically and effectively grow their businesses.

To learn more about Archer Atlas and how you can receive free online training and the business enhancing audio program, Four Steps to *Grow Your Business Exponentially*, visit ArcherAtlas.com.

Get Your Free Business Growth Kit Today

As a big "Thank You" for reading this chapter, I'd like to give you three FREE GIFTS to help you grow your clients, sales, and the overall bottom line of your business, even more.

1. You'll get 3 FREE chapters of the upcoming business book *ASK: 5 Proven Paths to More Clients, Revenue & Bottom Line Profits* before it's even released on Amazon and available to the public.

2. You'll get the audio program *4 Steps to Grow Your Business Exponentially*, along with its corresponding white paper and transcript, previously only available from my website at a cost of $197.

3. Not only that, you'll receive 3 FREE issues of *Archer Atlas's Marketing Made Easy Newsletter* and 3 FREE issues of *The Archer Atlas B2B Letter*, an additional $297 value.

These three free gifts—an almost $500 value in all—are yours today, just for reading this chapter.

To claim these free gifts, just head on over to our website at http://www.ArcherAtlas.com or shoot me an email at Archer@ArcherAtlas.com.

Chapter 14

Email Marketing That Works

Scott Dudley

Introduction to Email Marketing

Email marketing was actually one of the very first strategies used to drive traffic and advertise online. Along with banner advertising, it was the original method that online marketers used in the early-to-mid-1990s. Back in those days email was a novelty. People actually got excited when they received an email from someone - no matter who it was from.

The good old days of America Online (AOL) giving you an audio alert of "You've Got Mail" are legendary. Personally, I can remember hearing this alert many times, and then quickly opening the email to see what it was about, and who it was from.

But, before too long this excitement started to wear off as people's inboxes were bombarded with spam and marketing messages. It's not surprising that this happened though, considering the obvious advantages email provided, compared to the old fashioned postal system.

Old fashioned snail mail costs money, and it takes time to get to the person (and in some cases is never delivered). But email is free and is delivered instantly. And back in those days, emails could be sent to millions of people at a time (if you had a big enough list of email addresses).

As a result of this, spam filters were introduced to all the email programs. This was to filter out the garbage that a lot of spammers and dodgy marketers were sending out to thousands (or millions) of people. This resulted in the ISP's targeting the spammers and tightening up the rules considerably.

As well as the blatant spam though, many people were now receiving a lot of promotional emails from marketers. And they had to deal with loads of special offers and freebies. E-books and newsletters were the latest craze during this period.

Back then, just about any e-book (and a lot of them were garbage) had some sort of perceived value. It really didn't matter whom it was written by. And a lot of them were given away for free, simply as a bribe to get the opt in - and a new subscriber.

So, the inbox quickly became severely overcrowded with far too many emails coming in. This resulted in a lot emails simply being deleted or never even opened. Because of this, the average person is now much more careful to opt in to a marketer's list - and to also give them their email address. People have learnt their lesson over time. They know by opting in, it will just mean more emails to have to deal with.

With this in mind, you may be thinking that email marketing is dead and a waste of time. But it's only a waste of time if you're doing what nearly everybody else is doing. A huge majority of people that are sending out marketing emails are going about it completely the wrong way. No wonder most people end up getting poor results.

In this day and age it is crucial to stand out in the inbox. You MUST get the attention of your subscribers. The basic idea is you want people to be looking forward to receiving your emails, even to the point where they are disappointed if they don't hear from you.

Personally, there are a few marketers whose emails I really enjoy reading. And this is despite the fact they are almost always pitching something. You want your subscribers to become your raving fans - so to speak. It's true, it's not easy, and it requires a lot of practice to master. But it's worth the effort in the long run.

Most people get it completely wrong by either sending out blatant sales pitches or emails that are 100% content. I don't recommend either of these methods. There needs to be a happy medium reached between them.

Blatant sales pitches don't allow you to build a relationship with your subscribers. This strategy is all about short term sales. It's true, there are some so called "guru marketers" that make a lot of money by hammering their lists with sales pitch after sales pitch. However, the old saying "people hate to be sold to, but they love to buy" is very true.

Once a prospect realizes that your primary motive is to get them to whip out their wallet, the relationship is over. Your emails will either be deleted or ignored. And it's very likely they will unsubscribe from your list.

The end result of this is you lose them permanently. They don't want to hear from you anymore, particularly if they bought a product from you that was really poor quality. This type of selling usually results in a lot of refunds and bad feedback on online forums. You don't want to have to deal with this, especially if you're trying to build a sustainable long term business.

Interestingly enough, the other extreme is just as common. These are the people who give out loads and loads of fantastic content for free, working tirelessly to please their subscribers. They believe their subscribers will come to the conclusion of thinking "if their free stuff is this good, imagine how good their paid stuff must be".

Sadly, these marketers are wasting their time. Because of the massive amount of free content floating around on the internet nowadays, most people no longer crave it. The majority of this content is dull, dry and boring. And with a few rare exceptions, the average person is simply not interested in it. These days the masses prefer entertainment, not textbook like content.

It may have been a different story in the first decade of the internet, back when online content was still in its infancy. In those days, the world wasn't used to having a wealth of information instantly ready at their fingertips. But now, we have millions and millions of pages of free content to wade through. And who knows what percentage of this information is inaccurate and contain facts that are completely wrong?

Additionally, and without realizing it, these marketers are also training their subscribers to expect free content. When you finally get the "balls" to actually try to sell something, it usually results in abuse and complaints. If someone is getting all of this premium content for free, there is no incentive to ever pay for it. It's like shooting yourself in the foot.

It's not a bad idea to give away a bit of content to begin with, to establish trust and credibility with your subscribers. You want them to see you as their trusted advisor in your market; as someone who acts as their fiduciary by keeping their best interests at heart. Jay Abraham calls this the Strategy of Preeminence. I would highly suggest doing a Google search on this.

In my opinion, you shouldn't be giving away your very best secrets which are included in your products for sale. Obviously this is only relevant if you're selling information products. If you're not selling information products, there's no need to hold back your best secrets.

So what is the best way to write emails then?

Simply put, you need to strike the right balance between pitching and giving away content/information. But more importantly, you must present it in an ENTERTAINING way that is INTERESTING to read. This includes highlighting a problem your subscribers are likely to be experiencing, and to then provide them with a solution (which is your product or service).

We'll go into a lot more detail about how to do this a bit later in this chapter. For now, I will continue to cover the basics.

One huge benefit of email marketing is that it's extremely cost effective. Obviously sending emails is free (at least it is for the moment). So even if you have a list of 100,000 people to send to, it is not going to cost you a cent. The only cost involved is the monthly charge for the email marketing software.

Personally, I use Aweber. At the time of this writing they charge $19 a month, until you reach your first 500 subscribers. There are plenty of other good options available around this price range, too. There really is no excuse for not being able to afford email marketing at less than $1 a day.

The last thing I'll cover in the introduction is the possibility of becoming an email copywriter. This is a great way to get experience writing emails which sell. A skilled email copywriter is capable of writing captivating subject lines, entertaining and interesting body copy, as well as persuasive calls to action.

You see... the best way to get to the stage of writing sizzling emails for your own business, is simply to write a lot of emails. The more you write, the better you will get. This may mean working for someone else for free to begin with, and then gradually increasing your fees.

A good email copywriter could charge as much as $100 per email, and a professional could easily charge $1,000 or more per email. By offering your email skills to clients like this, you can open the door for long term deals, getting paid on a retainer.

Obviously, you will need to be producing excellent work and getting results to be considered for a long term role. You could also advertise your services online, and attract potential customers through pay per click advertising or SEO. It also helps if you have a proper website that shows off your work, either through blog posts, or a portfolio page.

The point is to be targeting clients with large lists, where you can provide plenty of value by significantly raising their bottom line. This is where the money is at. The idea should be to attract fewer clients that pay you high fees, instead of lots of clients who pay you low fees.

But having said this, I realize a large percentage of people reading this will have no interest in writing for someone else. So let's move on, and talk about building your list.

Building a List of Targeted Subscribers

To get maximum results for email marketing building and growing your email list needs to be a priority. For every subscriber you lose, you want to be continually adding new people. This aspect of the craft is just as important as writing really good emails. But don't be fooled into thinking that a large list is all you need to be successful.

A smaller but more responsive list will always be more useful to you than having a large list that has no interest in what you're selling. Having a large list in itself means nothing, especially if the majority on the list isn't interested in hearing from you.

Before you get started, it's really IMPORTANT to decide on precisely who your ideal target market is. You want to be crystal clear on the exact characteristics of this perfect prospect, so put some real thought into this exercise. Don't skip this step.

Some things to consider while doing this are:

- What problems are they experiencing which you can solve with your product or service?
- What age and gender are they?
- What part of the world do they come from?
- What is their average income?
- What are their hobbies/interests?
- What forums/blogs do they visit online?
- What movies/TV shows do they like?
- What frustrates them the most?
- And anything else along similar lines to the above.

The more relevant things you can take into consideration, the better. Take your time and uncover as many clues as possible. Dig deep, just like a detective.

Once you have done this, you should have an excellent idea of what type of "opt-in bribe" you need to create. But remember, it's harder than ever to get people to opt in and give you their email address. Unless you are offering something that is of real, genuine value and interest to them, you're going to struggle to build a list.

It was far easier back in the old days of the internet. All you had to do was offer them some sort of e-book or a subscription to your newsletter. Subscribing to a list was a novelty back in those days, but now people are highly skeptical. They know if they subscribe they're just going to get more emails in their inbox.

Once you have created your opt in bribe, you will need to design a landing page (also known as a capture page or a squeeze page) with an opt-in form on it. If you don't know how to do this yourself, you can easily find someone to outsource it to. There are plenty of programmers at Fiverr.com who will do this for you very inexpensively.

If you want to do it yourself, there's a great theme that you can buy for Wordpress, called OptimizePress. This makes it quick and easy if you're not very technically minded. Also, there is another system called LeadPages which is even easier to use - anybody can set up a nice looking, fully functional capture page using LeadPages.

Importantly, you'll need to think of an appealing headline to get the attention of your prospects. And include some bullet points detailing what benefits they're going to get by opting in. It's also a great idea to include a high resolution image to show a physical picture of what they will be getting as well.

You'll also need to set up a web page that redirects the prospect as soon as they have opted in. This is known as the thank you page. It's a great idea to put some sort of message on this page to thank them for subscribing - and to tell them what to do next (which is usually to check their inbox for the email you have just sent them).

This first follow up message is setup to go out immediately after someone opts in. You could call this a welcome message of sorts. In this message, give them a friendly welcome and talk a little about the gift you have just given them. Finish off by letting them know they can expect to get more useful tips and information in the future via email.

You want to be upfront and honest with them, right from the beginning. Let them know (in a tasteful way) you're going to be sending them emails daily (or whatever frequency you have chosen) to their inbox. As long as they clearly know your intentions, there should be no problem with any spam complaints or nasty email replies.

It's also important to have your opt-in form integrated properly with your email marketing software. Otherwise, the people that opt in won't be added to your list. If you already have a pre-written autoresponder sequence ready to go, make sure it's loaded inside your email marketing software.

You may be tempted to buy a list from a list-broker instead of going through the process of building a list. It's true, it is a lot faster and easier than building your own list, but it's not worth it. The results you will get from buying a list will almost always be dismal. I highly recommend you build your own list of targeted prospects that you develop a relationship with over time.

Obviously, it's much easier to sell to people that know, like and trust you. If you just buy a list and start emailing them, you're basically spamming. Very few people buy from spammers, and fewer become a long term customer of a spammer. Your goal should be to build a list of raving fans and long term customers, and to do this it is imperative you build a list from scratch and treat your subscribers really well.

To build your list you're going to need to drive traffic to your landing pages, and lots and lots of it. But we're not just talking about any old traffic; we're talking about targeted traffic that will be interested in receiving your opt-in bribe. You pretty much have two options here - either free or paid traffic.

Paid traffic is a lot faster, is usually instantaneous, but it's also expensive. Free traffic is a lot slower and it takes a lot of manual work to see any results. However, it's important to realize your time also has an opportunity cost. You could have spent this time doing many other things instead, so it's not actually free, is it?

Some of the paid traffic methods include:

- Pay Per Click (Google Adwords, Facebook, YouTube, Bing)
- Solo Ads
- Banner Ads

Some of the free traffic methods include:

- SEO
- Writing articles
- Blogging (or content marketing)
- Video marketing

A whole book can be written about traffic, and many have, but this subject is beyond the scope of this chapter. My advice would be to start with one of the paid traffic methods and to stick with it until you master it. Just start off with a low daily budget and then build it up as you get more confidence and see some results.

The worst thing you can do is to constantly change your traffic strategies, and continually move from one thing to the next. I can tell you this from personal experience. Focus and definiteness of purpose are the keys to learning any skill.

The Fundamentals of Email Marketing

The question that a lot of people ask is how often should you email your list? Many so called "gurus" will tell you that you shouldn't bother your subscribers too much, and it's best to send only one or two emails a week. There is some truth in this theory, but that's only IF you're sending out emails that are either really boring or just pure sales pitches.

But, if you're writing emails the way I'm going to explain to you, it's a completely different story. The whole crux of what I'm going to be showing you is to send out INTERESTING emails (which include a call to action) on a daily basis.

Yes, daily emails (or weekdays at least, you can have the weekends off).

It's true that you will get a lot more people unsubscribing if you are mailing daily, but you shouldn't let that affect you too much. Those that unsubscribe from your list are never going to become buyers anyway, so don't worry about it. They're just taking up unnecessary space on your email list. Don't forget the more subscribers on your list, the more you are charged for it. Remember the goal is to build a responsive list, not necessarily a large list.

So the big question is, how do you go about writing emails that are both interesting and that your subscribers will want to read? Well there's a word that sums it up in a nutshell - "infotainment."

Let's start off by taking a look at the dictionary definition of infotainment: "Broadcast material that is intended both to entertain and to inform."

Notice there is no mention of teaching in this definition. The fact is people are bored with reading emails that are written just like a textbook. Most teaching is really dry and puts the reader to sleep, so your goal is to make your emails both entertaining and informing. Another great idea is adding curiosity. Just remember, it's important to understand that EVERY email should contain some sort of call to action in it somewhere.

We'll go into more detail about how you actually structure the emails later in this chapter.

One important thing to consider with your email marketing is that you want to give yourself the best possible chance of having the emails opened. And this includes beating the spam filters. Most email marketing software programs include some sort of spam tool. This tool shows you how likely it is that the email is going to end up being sent straight to the spam section. In other words, how likely to never be seen.

Personally I use Aweber, and the spam filter they provide is called "Spam Assassin". It gives me a score out of 10 for how likely it is going to be flagged for spam when sent out. It will show me which words or phrases are considered as spam and should be changed. Any score over 3.5 is considered as spam according to Aweber. Your email marketing software should have something similar to this. My advice is to use it and to pay attention to it.

Some common words that alert spam filters are:

- free
- money
- commission
- million
- $
- save $

These are just a few obvious ones to avoid, and there are many more. Just remember that you should always check your spam score before sending out any email.

So the question now is whether to use autoresponders or broadcasts? My advice is to use both and to set up two separate lists for each. The first list is set up with your initial autoresponder sequence and drip feeds them emails (preferably daily) until it's finished. This sequence should be written to primarily build trust and confidence with your prospects. And yes, you should be selling something in these emails as well.

Once this initial sequence is finished you should setup your email marketing software to move them to your daily email list. So, the only people who are getting emails on this list are those that have already been sent all the emails in your autoresponder sequence.

Most email marketing software will allow you to automate this. You can just set it and forget it. This is fairly easy to do once you know how. Contact support of your company if unsure of how to do it.

For example, you may have a sequence of 50 emails set up initially in your autoresponder. During the first 50 days after subscribing the prospect will get one of those emails each day. Then, once the 50 days are over, they will start getting your daily broadcasts from that point onwards. The key here is to have your emails sent out with high frequency, ideally daily.

Another thing to consider is the choice of using either HTML in your emails or text. Personally I use the text option (with active links) because it looks a lot more personal. No images or fancy graphics. You'll find that HTML emails tend to look like they're being sent from companies or corporations. These are clearly advertising and are rarely opened because of it.

The plain text feel with active links looks just like one of their friends has sent it to them. Therefore, it has much more chance of being opened and read. But that is just my personal opinion. I'm sure it depends on which market you're in. The best solution is to test both options and to see what works best for you.

You can also try to use the HTML templates that most email marketing software programs provide for you. A word of caution: Those templates can sometimes look horrible when displayed in certain email programs. Services like Gmail automatically block images in emails to prevent possible viruses. In my opinion, it's best to just keep things simple.

When it comes to which email marketing software to use, it's important to realize that you get what you pay for. There are some email marketing providers that offer a free platform. But my advice is to stay away from these. The quality and reliability of a free email marketing provider is questionable. Just imagine building a list of around 40,000 subscribers only to find out the email marketing provider has closed down and gone out of business.

If they cease to exist, your 40,000 subscribers will also cease to exist (if you haven't backed them up) - along with your business. This is just common sense. If the email marketing provider you're with is not making ANY revenue, then it is fair to assume they are not taking security too seriously - or providing good customer service. There may be some exceptions, but personally I wouldn't trust an email marketing provider that gives its service away for free.

There are many paid options out there, some relatively cheap and some very expensive. The more expensive ones tend to provide a complete all in one integrated CRM solution - including a merchant account. Typically you would only use a high-end service like this if you have a lot of products and are making a lot of sales. These are mostly for the serious internet marketers out there who are already running successful businesses.

If you're just getting started, Aweber, GetResponse, iContact, or Constant Contact should do the job for you.

It's important to get your priorities right when sending out your emails. The average email marketer obsesses over things such as open rates and click-through rates. While it could be argued that these things are important to some degree, you should never forget THE PRIMARY GOAL IS TO MAKE SALES.

Put it this way: No matter how high your click-through rate is, you can't take a "click-through" to the bank and cash it. Getting all excited about having a 90% click-through rate is useless if no one buys. Bottom line... it is much smarter to be testing which emails have produced the most sales. Analyze these emails to see why they were successful. Once you can see a bit of a pattern emerging from the emails that converted well, you can quickly learn what works best.

The more emails you send, the easier this will become over time. In any case, measuring click-through rates and open rates is only statistically relevant if you are mailing to a huge list. Getting a click through rate of 75% from a list of 20 people is not even worth talking about. Having said this though, it is still important to get as many people as possible to open your emails.

Legendary copywriter Gary Halbert talked about old fashioned snail mail being sorted into two piles. An "A pile" and a "B pile". The "A pile" was mail that was definitely going to be opened such as bills, tax notices, or hand written letters from friends and family. The "B pile" was stuff that was clearly advertising and promotional material. The point was, the "B pile" was destined to end up in the trash bin without even being read.

So, when writing your emails you should be doing your best to get them into the "A pile" of your subscribers. There probably aren't any surefire methods that are guaranteed to work, but here are some suggestions:

1. Using your own name in the "From" field, instead of a company name or something else
2. Writing subject lines that are short, get the attention of the reader, and are curiosity provoking
3. Using plain text in your emails instead of HTML

Writing the Emails

First off, I suggest you pay careful attention to what is known as the AIDA formula. Every email you write should be checked against this formula. This is because if it is missing any of these elements it will more than likely bomb.

AIDA is simply an acronym for: Attention, Interest, Desire, Action.

ATTENTION comes from the subject line and the opening sentence of the body. Put simply, if you don't get the attention of the prospect, they're never going to bother opening your email, let alone read it. The key here is that it must relate somehow to the body of the email.

INTEREST builds up from a story, a fact, or something intriguing that the prospect is curious about. The subject line should have already grabbed their attention, so it's time to get them interested. Remove the fluff and get straight to the point here. The average attention span of your reader is very short.

DESIRE is where you start talking about how your product or service is going to solve a problem the prospect is experiencing. It is important that it is focused on the pains of your target market, and it should use language and terminology they are familiar with.

ACTION is simply asking for the order. You've already built up the desire in the prospect, now you just show them where they need to go to buy. Ideally you should be using some sort of urgency or scarcity to motivate them to do it now. Never use false scarcity though.

If you can manage to include all of the above in your email, there's a good chance you will make a lot of sales. As well as the AIDA formula, there's also a certain structure that I like to use to write the emails in the infotainment style that I was talking about before. It goes something like this:

- Subject line
- Entertainment piece
- Intersection (the joining sentence)
- Problem the prospect is experiencing
- Call To Action

Let me explain...

The subject line is arguably the most important part of the email, as this usually determines if the email is opened or not.

Obviously, if the email is not opened the body copy will never be read, and you've wasted your time. This is why it's crucial to spend a bit of time coming up with the right subject line. Don't just slap anything up and hope for the best.

Put some thought into it.

If you've thoroughly researched your target market, you should have a good idea of what your subscribers will and won't respond to. Dull,

244

boring subject lines are usually ignored, as are blatant sales pitches or advertisements. People don't want to spend all day reading email, and will usually only bother opening it if they know the sender, or if the subject line appeals to them.

Some classic ways of improving your open rates are to evoke curiosity or shock people. But the point is not to offend your subscribers; you want to tastefully stand out in the inbox.

So try to use something clever which is related to the content of the email. You NEVER want to use clever subject lines that are not related in any way to what you've written in the email. That will just annoy people and turn them off. Always pay off the subject line in the body copy.

One thing you can also do is split test your subject lines to see what performs better in your market. This is easily set up with your email marketing software and is well worth a try.

After the subject line the email starts off with some sort of form of entertainment. It could be anything. Such as:

- a joke
- a brief history lesson
- a famous quote
- a reference to a popular TV show or movie
- a TV or movie character
- a story about you, or someone you know
- something controversial
- something bizarre
- something shocking
- something to do with sex
- basically, anything that's interesting to the reader

But (and it's a big but), you need to tie the piece of entertainment into the problem your prospect has, which I will cover shortly. The sentence that joins the two is the part of the email that I call the intersection. It basically joins the dots between the entertainment and the problem.

The intersection leads you into where you start talking about one of the main problems that your target market has. However, the problem you discuss must be one that your product solves. If it is an information product you're selling, you should only be including a teaser for the product you are selling them. Remember, if you give them too much information, obviously they will not need to buy your product.

You want to build up a strong desire to buy what you're offering; this way the reader feels they've got something out of reading the email. And because it was also tied into some form of entertainment, it gets the brain's creative juices flowing - which is then the perfect opportunity to close with a relevant call to action to your product. If your product is positioned as the ideal solution to the problem you have just discussed, it's then just a matter of telling them where they have to go to get it, and this should just be by clicking the link provided in the email. Usually it is put right at the very end of the email, but it could also be put in the P.S. section - if you include a P.S. Remember though, you need to give them a good reason why they should click on your link. The best way to do this is to dig deep into the core benefits of your product, and to demonstrate how it's going to make your prospects life easier/better/more enjoyable/more profitable etc.

For most people, it will be a challenge to continually come up with topics to write about, especially on a long-term basis. The best way to do this is to simply be aware of what is happening around you and to figure out ways you can cleverly tie it into your product. For example, if something bad happens to you during the day, see how you can write about it. Find a way to tie it into your product somehow. Storytelling is absolutely perfect for this - whether it's a story about yourself or someone else you know. Other ways to find topics to write about include some of the following:

- current events or news
- trending topics on Twitter, Google News, or Yahoo News
- looking at forums related to your marketplace
- by continually writing down relevant ideas into a notebook and referring to it later
- by watching TV shows or movies to get ideas

The important thing is to always tie it into the problem that your product solves, but do it in a way that shows plenty of personality. Dry, boring emails, will not do the trick. For some people, this doesn't come naturally and can be a bit difficult at first.

The only way around it is to keep writing emails and to study how other people do it. Obviously you don't copy their exact words or style, but you can get some good ideas and model how they do it.

Some ways of spicing up your emails include:

- Words misspelling puposefully (kinda kool)
- slang
- metaphors
- idioms
- similes
- segues

The point is you've gotta (note the deliberately misspelled word) mix it up it a bit. Anything to spice up your writing. You want the reader to be genuinely interested in what you're writing about, and you want them to see you as being someone different from all the rest. Do your very best not to sound dry, dull and boring.

Don't concern yourself with losers who point out spelling or grammar mistakes. They are most likely never going to buy from you anyway. Remember, the whole point of your emails is to generate sales and long term customers. I'm not saying it's OK to be sloppy, you still need to proofread what you write. But don't worry about impressing the English teachers out there.

You want to pay attention to the words you're using to persuade people to take action. There are certain words that have been proven to be hypnotic in a way that gets into the head of the reader. According to Joe Vitale's excellent book, Hypnotic Writing, some of these words are:

- announcing
- astonishing
- at last
- exciting
- exclusive
- fantastic
- fascinating
- first
- free
- guaranteed
- incredible
- initial
- improved
- love
- limited
- offer
- powerful
- phenomenal
- revealing
- revolutionary
- special

247

- successful
- super
- time-sensitive
- unique
- urgent
- wonderful
- you
- breakthrough
- introducing
- new
- how to

By using hypnotic words, you're painting a picture inside the readers head - and building the emotion of desire. The more you can build the emotion of desire inside your prospect, the more likely they're going to take action and buy from you. The idea is to get the reader glued to your email, and to do your best to make sure they can't help but read the whole thing.

Just like Joe Sugarman says, you want your copy to be like a slippery slope. After reading the first sentence of the copy, you want them to be interested enough to read the second line of the copy, and so on and so on, until they reach your call to action in a buying frenzy.

One very effective method is what Dan Kennedy refers to as PROBLEM/AGITATION/SOLUTION.

Once you've talked about the problem they're experiencing, you then want to agitate them by describing how painful, annoying and frustrating it can be. You see, once the problem is agitated they're then more open to finding a solution.

There's a great deal of debate about how long your emails should be. In my opinion, there's really no exact amount of words you should be using. Generally though, it's a better idea to keep it under 300 or 400 words if possible.

That's not to say you can't make it longer, but the longer the email the more chance you have of losing their attention. Therefore, a long email is only effective if it's really well written and also of immense interest to the reader.

As I have said, the average person has a very short attention span. They're not interested in reading long drawn out emails, especially if it's the same old boring rubbish that most people send them. Very few writers are good enough to be writing long pieces which can hold the interest of the reader. With this in mind, it's usually best to keep them short and to the point. As your writing improves, you may want to consider making them longer.

You'll also find that short, punchy sentences and paragraphs enable you to hold the attention of the reader. Short sentences are generally much easier to digest and understand. They reduce confusion and get straight to the point. Some readers can get lost in long sentences, and they have trouble making sense of what you're trying to say. The old saying that "less is more" explains this perfectly.

Long paragraphs are even worse. Most readers take one look at a huge paragraph in an email and hit the delete button straight away. It just looks like too much work to bother reading, and it's hard on the eye as well. I recommend mixing up your paragraph lengths. Have some paragraphs just a few words, some one sentence only, and others can be two or three sentences.

When writing your paragraphs you want to use a conversational tone. In other words, write just like you talk. Use words and phrases you would use when having a normal conversation with someone. You don't want your email sounding all stiff like a textbook.

Textbook style writing is really boring and turns most people off. I recommend recording yourself reading your emails out aloud, then transcribe and edit the recording to clean it up. If you do this, you'll have an email written in a conversational tone.

This type of entertaining email written with your own personality should be aiming to either attract or repel people. Yes, you read that right. In some cases, you will want to repel people - because your subscribers should either love you or hate you, but not be lukewarm.

A lukewarm subscriber just hangs around without having any real interest in what you're offering. At least if a prospect hates you, they're going to be talking about you - even if it's in a bad way. And by them unsubscribing, your list stays fresh and responsive.

A great way to ensure a subscriber either loves you or hates you is to send out a controversial or shocking email; one that is heavily opinionated and about a popular current topic. This may result in getting hate mail back, but on the positive side you can use the hate mail as a topic for a future email.

It may come as a bit of a shock to be abused by your subscribers, but at least you know you don't want these people on your list. You can easily manually unsubscribe them if you need to.

Laser Targeting Your List with Segmentation

The last thing I will cover briefly in this chapter is list segmentation. This exercise allows you to laser target prospects fitting into a narrower subcategory of the niche you specialize in. It's perfect if you're thinking of doing a new product launch. A classic example of this would be if you have built a list of people who are interested in dog training.

Say, you're now considering creating a new product about dog training for Dobermans. You then send out an email to your main list asking those interested to click the link to an opt-in page and to opt-in.

By doing this, you build a sub list of people who are specifically interested in training Dobermans. In the future, you can market any products you create that are specifically about Dobermans to this list. The further you can dig into your niche, and the more you can laser target people, the better your results will be.

For example, you could dig even further and create a sub list of people who are interested in learning how to train male puppy Dobermans. In this case of course, the dogs are only puppies for a short period before they grow up. But even so, you get the idea.

Keep in mind that segmenting is not just for product launches. Sometimes you may want to resend an email to the people who never opened the original email. Quite often people have completely missed your email because their inbox was full.

By resending it (only to those who didn't open it before), you'll find that you'll get a lot more people opening it, than just sending it out once. Or, for whatever reason, you may want to send an email only to those people who did open the message. It might be some sort of follow up message to get their opinion.

The same sort of thing can be done for:

- links in an email that were either clicked or not clicked

- segmenting subscribers in a certain country of the world
- segmenting date ranges when subscribers have signed up
- and so on and so on

The possibilities are endless really, but the point is to use list segmentation as much as possible to enable you to target your customers a lot better.

About the Author

Scott Dudley has been marketing online since 2008 and started out promoting various network marketing and direct sales companies. During this period he was introduced to almost every aspect of internet marketing. At this stage of his career, he concentrated heavily on blogging and email marketing, and built up a large following using both mediums.

Then in early 2012, he decided to quit the biz op industry and focus solely on copywriting and email marketing. He completed the highly acclaimed AWAI copywriting course soon after, and was able to quickly build up a loyal client base.

Most of his work is based on writing emails that sell for his clients, but he also writes copy for opt in pages, sales letters, articles and reports. He also works on his own projects, and uses a simple sales funnel formula of just a squeeze page, sales letter and order page combined with relentless follow up via email marketing.

Scott has twice been features in Internet Marketing Magazine and has made many guest post appearances on major blogs.

If you'd like to learn more about the finer points of effective sales and marketing you can subscribe to his DAILY emails at http://scottdudley.net, or you can reach him on Skype at Scott_Dudley if you'd like to connect with him.

Chapter 15

Customer Control

HOW A SIMPLE STRATEGIC CUSTOMER RETENTION SYSTEM CAN HELP YOU ACHIEVE 30% REVENUE GROWTH EACH YEAR

Russ Holder

"A 5% increase in customer retention can result in a 25-95% increase in profitability."

Frederick Reichheld
"The Loyalty Effect" - Harvard Business Review Press

The Big Idea

Customer Control is a simple system for maintaining a business's most important asset: the customer. Customer Control is also the easiest way for an established business to create, manage and sustain growth, even in difficult business and economic conditions.

Gaining Customer Control doesn't happen by accident. It requires deliberate planning and intent focus on what really produces results... and that's where the Customer Control Model™ comes in.

Let me start off by quickly explaining what Customer Control is and is not...

What is Customer Control? It is a unique and powerful system for creating business growth through strategic customer retention.

Customer Control is not unethical or manipulative in any way. Although the name may sound controversial, Customer Control is based on a company providing and delivering value to their customers in a strategic way that maximizes customer lifetime value. With Customer Control, the growth of your business is within your control.

A few years ago I consulted with a small industrial supply company whose growth had stagnated at around the $10 million level. Competition in their market was fierce, with a dozen direct competitors in their local area. Customer Control has put them on path to achieve over 30% growth for their third straight year... all without having to spend additional money on new customer acquisition. There's a good chance that it can do the same for your business as well.

Trends Affecting Customer Retention

Building and growing a business is not as easy as it used to be. Business leaders and entrepreneurs in just about every industry and profession today face several trends that seem to be worsening as the Information Age progresses. Each one of these trends represents unique challenges, but to make matters worse, these trends tend to feed off of each other. These trends are:

Increasing Competition – If you compare your industry now to the way it was 20 years ago, you will find that there is 50-80% more competition today. This holds true in just about every industry and business category, and this trend isn't slowing. In a struggle to be heard in the crowd, businesses flood the market with their sales and marketing messages, causing...

Advertising Overload – The volume is staggering. Multiple organizations have researched this, stating that the average person is exposed to 3,000-5,000 advertisements or brand messages every day. Instead of becoming overwhelmed, we have developed a very unique defense mechanism I call "advertising radar", which allows us to detect and ignore these messages. Unfortunately, your marketing messages are also being ignored.

Marketing Incest – Most marketing within an industry or profession looks identical to all the other marketing within that industry or profession. Take a look at one of your industry publications and you will immediately see the proof. The important point to understand about marketing incest is that you will never stand out from the crowd by doing the same things that everyone else does.

Difficulty Reaching Your Market – Combine trends 1-3 and the result can be extremely frustrating. One of the biggest complaints I repeatedly hear is how difficult it has become to reach prospective customers in a meaningful way.

Declining Customer Loyalty – Customer loyalty has been on an insidious and consistent decline since the beginning of the Information Age. With so many options and all of the free information about products and services available on the internet, customers are more informed and empowered than ever before. You should also expect this trend to continue.

These trends can't be ignored. They are here to stay and we must learn to adapt in order to persist and grow our businesses. One of the least expensive and most effective ways for us to adjust to these trends is to gain more control of the customers we already have. The masters of business growth, the companies driving double-digit growth year after year, even in the most challenging market conditions, do this by having a more strategic approach toward customer retention that other companies.

One of the least expensive and most effective ways for us to adjust to these trends is to gain more control of the customers we already have.

The Easiest Path to Sustainable Growth

In this chapter I will introduce you to the Customer Control Model, a powerful system that will help you improve each of the four focus areas of customer retention. If your business model is based on repeat purchases, the result in business growth can be amazing.

The Customer Control Model simplifies a complex problem, helping large and small companies alike to thrive in today's competitive marketplace. Among countless business opportunities, Customer Control is very different in the fact that it's not optional… it's essential. If you are serious about increasing sales, profits and market share, Customer Control must become a priority.

According to the White House Office of Consumer Affairs, it is six to seven times more expensive to acquire a new customer than it is to keep a current one. Customer acquisition, however, is too often the first focus of companies looking to increase revenue, even though it is typically the single most expensive and inefficient process in which a company engages. Depending on the industry and maturity of the business, a company often spends 20-30% of their total revenue on marketing to generate business.

In his book "The Loyalty Effect" (Harvard Business Review Press), Frederick Reichheld shows us that a 5% increase in customer retention can result in a 25-95% increase in profitability across a variety of industries. **Additional research by Bain & Company indicates that a 10% rise in customer retention can yield a 30% increase in the value of the company.** When small customer retention improvements produce such significant results in profitability, why do so many companies not in their startup phase direct an inappropriate amount of their marketing efforts toward customer acquisition?

Strategic Customer Control

One of the biggest problems I see among small businesses is that they are often not as strategic as they need to be in their sales and marketing efforts. To gain control of the important functions and processes that drive revenue and profitability in a business, you must become very strategic in the way you both plan and execute your plan.

"Strategy without tactics is the slowest route to victory. Tactics without strategy is the noise before defeat."

Sun Tzu
"The Art of War"

I love this Sun Tzu quote because it is extremely applicable to business development and marketing. A strategy is a method or plan to achieve a desired goal. A tactic is a tool that you use to execute that plan. For us to achieve high levels of customer retention – Customer Control – we must first have an exceptional strategy. The tactics we choose come later. Too many well-meaning entrepreneurs, business leaders and marketers throw out customer retention tactics in a non-strategic way, hoping that something produces a noticeable result. When results aren't easily realized, they often give up and direct their marketing efforts elsewhere, never gaining any real momentum, and never achieving significant results.

In your efforts to create a strategic customer retention program – to gain Customer Control – you must make certain that your plan is:

1. **Focused**, keeping you constantly moving toward your overall customer retention goal.
2. **Comprehensive**, covering all four major facets of customer retention.
3. **Simple** enough to easily implement and manage.
4. **Flexible** enough to allow quick and easy adjustments.
5. **Revenue driven**, with all major elements directly supporting the company's growth goals.

Don't worry, creating a strategic customer retention program doesn't have to be difficult. Let me introduce you to your new best customer retention friend…

The Customer Control Model™ - Strategic Customer Retention Simplified

Four quadrants make up the Customer Control Model: customer buying lifetime, customer purchase frequency, customer attrition, and customer reactivation. When you follow the model to create your customer retention program, not only will you achieve all five of the previously mentioned guidelines, you will maximize your potential to generate revenue from your current customer base. I'll expand on each of these Customer Control quadrants shortly, but first we need you to do something very important.

Customer Control Model™

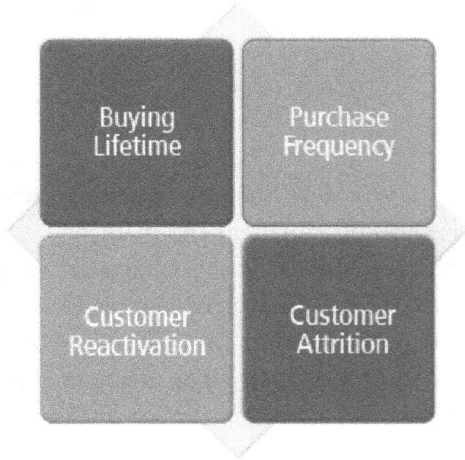

| Buying Lifetime | Purchase Frequency |
| Customer Reactivation | Customer Attrition |

Your Customer Values

Do you like math? Not everyone does, but you may find this drill very enjoyable if you imagine the numbers as deposits you're making into your bank account. There are a couple of numbers you need to understand to help you make informed and intelligent Customer Control decisions. I'm going to help you zero in on these numbers with a few examples and a tool I created just for you.

The reward for going through this process is definitely worth your while. You are going to learn a how to apply a powerful system to grow your business that can be worth millions of dollars to you over the next few years, but it's imperative that you know your numbers.

What is a customer worth to your business? What are they worth to you in revenue and profits, over a year and a lifetime? These numbers aren't difficult to calculate, and I'm going to make it very easy for you to determine yours with the...

Now that you have your Customer Control Calculator, let's calculate your customer values. I'll use simple numbers for the example in this chapter, but you should use actual numbers from your business to make this information personal and valuable to you. The numbers you need for these calculations are:

1. Average Transaction Value – the dollar amount of your average sale.

2. Customer Purchase Frequency – how often a typical customer purchases from you over a period of time (typically annually).

3. Customer Buying Lifetime – how long your typical customer continues to actively purchase from you.

4. Profit Margin – your average profit margin per sale.

For the purpose of our example, let's create a fictitious business that I'll call Customer Control Potential, Inc., or CCP Inc. Here's how their numbers look:

- Average Transaction Value: $50

- Customer Purchase Frequency: 10 per year

- Customer Buying Lifetime: 5 years

- Profit Margin: 50%

The typical customer for CCP Inc. is worth $500 per year (Annual Customer Value in Revenue) and $2,500 over their buying lifetime of 5 years (Lifetime Customer Value in Revenue). Apply the 50% profit margin to that calculation and we know that each customer is worth on average $250 per year in profits (Annual Customer Value in Profit) and $1,250 over their lifetime (Lifetime Customer Value in Profit). Here's how it looks on paper:

Customer Values – Preferred Method	
Average Transaction Value:	$50
Customer Purchase Frequency:	10
Customer Buying Lifetime:	5 years
Annual Customer Value – Revenue:	**$500**
Lifetime Customer Value – Revenue:	**$2,500**
Profit Margin:	50%
Annual Customer Value – Profit:	**$250**
Lifetime Customer Value – Profit:	**$1,250**

There's another simple way to estimate your customers values. Divide your annual gross sales by the number of customers that purchased from you last year. The numbers should be the same.

Customer Values – Secondary Method	
Annual Gross Sales:	$1,000,000
Number of Active Customers in the Last Year:	2,000
Annual Customer Value:	**$500**

Either way you choose, these calculations should get you close to your actual customer values. Equipped with this information you are now ready to explore the Customer Control Model.

Using the Customer Control Calculator – Navigate to the tab labeled "Customer Values" at the bottom of the calculator. Enter your information in the orange boxes. If you haven't downloaded your free calculator yet, get it now at www.RussHolder.com/CustomerControl.

Customer Buying Lifetime

Customer Buying Lifetime is the first quadrant in the Customer Control Model, and it is often the limited way people think about customer retention. The concept is simple and logical: the longer customers continue to do business with you, the more products and services you have the opportunity to sell them.

I find it productive to think about customers like this: Not only are your customers your most valuable business asset, they are also your competition's best prospects. You have to assume that your competitors will try to steal them away from you at their first chance. Don't give them that opportunity.

A common mistake is to think that good customer service is all that it takes to keep your customers coming back, but it's not enough. More than 200 million Americans each year stop doing business with companies they were satisfied with. Additionally, more than 60% of so called "satisfied" customers switch companies and brands regularly.

The Cost of Poor Customer Service

According to HelpScout, **it takes 12 positive experiences to make up for one unresolved negative experience**, and these negative experiences can have a crippling effect on businesses.

In fact, Genesys estimates that **$83 billion is lost by US businesses each year due to poor customer service**.

Because the cost of losing your customers is so high, you can't afford not to "thrill" them. What about your customers? Are your customers more than satisfied? Are they thrilled with the products, services and customer service you provide them? How do you know? If there were a problem, what do you do to remedy it?

Maybe you have heard about the differences between transactional and relationship buyers. Transactional buyers purchase entirely on the economics of the transaction, and they will leave you for a competitor to save a dollar. Studies by Dr. Paul Wang of Northwestern University show that only 15-20% of buyers are strictly transaction buyers, while 80-85% prefer to have a relationship with the company they do business with. These relationship buyers have the potential to remain loyal to you for a long time, so you need to do everything you can to make them "thrilled" to be your customer.

How to Increase Customer Buying Lifetime

There are three key areas you must concentrate on to increase customer buying lifetime:

1. Amazing customer service

2. Offering products and services your customers want

3. Consistent communication of value

Although I've already mentioned customer service, there's something else I want to touch on. We all know that delivering excellent customer service is important to increase a customer's buying lifetime, and we've all heard that we should "under-promise and over-deliver." The problem is that many companies who think they give great customer service really do not. According to research conducted by Forrester in 2012, only 37% of US companies earned a customer experience index rating of good or excellent, but over 60% believed they were doing a good or excellent job. That's quite a gap.

The second key to extending your customer's buying lifetime is to make certain that you're offering the products and services that your customers want. If your customers want something that you don't offer, then they have to go elsewhere to get it, and bad things can happen when you lose control of the buying process.

One consistent theme you will hear throughout Customer Control is the phrase "consistent communication of value." You need to communicate to all of your customers (active, inactive, and prospective) on a consistent basis, and they need to perceive all of these communications as having real value.

There is a term often used in the marketing world called "top-of-mind awareness", also known by the acronym TOMA. About 50% of all advertising dollars are spent to increase top-of-mind awareness, and in 2013 that equated to $85 billion. Why is so much money spent to build and maintain awareness? Because the phrase "out of sight, out of mind" applies perfectly to marketing, especially customer retention.

When you think about all the time and money you invest acquiring customers, you can't afford to let them forget about you. And like it or not, they will forget about you. Studies show that for each month without meaningful contact with a customer you can lose about 10% of your top-of-mind awareness, meaning that you can be completely forgotten in less than a year.

So, the key to top-of-mind awareness is consistent and meaningful contact with your customers, or consistent communication of value. Once again, this doesn't have to be difficult, just provide them with information that is important to them. Add to that amazing customer service, over-delivering on your promises, and offering products and services that your customers want, and you're on your way to making great improvements in increasing customer buying lifetime.

The tactical tools that you use to increase customer buying lifetime will vary based on the business and industry. These simple questions should get you started on your plan:

1. What can you do to increase the buying lifetime of a customer in your business?
2. What can you do to thrill your customers with amazing customer service?
   - What are your different points of customer contact?
   - What can you do to make those contacts more enjoyable and memorable for your customers?
3. What can you do to over-deliver on your promises?
4. What can you do to provide them with more of the products and services that they want?
   - What products and services do your customers purchase before, during, and after purchasing from you?
   - What can you do to keep them from going to other sources to get them?
   - Can you offer any of these other products and services to them, or can you strategically align your business with another that provides these products and services?
5. How can you consistently communicate value to your customers?
   - What tools do you use to communicate with them?
   - What tools could you use?

- Do your customers consider your communications with them meaningful?

Doing the Math

By providing amazing customer service, offering products and services that your customers want, and consistently communicating value to them, you can make significant improvements in extending your customer's buying lifetime. Most often a 20% increase is not difficult, and I've seen improvements of 50-100% with a strong effort.

Let's take a look at our example company, CCP Inc., and apply a conservative improvement of 20% to their Customer Buying Lifetime.

Customer Buying Lifetime		
Activity	**Current**	**+20%**
Customer Buying Lifetime:	5 years	6 years

A 20% improvement adds a year to the buying lifetime of a customer. This will have a major impact on the long-term success of a business in both their number of active customers and Customer Lifetime Value.

What about your business? Could you extend your customer's buying lifetime by 20% or more? What do you think is possible? Enter your potential in your Customer Control Calculator now.

Using the Customer Control Calculator – Navigate to the tab labeled "Buying Lifetime" at the bottom of the calculator. Enter the improvement you think is possible in the orange box. If you haven't downloaded your free calculator yet, get it now at www.RussHolder.com/CustomerControl.

Customer Purchase Frequency

The second quadrant of the Customer Control Model is Customer Purchase Frequency, and it simply refers to how many times a customer purchases from you over a period of time, typically annually.

There are two primary reasons why the concept of Customer Purchase Frequency is important:

1. If you can get your customers to purchase from you more often over a period of time, your business should grow. If your business model is based on repeat purchases, then increasing Customer Purchase Frequency is crucial to long-term success.

2. The longer your customers go between purchases from you, the greater chance they have of buying from your competitors. If your customers buy from one of your competitors, there's a good chance they will never come back.

The approach to increasing customer purchase frequency is similar to that of increasing customer buying lifetime: offer more products and services that your customers want, and consistently communicate value to them.

Providing value in your communications with customers can be accomplished in many ways. It can be a sales person following up with clients with useful information regarding your offering, or even making them a special offer. It can be a print or email newsletter keeping your customers abreast of industry trends and events, or even new products and services. The important point is that your customers must find this information valuable, and that you communicate often enough to build and maintain top-of-mind awareness.

The options you choose to implement in your business will vary greatly depending on your industry and markets, but here are a few that can produce excellent results in improved purchase frequency:

- Print and email newsletters
- Customer satisfaction and feedback surveys to show that you care about doing an excellent job for them
- New products/services and their benefits
- Providing automatic re-order options
- Strategic follow up from the sales team

Doing the Math

Could you increase purchase frequency by 15% if you started using tools such as newsletters, emails, surveys, and phone calls to consistently communicate value to your active, inactive and prospective customers? If you offer products and services that can be purchased on a regular basis, I've found that improvements between 10-30% are common.

Let's calculate your potential. CCP Inc. currently averages 10 purchases per year from their active customers. A 15% improvement would increase Customer Purchase Frequency to 11.5 annual purchases.

Customer Purchase Frequency		
Activity	**Current**	**+15%**
Customer Purchase Frequency (annually):	10	11.5

If you don't know your current Customer Purchase Frequency, you can calculate it by dividing your total number of transactions by your number of active customers. For example, if 2,000 active customers made 20,000 total transactions, then your average Customer Purchase Frequency is 10 purchases per year.

Enter your potential improvement into your calculator now.

Using the Customer Control Calculator – Navigate to the tab labeled "Purchase Frequency" at the bottom of the calculator. Enter the improvement you think is possible in the orange box. If you haven't downloaded your free calculator yet, get it now at www.RussHolder.com/CustomerControl.

Customer Attrition

Customer Attrition is often called customer churn or customer turnover, and it is the exact opposite of customer retention. It is the number of customers you lose or that become inactive over a period of time. For many failing and under-performing businesses, Customer Attrition is their silent killer.

The most important thing to understand about Customer Attrition is the detrimental effect is has on the growth of your business. If you examine your customer database, there's a good chance you will find that 20-40% of your customers stop doing business with you each year. The actual attrition rate varies greatly from one business to another, but it typically falls into the 20-40% range. Don't believe yours is that high? I implore you to find out exactly what your number is. This is a number you need to know, so research it for yourself.

Customer Attrition's Effect on Business Growth

Here's an enlightening way to think about Customer Attrition and how it stifles the growth and profitability of your business:

- The average business will lose 20-40% of their customers each year.
- This equates to 100% customer turnover every 2.5 – 5 years.
- **By doing nothing more than reducing Customer Attrition by 50%, your sales will double every 5-10 years.**

How to Reduce Customer Attrition

The steps to reduce Customer Attrition are simple: first, discover your actual Customer Attrition Rate. Second, find out why your customers left you. The US Small Business Administration and Chamber of Commerce released some very interesting statistics about why customers quit purchasing from a business:

- 1% die
- 3% leave the geographical area
- 5% actively seek alternative solutions
- 9% are lured away by competitors
- 14% are dissatisfied with the product or service
- 68% are unhappy with customer service

This research shows us that 82% of your lost customers are unhappy with you. Unfortunately, unhappy customers don't always complain. The majority leave without ever giving you the opportunity to make things right with them. In fact, a study by the Research

Institute of America found that 96% of your unsatisfied customers will never say anything to you about their discontent.

Most companies can greatly reduce Customer Attrition with focus on three critical areas that should sound familiar to you:

1. Excelling at customer service
2. Over-delivering on your promises
3. Consistently communicating value to customers

When it comes to customer retention, many of the most successful companies I've worked with excel at delivering more than what is expected from them. Under-delivering often means a lost customer, but over-delivering results in loyal customers.

Showing your customers how important they are to you can also go a long way in reducing attrition. Having preferred customer sales or discounts, customer appreciation sales or events, and customer rewards for remaining active customers for a certain period of time can accomplish this objective. They're your customers, and you should know them better than anyone else, so get creative. What can you do to reduce customer attrition in your business?

Doing the Math

Of the 20-40% of customers lost to attrition every year, I've found that most businesses can reduce that number by 20-40%. Those numbers are the same, and I don't want this to be confusing, so let's go through a calculation together with our fictitious company CCP Inc.

Reducing Customer Attrition	
Number of Active Customers:	2,000
Customer Attrition (Churn Rate):	25%
Customer Lost to Attrition Annually:	500
Annual Customer Value – Revenue:	$500
Sales Lost Annually Due to Customer Attrition:	**$250,000**
Customer Retained by Reducing Attrition by 20%	**100**
Sales Resulting from Reduced Attrition of 20%:	**$50,000**

CC Potential, Inc. has 2,000 active customers, and they lose 25% of them each year to attrition, resulting in a total of 500 lost customers annually. Each customer averages $500 a year in purchases, which means $250,000 of sales are lost annually because of attrition.

If you can reduce Customer Attrition by 20%, which is a conservative number, it's like saving 100 customers because they remain active and continue purchasing from you. Maintaining their current Annual Customer Value of Revenue equates to $50,000 of sales. All of this is a result of reducing customer attrition by only 20%.

Using the Customer Control Calculator – Navigate to the tab labeled "Attrition" at the bottom of the calculator. The top section of the calculator shows you how much money you're losing each year because of customer attrition. The bottom section show you how much money you can win back by reducing attrition. In the orange box in the middle of the page enter how much you think you can reduce attrition in your company. If you haven't downloaded your free calculator yet, get it now at www.RussHolder.com/CustomerControl.

Customer Reactivation

Now it's time to take action and win your lost customers back. This is called Customer Reactivation, the fourth quadrant of the Customer Control Model, and it represents a tremendous opportunity to grow your business.

Since the typical business loses between 20-40% of their customers annually, every business that has been around for a few years has inactive customers. Let's say that your business is better than most and your attrition rate is only 20%. If you have had an average of 2,000 active customers throughout this time, then you've lost around 400 customers per year, or 1,200 customers over the last three years.

These inactive customers haven't purchased from you recently, but that doesn't mean that they won't purchase from you again. At one time they liked your business, but something has changed. Inactive customers are almost always easier to sell to than a prospective customer with whom you have no relationship. Additionally, you already know how to contact them, so there is less time and cost associated with communicating with them and establishing a relationship.

How to Reactivate Your Inactive Customers

To reactivate your inactive customers you must first know who they are. Once you have your list of customers who haven't purchased from you recently, you now need to communicate with them the following message:

1. Thank them for doing business with you in the past.
2. Remind them of the benefits they received from you.
3. Take responsibility for having "neglected" them and make it clear that you will do whatever it takes to remedy any problems.
4. Present a special limited time offer that your inactive customers will find difficult to pass up.

Many customer reactivation attempts fail because they either don't take responsibility for neglecting them, or they don't make a strong enough reactivation offer. Remember, the first goal is to get them to become an active customer again. Then you will be able to work them back into your sales process and gain additional profit from them. Even if the reactivation sale doesn't make you any profits, you're getting them back into the habit of doing business with you.

Customer Reactivation can have an incredible impact on the growth of your business. Contingent on the industry, business and offer, I regularly run reactivation campaigns that close between 10-25%. I have a colleague who ran a reactivation offer that pulled an incredible 75%. Let me re-emphasize that making a powerful offer is key.

Depending on how often your typical customer purchases from you, most businesses can run reactivation campaigns every year. Some businesses can run them every quarter. Your first campaign should produce the greatest results, but keep testing new and motivating offers and you should see results every time.

Doing the Math

How many inactive customers do you have in your database? You probably have considerably more than the total of three years of attrition. For our example, CCP Inc. has a total of 3,000 inactive customers. Let's see what happens if we reactivate just 10% of them.

Customer Reactivation	
Number of Inactive Customers:	3,000
Customers Reactivated at 10%:	**300**
Annual Customer Value in Revenue:	$500
Sales from Customer Reactivation:	**$150,000**

Reactivating 10% of their inactive customers brought 300 customers back. Since each customer is worth $500 a year in sales, their customer reactivation efforts are worth $150,000 to them over the next year.

What can you do to win back customers in your business? Go to your Customer Control Calculator now to enter your data.

Using the Customer Control Calculator – Navigate to the tab labeled "Reactivation" at the bottom of the calculator. Enter the percentage of customers you think you can reactivate in the orange box. If you haven't downloaded your free calculator yet, get it now at www.RussHolder.com/CustomerControl.

Your Potential with Customer Control

Now that you have an understanding of Customer Control, let's see what real potential lies in taking control of customer retention in your company. A strategic and comprehensive customer retention program based on the Customer Control Model produces an incredible amount of marketing synergy. Take a look at the example below for our fictitious company, CCP Inc:

Customer Control = Business Growth

Activity	Current	Projected
Average Transaction Value:	$50	$50
Purchase Frequency:	10	11.5
Annual Customer Value – Revenue:	**$500**	**$575**
Customer Buying Lifetime:	5 years	6 years
Lifetime Customer Value – Revenue:	**$2,500**	**$3,450**
Customers Gained from Reduced Attrition:	NA	100
Customers Gained from Reactivation:	NA	300
Total Number of Active Customers:	**2,000**	**2,400**
Annual Sales from Active Customers:	**$1,000,000**	**$1,380,000**

These small improvements in each of the Customer Control quadrants add up. For our fictitious company Customer Control Potential, Inc., it totaled 38% growth… and that's not including the cumulative effect of implementing your Customer Control program year after year. If you would like to see those numbers, they are listed on the "Putting It All Together" tab of the Customer Control Calculator.

Put Customer Control to Work in Your Business

I tried to make the example in this chapter a typical one, and I wasn't very aggressive with improvements. You may not be able to achieve 38% annual growth with Customer Control, but could you do half of that? Would a strategic customer retention program be worth your effort if it only generated 19% growth for your company?

What does your Customer Control Calculator say is possible? Check out the red tab labelled "Putting It All Together", paying special attention to the Cumulative Growth section. That's why I say Customer Control is not an option… it's essential to your business success.

How much growth could you achieve over the next few years with a comprehensive customer retention program? What would it mean to you in increased revenue and profit?

Actually, here's a better question to ask yourself: what would be the cost of not putting Customer Control to work for your business? How much will you lose in sales, profits, and lost customers over the next year or two? What will it cost over the lifetime of your business? If you are a stakeholder in a private company and selling the business for maximum value is your exit strategy, what would you lose?

Start now and do something. With the Customer Control Model small improvements add up and the results build on each other year after year. Use the questions below to assist in your Customer Control planning. Good luck with your future Customer Control efforts, and please don't hesitate to contact my office if we can assist you.

Customer Control Quarterly Planning

- What can you do to improve customer buying lifetime?
- What can you do to improve customer purchase frequency?
- What can you do to reduce customer attrition?
- What can you do to reactivate your inactive customers?
- In what ways can you improve or excel at customer service?
- How can you over-deliver on your promises to your customers?
- How can you offer more of the products and services that your customers want?
- What can you do over the next quarter to consistently communicate value to your active, inactive and prospective customers?

About the Author

Russ Holder is a leading business development and marketing expert and the best-selling author of *Maximizing Business Growth* and *20 Reasons Why Your Sales Stink*. However, Russ is best known for his skills at helping companies strategically grow in competitive marketplaces.

Based on 17 years of intense experience in consulting with over 200 companies in 40-plus industries and business categories, Russ has served as a strategic advisor to leaders of high growth businesses worldwide, including multiple members of both the Fortune and Inc. 500 lists.

With an intent focus on producing results in sales, profits and market share, Russ developed his proprietary TriFecta Exponential Growth Model®, Sales Success Circle™, Stealth Selling System, and Customer Control Model. They serve as a ROI-focused framework that creates marketing synergy and substantial growth for his clients.

If you're interested in learning more about Russ Holder's business development programs, the next step would be to schedule a brief phone conversation with us so we can learn more about your business.

We only take clients whose opportunities or challenges we feel comfortable addressing. Since these differ for every client situation, we respectfully ask to learn more about you before making any commitments as to how we might be able to help.

To contact us, simply use the information below:

- Web: www.RussHolder.com
- Email: Russ@RussHolder.com
- Phone: (225) 308-3323

Connect with Russ Holder:

- LinkedIn: http://www.linkedin.com/in/russholder
- Facebook: https://www.facebook.com/russ.holder
- Twitter: https://twitter.com/russholder
- Google+: https://plus.google.com/+RussHolder/posts

FREE Resources from Russ Holder

For free tools to help you gain Customer Control in your business, to www.RussHolder.com/CustomerControl.

- The Customer Control Calculator

- "Do You Have Customer Control?" quiz

- The audio program "Growing Your Business During an Economic Meltdown"

- A subscription to the Growing to Extremes Memo

Also, if there is anything I can do for you, you can reach me through my website www.RussHolder.com, or you can call my office at (225) 308-3233.

Can You Do Us a Favor?

Thank you so much for reading our book. We hope that you both enjoyed it and found the content useful. More than that, we hope that you are successful in applying it to help you reach higher levels in your business.

As you probably know, many people look at reviews on Amazon.com before they decide to purchase a book. **If you liked any aspect of this book, could you please take a minute to leave a review on Amazon.com?**

- Maybe you really liked one of the chapters written by a specific author? If so, please let others know what you liked.

- Did you like the book as a whole, and feel like it offered many practical tips for improving your business. Again, please let us know what you liked in a review.

You can leave your review right now by following this link: http://www.amazon.com/Going-Up-Strategies-Reaching-Business-ebook/dp/B00JU79F3M.

The 60 seconds it will take would mean a great deal to us and to the future readers of this book.

Thank you so much,

The Authors of *Going Up*

www.ingramcontent.com/pod-product-compliance
Lightning Source LLC
Chambersburg PA
CBHW060543200326
41521CB00007B/471